Prais

'This is a story you think you... ...
you don't ... Not so much ... ...
epic, farce and satire rolled into one. ... ...f
battles and banquets, as densely populated and richly depicted as
Game of Thrones'
Rachel Cunliffe, *The Times*

'Lets us see how power really worked, in public and private. We
glimpse the emperors at work and at play, in the dining room and
in the bedroom. And we see how even they, despite the sycophants,
were often prisoners, not architects, of the system. One false step
and it would all be over ... Stothard tells this story superbly'
Dominic Sandbrook, *Sunday Times*

'Profound scholarship written with the verve and expertise of an
accomplished novelist. On every page lapidary phrases evoke the
reality of life in the ancient world ... Wonderful, evocative stuff!'
Harry Sidebottom, *Daily Telegraph*

'A brilliant picture of the vibrant realities of life in the ancient world
... Marvellous'
Roger Alton, *Daily Mail*

'Illustrates how, with some paternal scheming, a relatively ordinary
man could push his way through the corridors of power and emerge
on top ... This hugely readable novel-like account is a *Succession* for
the Julio-Claudian years'
Sir Michael Fallon, Founder of the Parliamentary Classics Group

PETER STOTHARD is an author, journalist and critic. He is a former editor of *The Times* and of the *Times Literary Supplement*. He lives in Cambridge.

Also by Peter Stothard

Thirty Days
On the Spartacus Road
Alexandria
The Senecans
The Last Assassin
Crassus

PALATINE

AN ALTERNATIVE HISTORY OF THE CAESARS

PETER STOTHARD

WEIDENFELD & NICOLSON

First published in Great Britain in 2023 by Weidenfeld & Nicolson
This paperback edition first published in 2024 by
Weidenfeld & Nicolson,
an imprint of The Orion Publishing Group Ltd
Carmelite House, 50 Victoria Embankment
London EC4Y 0DZ

An Hachette UK Company

1 3 5 7 9 10 8 6 4 2

A CIP catalogue record for this book is
available from the British Library.

ISBN (Mass Market Paperback) 978 1 4746 2101 4
ISBN (eBook) 978 1 4746 2102 1
ISBN (Audio) 978 1 4746 2103 8

Typeset by Input Data Services Ltd, Bridgwater, Somerset

Printed in Great Britain by Clays Ltd, Elcograf S.p.A.

www.weidenfeldandnicolson.co.uk
www.orionbooks.co.uk

To Adam and Eliza

There is a high road called the Milky Way. This way the gods pass to the halls of the mighty Jupiter. To right and left are the houses of the greater gods, doors open and crowded. The lesser gods live elsewhere. This is the place I would not fear to call high heaven's Palatine.

Ovid, *Metamorphoses* (8 CE)

CONTENTS

MAIN CHARACTERS

THE VITELLII

PUBLIUS VITELLIUS (*c.*40 BCE–*c.*30 CE), palace official from the south of Italy, later a personal procurator for Augustus.

LUCIUS VITELLIUS (*c.*10 BCE–51 CE), son of Publius, consummate courtier for three emperors and their wives and three times consul.

PUBLIUS VITELLIUS (*c.*12 BCE–*c.*31 CE), brother of Lucius, soldier, lawyer.

VITELLIA (*c.*6 BCE–*c.*45 CE), sister of Lucius and Publius, mother of Aulus Plautius, leader of the conquest of Britain.

SEXTILIA (*c.*5 BCE–69 CE), wife of Lucius, mother of Aulus and the younger Lucius.

AULUS VITELLIUS (*c.*12 CE–69), son of Lucius and Sextilia, master of the dining table, eighth emperor of Rome.

LUCIUS VITELLIUS (*c.*16 CE–69), son of Lucius and Sextilia, family enforcer.

PETRONIA, first wife of Aulus Vitellius.

GALERIA FUNDANA, second wife of Aulus Vitellius.

GERMANICUS VITELLIUS, son and heir to Aulus Vitellius.

VITELLIA, daughter to Aulus Vitellius.

AT THE EMPERORS' COURT

PALLAS, Palatine treasurer (*c.*1 CE–62), ally of Lucius Vitellius, former slave.

NARCISSUS (*c.*1 CE–54), palace official in charge of correspondence for Claudius, enemy of Pallas, former slave.

CALLISTUS (*c.*5 CE–*c.*50), correspondence secretary of Caligula and alleged conspirator in his death, former slave.

RUBELLIUS BLANDUS (*c.*25 BCE–*c.*40 CE), provincial courtier who caused a scandal by marrying into the imperial family.

GNAEUS CALPURNIUS PISO (44/3 BCE–20 CE), grandee of the senate prosecuted by Publius Vitellius for murder.

PLANCINA, wife of Piso.

LUCIUS AELIUS SEJANUS (20 BCE–31 CE), captain of the palace guard, chief courtier to Tiberius, patron of Publius Vitellius.

THRASYLLUS (*c.*20 BCE–*c.*35 CE), Greek-Egyptian court astrologer to Tiberius in Rome and Capri.

AKA II OF COMMAGENE, wife of Thrasyllus.

ENNIA THRASYLLA, Thrasyllus's granddaughter, married to Sejanus's deputy and successor, Macro.

MARCUS GAVIUS APICIUS (*c.*10 BCE–*c.*35 CE), court gourmet and attributed author of luxury Roman recipes.

APICATA, wife of Sejanus and said to be daughter of Apicius.

'TIBERIUS CLAUDIUS LIBERTUS', father of Claudius Etruscus, uncertainly named freed slave from Smyrna.

CAECINA ALIENUS, young and colourful commander for Aulus Vitellius.

FABIUS VALENS, older, dissolute commander for Aulus Vitellius.

CAENIS (c.20 CE–74), former slave of Antonia, long-time mistress of Vespasian.

EPAPHRODITUS, former slave and correspondence secretary to Nero, owner of the philosopher slave Epictetus.

WRITERS

QUINTUS HORATIUS FLACCUS (Horace) (65 BCE–8 BCE) son of an ex-slave, lyric poet and favourite of Augustus who avoided too close an association with the Palatine court.

PUBLIUS OVIDIUS NASO (Ovid) (43 BCE–17/18 CE), exiled for unspecified, probably sexual, offences within the court.

PHAEDRUS (first century CE), satirist and adapter of Aesop's fables.

CLUTORIUS PRISCUS (c.20 BCE–21 CE), professional flatterer poet, paid and executed for his panegyrics.

SILIUS ITALICUS (c.26 CE–101), friend and adviser to Aulus Vitellius, author of the longest surviving Latin poem.

CLUVIUS RUFUS (*c*.20 CE–*c*.70), friend and adviser to Aulus Vitellius, author of a lost political account of the early empire and a history of acting.

GRATTIUS FALISCUS (*fl c*.20 BCE–*c*.15 CE) author of *Cynegeticon*, a poem on breeding dogs and hunting.

IMPERIAL FAMILY

JULIA LIVIA (5/7 CE–43), granddaughter of Tiberius, married to Nero, son of Germanicus, and then to Rubellius Plautus.

LIVIA (59/8 BCE–29 CE), mother of Tiberius, creator with Augustus of the *domus Caesaris*.

AGRIPPINA THE ELDER (14 BCE–33 CE), granddaughter of Augustus, wife of Germanicus, starved to death on orders of Tiberius.

GERMANICUS (15 BCE–19 CE), first heir to Tiberius, patron of Publius Vitellius.

AGRIPPINA THE YOUNGER (15 CE–59), daughter of Germanicus and Agrippina the Elder, married to the Emperor Claudius with help from Lucius Vitellius, murdered by her son, the Emperor Nero.

ANTONIA (36 BCE–37 CE), niece of Augustus, patron of Lucius Vitellius and Pallas.

DRUSUS JULIUS CAESAR (14 BCE–23 CE), son and heir of Tiberius, subject of premature obituary panegyric by Clutorius Priscus.

JUNIA CALVINA (*c*.25 CE–*c*.80), great-great-granddaughter of Augustus, first wife of the younger Lucius Vitellius

EMPERORS

AUGUSTUS (63 BCE–14 CE)

TIBERIUS (42 BCE–37 CE)

CALIGULA (12 CE–41)

CLAUDIUS (10 BCE–54 CE)

NERO (37 CE–68)

GALBA (3 BCE–69 CE)

OTHO (32 CE–69)

VITELLIUS (12/15 CE–69)

VESPASIAN (9 CE–79)

THE VITELLII

PUBLIUS VITELLIUS

Aulus   Quintus   **PUBLIUS**

VITELLIA

LUCIUS = SEXTILIA   Scribonia = AUGUSTUS ═══

Agrippa = JULIA ═══

Petronia = AULUS

Petronianus

Lucius = JULIA   Gaius
Aemilius
Paulus

GALERIA

Marcus = Aemilia
Junius   Lepida
Silanus

Vitellia   VITELLIUS
GERMANICUS

LUCIUS ═══ JUNIA
CALVINA

TRIARIA

THE JULIO-CLAUDIANS

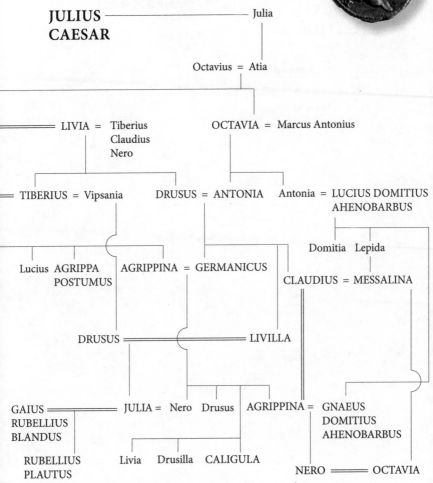

BRITANNIA
GERMANIA
GERMANIA INFERIOR
RHINE
COLONIA AGRIPPINENSIS
GERMANIA SUPERIOR
GALLIA
DANUBE
PANNONIA
LUGDUNUM
BEDRIACUM
PO
HISPANIA
TIBER
ITALIA
CORSICA
ROME
TIBUR
CAPRI
NOLA
CARTHAGE
MEDITERRA

THE·ROMAN·WORLD
IN·69·CE

BLACK SEA

•TOMIS

DANUBE

PONTUS

MACEDONIA

ARMENIA

COMMAGENE

ASIA

•ATHENS

•ANTIOCH

SYRIA

JUDAEA

NEAN SEA

JERUSALEM•

•ALEXANDRIA

INTRODUCTION

This is a view of the early Roman Empire that its own historians never wanted us to see. Set inside the houses of the Palatine hill, high on the edge of the ancient Forum, it is a book about two men in particular, a father and son, also a brother and others from the chorus-line in the theatre of imperial Roman life, some with ambitions for bigger parts themselves, almost all of them in one way or another reviled. Many of the characters, thanks to writers over 2,000 years, have been dismissed as poisoners of bodies and minds, informers, selfish gorgers, fabulists, fakes and facile toadies, bureaucrats at best. But Rome, like many later cities and states for which it set the standard, lived by men and women such as these.

Palatine shows the birth of Western bureaucracy. It is a history of the big rooms seen from the small, of the top table told from the lower tables. Its themes are flattery and gluttony, charges that need often to be challenged. Its events include the Roman invasion of Britain and Jewish unrest in the time of Christ but, until its final climactic year of four rivals fighting for the throne, it is a tale of peace more than war. It is a story of a single ruling household and of tactics for domestic times. It is a resonant story for our own times, of dimming memories of a glorious past, downwardly mobile aristocrats, sideways-moving provincials, upwardly advancing immigrants, personal excesses within the wheels of a powerful, often incomprehensible, machine.

It describes a world in flux, a Roman imperial world seen through the eyes of men and women on a hill that gave its name to every palace that followed. Amid a cast of slaves and former slaves, self-appointed lawyers, chancer arrivistes and the fabulously extravagant, it includes the lives of an old-fashioned soldier, snared in the politics of the new age, an exceptionally sycophantic courtier of that age, and a genial sluggard who became a notorious emperor of the banqueting table. Vitellius was their family name.

The most significant at the start of this history was the future emperor's uncle, Publius Vitellius (*c.*12 BCE–31 CE), an ambitious man of the army, not as clever or lucky as he needed to be. The longest-lasting was the father, Lucius Vitellius (*c.*10 BCE–51 CE), one of those quiet flatterers recognisable in many eras, a placid toad of the palace corridors, who lived and died in imperial service, ever more powerful as he lived through the successive reigns of Tiberius, Caligula and Claudius. Both were players on a stage newly distorted by one-man rule, its demands needing to be managed, its aims and rules rarely clear.

It was Lucius's son, Aulus Vitellius (12 CE–69) who briefly became an emperor of the Roman world, who was despised by everyone who told his story, and who, against tough competition from both predecessors and successors, set his own standards for the vice of gluttony. Aulus had a brother, brutal and mostly loyal, who was called Lucius like his father. Over half a century, one of the most important periods in the whole history of empire, the Vitellii competed against other ambitious bureaucrats, among the first in Europe to earn the title 'public servants'.

Images of the Vitellii exist only as traces. A fat-faced portrait bust in Venice, the so-called 'Grimani Vitellius', became an artist's model for gluttons. Publius the uncle, for all his efforts in the field and duties in the law courts, did not leave any picture for the history books. Nor is there an image of Lucius the father from his own lifetime: the man who rose silently in the treacherous court of Tiberius, who humoured Caligula's desire to be called a god, who both flattered and prosecuted the notorious empress Messalina was a great effacer of himself.

Lucius was one of those Romans who made the Rome of the early emperors what it was. He worked behind the scenery. He held the highest offices abroad as well as at home, but the man who failed to control Pontius Pilate in Judaea was in every way an unassuming provincial governor and slipped quietly out of every future. Lucius ran Rome while Claudius was pretending to conquer Britain, three times held the consulship, the highest office of old Rome, but, as a knowing survivor of show trials and purges, did not seek credit for himself except in imperial gratitude.

Lucius skilfully used the opportunities of a new era when a few family houses became a single house, a symbol of power as well as a fact of architecture. The imperial Palatine was the house of all power, its dining tables the place of diplomacy, political decisions and death sentences. The Roman Forum, once fought over so fiercely in fiery speech, had become almost a museum. The court was taking its place.

Different kinds of characters were beginning to make history. The Vitellii were just one family among many. A few of the newcomers were writers themselves. Most were not. Most became instead the victims of writers. *Palatine* is a different history of Rome under the descendants of Julius Caesar. It is a book less about the larger-than-life than about almost everyone else.

PART ONE

Seldom has anyone honourably bought loyalty to the extent that Vitellius bought loyalty with worthlessness.

Tacitus (*c.*105 CE)

1

IN THE PALACE DOGHOUSE

In December 69 CE, on one of the last days in a calendar like no other, only a mattress and a wooden door stood between the pale winter light and the panting body of that year's third emperor of Rome. The mattress smelt of dogs, but most of the dogs had gone. This was a small room in a palace of large rooms, but even its smallest rooms looked large to Aulus Vitellius when there was no one left behind.

Not long ago there had been many palace dogs, intimidating, entertaining, scavenging whatever meat had fallen from the loaded tables. Dogs knew how to get what they wanted with the lick of a flattering tongue and the low look of a deep-brown eye. So did the household staff, the lowest and the highest of them. Now they were gone.

Outside in the smoking streets of Rome there were dogs from near and far, some from thousands of miles away, from Britain, Syria, Africa, Greece, the endless steppes, the Danube and the Rhine. Each breed had its virtues and vices, wild bravery for the British, caution for Ukrainians, gluttony for most, fastidiousness for a few. Corinthian dogs were great sniffers of pigs.

In recent years there were rumours of racing dogs. Aulus had once been the governor of Africa and knew all about the dogs of Rome's old enemy, Carthage. Dogs from Cologne, known to all his soldiers from the northern frontier, preferred hares; if anyone were hungry enough to eat dog meat, it tasted like hare. He was not that hungry yet.

Every country had its own unique kind of dog. That was one of the reasons for visiting and invading other countries. Servants too had their special characteristics of places ruled by Rome. But all the living creatures that normally occupied the palace seemed to have

gone or, if not gone, were hiding, as he himself was hiding, from the
hunters beyond the mattress, bed and door. The guard dogs might
already have found new masters among the soldiers from the east
whose leader wanted him dead. He did not know.

Aulus's grandfather and uncle had known these dark halls well.
His father, Lucius, had been their most faithful servant, celebrated
in marble for his service, a diplomat and courtier, flattering when
he had to be, ferocious only very rarely, carefully commanding
fellow flatterers and rivals, ambassadors, conmen and cooks, even
ruling the whole city and far beyond when the fourth emperor of
Rome was away on his conquest of Britain.

That perilous regency – only a few months – had been a memorable part of Aulus's education, but none of his family had otherwise ever seen much purpose in educating him. Certainly, neither
of his parents ever thought that their son might be Rome's eighth
emperor. His mother, Sextilia, was pessimistic at his birth and
merely amused when, urged on by senators and soldiers, he added
the names Germanicus Augustus to his own. She never knew that
he was back now, in power no longer, with only the names she had
given him. Sextilia was dead, the news reaching him only a little
ahead of his hunters.

Unshaven inside a kennel, even in a palatial kennel with a
fortune in gold coins around his waist, he did not look like a son
to make a mother proud. He had always been tall, a virtue for a
Roman, but his limbs were loose and his stomach huge, his money
belt stretched tight. He had a deep scar on his thigh, testimony to
the dangers of chariot-racing with Caligula. He limped. He was
famed for gluttony. He was prone to belching loudly, a virtue to
those, including some very sophisticated thinkers, who thought a
man should always follow nature. The grander disagreed with his
philosophy of the fart.

He had for half a year been a popular leader of an ungovernable
army, men who had marched out of Germany for miles of murder,
looting and eating, men who had, merely by mistake, just burnt
Rome's most holy place, the temple of I.O.M., Jupiter Optimus Maximus, the Best and Greatest. Aulus had not had many jobs in his

life, and in one of them men had accused him of swapping precious temple ornaments for cheap replacements. That seemed unlikely now to be the desecration that anyone would remember him for. He was no Nero, an emperor forever blamed for theft and fire, merely one of Nero's friends. Anyway, maybe the latest burning had been his rival's fault. The Vitellians were not the only ungovernable army out in the streets of Rome in the winter of 69 CE. The acrid smoke from cracked marble still seeped into the palace.

From the Rhine to the Tiber he had ridden the waves of his popularity like a drunken sailor whose destination was chosen by chance. He had wanted to be a worthy successor to Nero. The massive walls of Cologne, birthplace of Nero's much-feared mother, Agrippina, had been his first capital. His final choices had only been where to hide, his family house in Rome or in the country, and whom to bring with him, his baker or his cook or both.

Even his friend, Silius, had gone. Silius Italicus had been consul when Nero died, a writer who had turned words into vast wealth in the law courts. He was a flatterer and a fighter who owned many houses where he too could be hiding. He was a collector of poetry and a poet himself, with ambitions for a long writing life if he could survive this latest wound in the body of Rome. Silius saw wounds everywhere, blood flowing from the swords and spears of ancient Carthage, from the dogs of Crete and Sparta, a nostalgist for the days when Roman soldiers fought Hannibal and not each other.

An emperor without a cook, a baker and without even a poet was no emperor at all. He did not want to be in his family homes. The palace had lured him back to the rooms where he had done the best he could. There were so many rooms, once the places for so many of the once enslaved, Greeks called Claudius and Claudia, Julius and Julia, the bread-makers and poisoners, shoppers and shit-shifters who proudly bore Roman names.

Here was the office of Pallas, the controller of the cash, of Polybius, who wrote poetry for posterity and letters back to kings, of the accountants and clerks whose names he had forgotten or never known. Not far away were the rooms of Beryllus, the little man who took so much money in bribes to deny the Jews, of Posides, the most potent eunuch at the court, of other eunuchs who made beds or offered their bodies in them, of fish-scalers, book-gluers, hair-dressers, of Halotus, the food-taster who sometimes stopped poi-sonings and sometimes did not, of Locusta, mistress of the deadly atropine, and Crispinilla, African costume mistress and mistress of so much more. There was the room of Doryphorus, dead critic of Nero's mistress, of Epaphroditus the detective, of Narcissus, that unforgettable name, the places for so many forgotten names. Now he was alone. It was not yet clear how close the danger had yet come. Every sound in the bitter air was muffled by the blankets that blocked his door.

There were so many clashing noises. This was the season of Sat-urnalia, the time of parties and public gambling, the brief pretence that everyone shared the same ancient liberty. From his dark room of the dogs any scream or cry could be a soldier's or a celebrating slave's. The soldiers of his rival might be celebrating too. Slaves might be killers. This was the time for reversing roles – even in this year, when the rise and fall of three emperors had been just a few of Rome's reverses.

There was a crash and a cry, then screams dulled by walls, silences punctured by the clang of iron, the sharp smell of smoke when wood burns stone. The kennel door opened. Empty rooms loomed before his eyes. The bed and mattress gave way, a rushing sound followed by a crash. An officer grabbed him by what was almost a beard. There was the sharp pain of a dog bite. It was a December of dogs.

2

MR GLUTTON AND MR FOOL

Aulus Vitellius's whole life was of one emperor following another – Augustus, then Tiberius, then Caligula, then Claudius, then Nero. He knew no other form of government. The age of rule by the senate and popular assemblies, the S and P of the SPQR on his soldiers' standards, ended in vicious violence half a century before his birth. Recent history was not required reading in the schools of Rome. Heroic antiquity was preferred.

Aulus could not remember the first succession, the hot southern Italian morning in the last week of the first emperor's life, August 14 CE. He was only two years old at the time, but he knew the stories. Everyone on the Palatine knew the stories.

A prized personal slave, one of hundreds in the imperial service, had the honour of the last combing of Augustus's hair, the last holding of a bronze mirror before his Roman nose and thick, grey eyebrows (so very different from his official portraits), the last encouragements in his struggle to ensure that neither sickness of stomach nor foreboding of death would be on show to his friends. It was important to keep up appearances when one man's appearance had become the reality of Roman power.

Aulus's brother Lucius was not yet born. His father, Lucius Vitellius, was around twenty-five years old and making his careful way, alongside Publius and two other brothers, in the imperial systems of Rome. His grandfather, also called Publius Vitellius, was a procurator, a personal representative of the emperor in the same service. He was around fifty-five and still remembered the aftermath of the assassination of Julius Caesar, when the Roman republic had failed its last test before monarchy began.

The health of Emperor Caesar Augustus mattered most to those in the household which he had built and ruled since then, helped by the elder Publius and a growing host of servants who had become public servants too. Within this *domus Caesaris*, Caesar's house and household, the master had attached the rule of Europe's greatest city, where his health also mattered, a country, Italy, where it mattered to a degree, and a wider empire, from Germany to Jerusalem and beyond, where in many places, whatever the public servants might pretend, it mattered hardly at all.

In a small room at Nola, at the western edge of Naples, on the landward side of Mount Vesuvius, it mattered to everyone. This was Augustus's palace, his *palatium*, whether he was on the Palatine hill in Rome or not. This was a modest part of his court in a modest part of his domain, but the name of where he lived and worked was always the same. The season was high summer. In the end there were no consoling sea breezes for the dying emperor, only men and women with fans made from leaves and silk, the slave with the comb and mirror, other slaves, doctors, cooks, other companions on the road who were free men but hardly free, all part of the travelling court which for fifty years had judged, taxed, threatened, used the minimum of force and turned the moving parts of the world.

The day was not yet at its hottest, the nineteenth day of August, the day on which the man who had given the month its name was home at his father's modest house. Born in 63 BCE, the son of a man of respectable success, adopted two decades later to be the son of the new god, Julius Caesar, Augustus had won his domination by diplomacy and force. As death came close in his seventy-eighth year he was back in the room where his natural father had died, where his own life, as the heir of Caesar, was entering its final hours. It was as if he were in a family hospital, a family theatre, staffed by retainers who owed him their every place in a family play.

He checked on the health of his chosen successor's granddaughter, nine years old and one of many called Julia, who was ill. The combing of his hair, the tilting of his mirror, the ointment for his weak left eye, the suggestion that he should thrust forward his jaw for his final speech, perhaps the very shutting of his stricken jaw: all help came from those who were his servants. He no longer had any equals. In the nearby towns, in Naples, Pompeii, Puteoli and Cumae, he was already worshipped almost as a god.

Augustus spoke as firmly as he could. He was never a strong speaker, just as he was never a strong fighter. He preferred to use others to win his battles and debates, to give him the authority that he reflected to the world. His last words, his hair and jaw in place, his eyebrows in a trimmed unbroken line, conveyed the modesty that he most liked to display. He saw himself as a common actor, taking the curtain-call of a comic play among the stock characters beloved by Roman audiences, Mr Glutton, the fat man, Mr Fool, the village idiot, Mr Chew, the ponderous sloth and Mr Toad, the flatterer.

Like the players of a travelling farce, when their night's work was done, the world's most powerful man asked for affirmation. Had he done well? Had he played his part? That was the last question he asked. If he had done his best, let him be given applause in return. Hands clapped like the clattering of tiles. Back in Rome the vaster mass of his palace servants, a class that extended from slaves to senators, each had their own anticipated role for the future. But not till the news came from Nola could the next act begin.

The original home of the Vitellii was only a few miles from Nola, at Nuceria on the south-east side of Vesuvius. In 14 CE they were still a family known by few, their ancestry, noble or otherwise, not yet even imagined. For four centuries Roman history had been a history of great families competing for votes and military glory, competing with gladiatorial spectacles and free food for voters, with cash and land for soldiers. At the beginning of the first century CE the Vitellii were not from one of those families. They did not pretend that when Romulus and Remus sucked wolf's milk on the Palatine, fighting each other before Rome's foundation, some Vitellian ancestor had been a spectator. But this was less of a disadvantage than it once had been.

Aulus's grandfather, Publius, held a mid-level place in the family that was already supreme over all rivals. He was one of Augustus's many procurators, part official, part servant, in the household of which the emperor was head, the only household that mattered, a fact that the Vitellii accepted faster than others who were grander.

This elder Publius had a brother, Quintus, who wrecked his prospects by fighting as a gladiator. Nuceria, like Nola, was rich from gladiator-training and less than 100 years before had been sacked in revenge by Spartacus and his slave army. Gladiators had glamour, but mostly the Vitellii were rising in more conventional ways, quietly, faithfully, sometimes ambiguously, and mostly with very great care.

From his middle-ranking place in the *domus Caesaris*, the modest procurator, Publius Vitellius, saw the advance of all his sons, Aulus, Quintus, Publius and Lucius – and a daughter, Vitellia. The repetition of the same names through the generations was not confusing on the Palatine hill. It was what Romans aiming at lineage routinely did.

Publius, the modest old servant, saw his son Lucius become close to Antonia, daughter of Augustus's sister, one of the women closest to the emperor. Lucius's friendship at court with Augustus's powerful and independent niece was his first step on the household ladder. Antonia was famed for choosing her partisans with care and she was there to help when Lucius went on to have two sons of his own, Aulus, the second Lucius, and another daughter, Vitellia.

After Aulus was born, as was the common custom, Lucius and his wife, Sextilia, ordered auguries to be taken for the boy. The reports were discouraging, particularly if he ever were to command an army. Lucius took careful note. He may not himself have believed in auguries, but prophets, soothsayers and sibyls were everywhere in Rome and Lucius was a very practical man. Sometimes emperors sought their advice and sometimes they banned them. Sometimes it became a crime to see the future and a safer course to keep people pinned in the present tense of their lives. Whatever his belief, Lucius acted as though the prophecies were true. Sextilia, breaking the imperial pattern of mothers fighting fiercely for their sons, was even more sceptical of Aulus's prospects in life.

3

SUCCESSION

From the death room in Nola in 14 CE news came only slowly back to the houses of the Palatine. Colonnades, corridors and tunnels connected what had once been separate homes but increasingly were one. It was a network of offices, dining rooms and halls in which truth was power and rumour spread like fire.

This was one of the three principal places of Rome's foundation, a steep hill where the marshes of the Tiber could most easily be crossed before anyone had ever thought of Rome. It was made from rough volcanic rock, lava and pebbles in a natural concrete that had been easy to carve for defensive walls.

According to myths much encouraged by Augustus, a small hut of reed and straw had been a home to Romulus there. This was a place of survival by suckling a wild beast under a fig tree. In the more certain history of the city it had become the home of the exotic goddess *Magna Mater*, and the eunuch priests who had saved Rome from Hannibal.

In the age of Julius Caesar the Palatine became a site for the rich to build luxurious houses and to look down on the Forum below. Some of those clinging to power in the old world that the Caesars had ended still had houses there. Many more did not, their homes belonging instead to newcomers, provincials, those who had arrived in Rome as slaves, the disrupters of old rules, the builders of empire.

Publius and Lucius Vitellius were born into imperial service and were in their late twenties in that August when Augustus's life was over. They were two ambitious young men who knew that Tiberius, the emperor's adopted son, the elder son of his wife Livia's previous marriage, was ready to take the throne. But, like everyone else at court, there was much that they did not know.

Their likely next master was aged fifty-six, an old man in the eyes of Rome, a pimply, surly soldier with a prominent chin, his upper lip hanging over the lower, a learned man but ponderous in speech, a heavy drinker, short-sighted, needing his own serious attention from a hair-dressing slave. It was common knowledge that Augustus had taken some time to accept this succession. He had forced Tiberius away from Rome for years, far from the halls and tunnels of his court, as a general in Germany and the Balkans or a retiree in island retreats. Each man was forever suspicious of the other. No one could rule out a last betrayal.

Around Vesuvius, local loyalists recognised both the emperor and his heir. Drinking cups were perfect for reinforcing the ambiguity. Along the lip of an Augustus cup might run pictures of the emperor's kindness to captured barbarians and his easy manner with Mars and Venus and other Roman gods. On a Tiberius cup there could be scenes of the next emperor sacrificing before a triumph, celebrating in Augustus's own chariots, listening attentively to the slave whose job was to remind the victor of his mortality. The owners of these cups could toast the imperial line with every quaff of wine and, if by any chance the line took a different direction, they could order their silversmiths to adapt. Adaptability was the key to survival everywhere, the more essential a key the closer the loyalist was to the imperial court itself.

After weeks of uncertainty in Rome there came new word from Nola to the servants of the emperor's bedchamber and banqueting halls. Augustus and Tiberius, it seemed, had met and talked before the comic-play farewell, the stomach-cursed emperor patronising his stolid stepson for the last time: 'O unfortunate Roman people to be chewed by such slow jaws.'

Exactly what had he meant by that? That Tiberius was a dullard, that he deliberated too long and acted too slowly, that he treated people like produce to be eaten, like objects to be exploited? Or was his comment a joke, just another line from the comic play on his mind as he faced his death? It was the job of the courtier to offer answers to such questions, whispering from the inside to those waiting outside.

It seemed quite likely a joke. The area around Nola was the home of comedy as well as killing in the arena. Both arts were practised sometimes by rich as well as poor. Thirty years before, the playboy consul Lucius Ahenobarbus, once married to the sister of Lucius Vitellius's patron, Antonia, was encouraging the most respectable rich men and their wives to play parts. Coarse wit entertained the highest tables.

On the nearby island of Capri, which Augustus had purchased for Rome and for his family, Greeks and Italians sang rumbustious comic musicals called the *phlyakes*. The most popular farces were called *Atellane*, after a town barely ten miles away. For fifteen minutes at a time, rarely more, and on temporary stages that travelled with their players, people of all ranks were used to watching men in masks mix the language of food, sex and the latest news, stock characters in stock plots, the slow and stupid, the guileful and the gluttonous – reassurance that everywhere and at all times the powerful pretended, the powerless laughed and life was more or less the same.

The high-summer heat beneath Mount Vesuvius was a haze between what was official news and household gossip. There was 'a sale of smoke', the name for the flow of rumour from the house of the Caesars. Lead drains softened, wood gables sweated, marble paths channelled water and lies. The body of Augustus cooled slowly for some hours, stiffening in the dampness of death, ringed by slaves in a tight noose of security, before the approved account of what had happened left Nola.

4

CARE FOR WHAT WE EAT

Augustus's wife, Livia, even more the matriarch when her husband was dying, controlled the time of death with a fig laced in deadly nightshade, atropine, as it was called in Greek after the Fate who cut the last thread of human life, belladonna as it became known for its use in giving women beautiful big eyes. Or so it was said.

Atropine was a popular drug for poisoners. It had long had its place in the line of the Caesars. The Egyptian queen Cleopatra, lover of Julius Caesar, loved the nightshade as both a cosmetic and a killer. It was Cleopatra's defeat that had brought Augustus to his decades of power before an end maybe hastened by her signature make-up in his fruit.

Poisoning was not easy. Like so much else, from putting on a toga in the morning to preparing for bed, it required trusted staff (some four or five slaves for the toga alone). Few could ever be trusted enough. It was never certain that Livia was a poisoner. She had a luxurious garden of rare herbs and a decorated dining room which reminded her guests of her opportunities to poison them as they ate. She had many enemies who might have made up the story, not least Tiberius himself.

The fig is less a matter of maybe. Augustus enjoyed the produce of his own gardens as the Roman aristocracy long had done, liking to praise the produce of Italy and, by patriotic contrast, diminish that of everywhere else. There were popularly believed reasons why food grown in Italy was finer than any other. The precious metals under its soil were not mined. They were left untouched to add flavour to vegetables and fruit. Augustus knew that there was no gold or silver or even copper and tin in Italy. If there had been it would most certainly have been extracted for sale, not left to make sweeter figs. But many patriots preferred the myth.

Food was part of an individual's character and the character of a whole people. A tongue was for talking and for eating. In street language, poetry and the farces of the stage, it was for sex. The Latin tongue was as special for the Romans as their land. The flatterer and the glutton, the names already beginning their life on the Palatine, were extremes of the same use of the *lingua Latina*.

Augustus liked it to be known that small figs and second-class bread were the staple of his diet at home. This was one of many self-conscious Roman virtues that for a while survived the rise of empire while others faded. The poet Horace, often a promoter of Augustus's ideals, was the son of a former slave and seller of cheap salted meat and fish. He wrote of how the simple vegetables from his farm outdid the feasts of kings. Horace was a pioneer of the satire, a word originally meaning the most mundane mincemeat, and invited grandees in elegant verse to his modest table, gently mocking the fashion for goose liver stuffed with figs. Love of plain country food was the official story from the court for the world outside, whatever the luxuries that its cooks could provide from all ends of the empire.

In 14 CE, whatever the roles of figs and belladonna, Livia delayed the death notice until her son had his preparations in place. For ten years Tiberius had been also Augustus's son. Together, Tiberius and Livia were left with the reins with which to rule and the servants who would help to hold them.

Rome's first emperor left a will prepared in part by his former slaves, Hilarion and Polybius. He bequeathed a household account book of the empire, along with a warning that its responsibilities not be expanded. His private legacy ranged from the tax due from provinces to the list of slaves and other former slaves, those who bore his name and from whom his successor could demand account. There was money in the treasury, not a huge sum since Augustus had not been a hoarder, and a successful economy based on high public expenditure and imperial taxes. There were poets and historians who knew their patriotic duty. It was not yet clear how Tiberius stood towards his political, economic or cultural inheritance.

Although there was nervousness on the Palatine and ignorance in the empire far away, the news of Tiberius's succession was at least the outcome most expected. The Vitellii depended on the succession of a Caesar. Already it was important for the men and women of the palace to be able to think beyond weeks and months towards far-extending years of family rule, consolidating gains and keeping rivals out.

Augustus's adoption of Tiberius in 4 CE, though guaranteeing nothing at first, had signalled his intentions for a hereditary monarchy. The legitimacy that he had won by himself in civil war and subsequent peace would continue through his descendants. What he could not decide was whether that first descendant needed to be a man like himself, inventive, original, an inspirer; or whether his hard-won legacy would best be served by a plodder, a consolidator, a man who slowly chewed his food.

There were other choices from within his own family, but the number was small and had shrunk over his reign. He had a massive mausoleum for himself, but few to follow him inside it. He had no son of his own and the eldest son of his sister was already buried there. A list of his achievements in bronze and marble, his *Res Gestae*, 'What I achieved in my life', stood at the gates as though a courtier permanently flattering his person. But the best chance of real permanence would be successors who owed their place to him alone.

Augustus had only one natural child, Julia, the daughter of a brief second marriage made to cement a political alliance in his rise to power and ending in divorce within days of her birth. There was never a suggestion that a woman could inherit in her own right. Julia had been strategically engaged, married and remarried – eventually to Tiberius – with results as unhappy as her mother's. For the past sixteen years she had stood condemned as a dangerous adulteress, the danger political more than moral. In 14 CE she was still in exile, allegedly starving. Not even the palace servants knew precisely why.

Before her disgrace Julia had produced five children as the wife of Augustus's greatest general, Agrippa, three sons, two of them dead at eighteen and twenty-three – one judged by her father as hardly better than a beast – and two daughters. From her marriage to Tiberius there had been only one child, a son, who had died soon after birth. After that her links to ambitious men at the court aroused Augustus's constant suspicions.

The emperor who wanted a dynasty had been peculiarly implacable against the one woman who could directly give it to him. Even Ovid, Rome's most popular poet, was in exile, and for mysterious reasons connected to Julia and her daughters. Ovid was a supreme artist in many forms. His works included not just *Metamorphoses*, an erotic literary guide to the borders between gods, men and beasts, but *Ars Amatoria* (*The Art of Love*), practical poetic advice for male and female seducers. The Augustus who promoted virtuous eating habits did not mind the higher literature but did not, it was said, want the sex guide.

Ovid was in a world of art way above the bawdy street farces of the Glutton and the Chewer, but he used the same sexual ambiguities when it suited him, more subtly but more woundingly too. In an archery competition Ovid's word for bow was not just a bow. No part was just a part, no service just a job, and a goal was an ejaculation as much as any other end in mind. Ovid had many enemies: those he had hurt, those he had let down and those who had read his poems with guilts about themselves.

The author of *The Art of Love* was an early victim of the courtly truth that what was amusing when the emperor was relaxed, might be treason when courtiers whispered that he needed to assert himself. Some connected Ovid specifically to the immoralities of the imperial family. In as much as anyone could be sure, that was enough for him to be exiled to the Black Sea and still be there at Augustus's death.

The elder Julia was her father's first and last hope of his own descendants, but no part of his future plans. She had not even known that her father was dying at Nola. She knew only that two of her surviving children were also exiled. Her son, Agrippa Postumus, named after her husband, Agrippa, and born after his death, stood condemned by Augustus as a waste of Palatine space. His strength of body was not matched by strength of mind: he liked not just to fish but to style himself Neptune. There was also her namesake daughter, condemned on similar sexual political charges to her own.

Instead, Julia's estranged husband, Tiberius, was at the head of the succession race and for further reassurance for the future he had a nephew, Germanicus, son of Antonia and his brother, Drusus, who carried the bloodline of Augustus and stood next in line. Germanicus was famously unlike Tiberius. In the summer of 14 CE he was in Gaul keeping the peace for tax collection. He was charismatic, popular and also neatly married to Julia's other daughter Agrippina, the only grandchild of Augustus neither dead nor banished from Rome.

This was a complex structure of exclusions, inclusions, expectations and hopes. Adopting Tiberius, after the early deaths of Julia's elder sons, his direct male heirs, was part of a programme of merging the emperor's Julian family, grown smaller by ill luck and ill feeling, with Livia's own much larger, and historically more eminent, Claudians. The whole was the Julio-Claudian house, but the Julian side, as Augustus knew, lacked the numbers to stay equal over time. A ruling family headed by Tiberius, with Livia still in place and Germanicus ahead, was a reasonable certainty for those who served the increasingly Claudian house of Julius Caesar's heirs.

It was not clear, however, what sort of ruler Tiberius would be, or how the court would have to adjust to him. Charisma had been the oil in the old machine. Augustus was a populist. The people and the army had backed him against the aristocratic senators who had murdered Julius Caesar. He had returned the favour with public works and the always careful acknowledgement that the people had the power. His family story and personal charms had made the system run. Tiberius was not a populist. He was not a charismatic man. There needed to be new ways to make the running smooth.

Those who worked in libraries could already know about the theory of flattery. In a house of Julius Caesar's family on the Bay of Naples there were at least three different theoretical studies on rivalries for a master's attention, whether the opposite of flattery was frankness or friendship, the kinds of scholastic dispute which enlivened debates after dinner. But there were few readers, and no clear route from theory to practice for anyone who did read. The whim of the master overseeing the discussion was the way that mattered.

Meanwhile, at her father's death, in her exile from the halls of the Palatine, the elder Julia was already part of half-forgotten history. The only daughter of the Emperor Augustus was already fading away, at first both alive and remembered, then alive but dead in the household memory, then hardly more than a ghost, not visited, not even visible with a backward look. She was allowed her last starving breath in the year of her husband's arrival on the throne. Agrippa Postumus, her son who called himself Neptune, died in that year too, leaving few mourners.

5

A WOLF BY ITS EARS

For the servants of the *domus Caesaris*, as for any Roman house-hold, the hereditary succession of a new head was in one way as normal as death itself: a son replaced a father and the house went on, upwards or downwards depending on the skill and fortune of the next generation. So it was with the Vitellii. But it was novel, even strange, for this process to apply to everywhere and everyone. Rome had occasionally been ruled by autocrats before, appointed for emergencies or the pretence of emergency; never in the 500 years since it expelled its kings had it experienced autocrats in a dynastic succession.

The powers of most officials lasted only a year, were awarded by election and were shared. The assassins of Julius Caesar had killed – and died – in order to keep that principle alive. Augustus ruled under the standard of ending civil war and stopping its return. He flattered the citizens of Rome, the high and the low, that they were still the ones in charge and that he was merely a *princeps*, their first citizen, the head of Caesar's house. They, in return, gave him respect that at some points came close to worship. It was a double deceit which the months after his death made all too clear. Augustus's legitimacy came from victory in war and the concealment of a military coup in comfortable disguise; Tiberius's right to rule – or even to be considered for rule – came only by being the son of the emperor's wife.

After the news from Nola there were immediate army revolts, disputes over pay and conditions of service, signs of more than mere disquiet. Even the celebration of a new festival for Augustus produced riots over actors' pay. Troops restored order, but they could not run an empire. The occupants of the Palatine needed new rules, new conventions, new flexibilities to manage an empire in the manner of a house.

Tiberius was reluctant to show the way. This simple indecision, the truth that he was not like Augustus, may have been the very reason why Augustus had chosen him. Germanicus would have been more likely to bring ideas and energy, but energy was arguably not what was most required. Consolidation and caution were more important.

In his military middle age, on the borders of the empire, Tiberius had grown used to the predictable obedience that comes with army rules. He had enjoyed too the simplicities of leisured life in island Greece. Even early in his reign he spoke of wanting to retire and of returning Rome from his one-man rule to rule by the few and the many. But he was 'holding a wolf by its ears', he sighed. Was it safer to keep holding the wolf and endure its struggle or to let the wolf go and risk the jaws of civil war? He could not let it go.

Any Caesar, any ordinary, unexceptional Caesar, however sluggish, however dull, was the way by which the destruction of war would be kept at bay. That seemed to have been Augustus's dying view. Peace might bring its own problems, but the household could deal with those. The staff could adapt. The lesson for anyone with an Augustus cup and a Tiberius cup was that there was new power but still also old power: the emperor among the gods would still be watching from around the rim.

For those on the Palatine adjustment was not simple. There were many different players, the surviving remains of Augustus's way of rule, the falling but not yet fallen and the rising, whose path was hard to see. There was still a cadre of senior men of the senate whose authority Tiberius said he wanted to restore but whose restored authority he feared. New men might aim to supplant them, but no one could be sure of when and how.

Even execution and exile could not destroy threats from those using his own family name. A man in Gaul had claimed to be Julia's fisherman son, Agrippa Postumus. The impostor was a former slave of Postumus who had succeeded in raising a small army, though not in protecting his infant court from a Palatine spy. This pseudo-Agrippa, once captured, saw no purpose in flattering Tiberius. Tortured on the rack and with no prospect of survival, he revealed

the names of none of his fellow conspirators, replying to the emper-
or's own question 'How did you come to be Agrippa?' with the
answer 'The same way that you became Caesar.'

This was an irresistible story, also a dangerous one to tell,
descending, as it did, into the deepest source of Tiberius's insecurity. The favour of the new master was the currency that courtiers
needed most, a fact to be hidden by a range of face-saving deceits.
Under Augustus's one-man rule it had become normal to pretend
that he was only the *princeps*, the first among equals. The pretence
required for Tiberius was already different.

When Augustus concealed his autocracy, he first cowed the senators with memories of the civil bloodshed he had ended, secondly
encouraged the second order of society, the *equites* or businessmen
knights, with commercial opportunities in a booming economy of
public works at home and abroad, some of it overseen by Tiberius.
And thirdly he empowered a small household bureaucracy.

That domestic office, promoting little overall policy but answering queries from across the empire, was where Lucius Vitellius
aimed to thrive. The new emperor would be known not just for
what he did (in a time of peace there were fewer opportunities for
doing) but for what he might possibly do, or what people thought
he might do. The Palatine currency was in signs and words, not just
on the coinage itself but in letters that were answered and, hardly
less important, those that were not.

Many of Lucius's colleagues were slaves and former slaves, men
and women whose names were the same as their master's: a 'Tiberius Julius', not so long ago enslaved in the Asian port of Smyrna,
might be as unique in his skills as he was nominally indistinguishable from many others. These men understood the minds of the
emperor's subjects much better than did those of the old Roman
military and political class. They knew the local codes.

The enslaved could be free. The Palatine household was no
different from those on the city's other hills. Romans for the most
part did not see slavery as an unchangeable state of nature. A Greek
nurse, bought and sold in Athens, had more chance of freedom in
Rome than if she had stayed at home. She could be a Claudia, like

her mistress. There were promotions, jobs bought and sold. 'Sales of smoke' might mean the passing-on of news or the offer of appointments that never quite happened. The seeds of later bureaucracies were there at these beginnings.

Lucius Vitellius was skilled at picking winners. He had the example of his father, the first of his family with a career at Rome, a man whose status rose to that of procurator, one of the many overseeing domestic tax receipts, sometimes doing the same job abroad in large provinces governed by senators or even a few small ones which they could govern themselves. The prefects in charge of Egypt, the corn supply and the city guard also reported directly to Augustus, a policy designed to stop unreliable senators having too much independent power. It was uncertain whether Tiberius would work in the same way, whether the system would work properly if he did and how much, beyond the Palatine itself, it really mattered who was emperor.

The exiled Ovid, desperate for return, saw his salvation in the whole *domus Caesaris*, not in the new sole occupant of the throne. In his *Metamorphoses*, his epic of possibility and change, he had compared the Palatine to the home of the Olympian gods. Soon after Augustus's death Ovid sent a poem to Rome praising not the ascent of Tiberius to the throne but the ascent of Augustus to those heavens beyond the Milky Way. He asked for it to be recited in the palace, to be heard by hundreds as well as read by the few.

This stratagem did not help Ovid: his crime, whatever it was, was not so easily forgiven. But although he had been outlawed for six years and could sense the political wind of Rome only by letters and visitors, his general sense was acute. There was an important pretence at Rome that Augustus was still the primary figure in politics – even after his death.

At the same time, however, Tiberius held power's reins and might choose to pull them one way or another. This was the new reality of one man, one house. Proximity to Tiberius brought the chance to learn about the new power – at dinners, at diplomatic meetings, at visits to soldiers. Food and force fuelled the machine. Flattery greased it.

Tiberius was not a confident populist like Augustus. He was not a charismatic leader. He avoided crowds. He wanted to trust those immediately around him, and if people failed the test, he would find others. Flattery quickly became the new oil, applied from those close below rather than flowing down from above. That was the beginning of the household's slippery truth.

Early every morning the Vitellii became part of a packed crowd of permitted admirers, a *salutatio* at which Tiberius showed himself in the portico of the palace, reviving the tradition of Augustus, who had strictly enforced attendance in formal dress except on days when the senate was sitting. This was the political theatre for Augustus the actor, also the place where his body had been brought to lie in state. It was as though he had never left.

Augustus never said goodbye to the Palatine. At the end of his life he had been too ill to take the *salutatio*. At Nola he had made his final bow only in his mind and to a very few, seeking an answer in applause to the question of how well he had performed.

The restoration of the *salutatio* by Tiberius was both the same and not the same. There was no stardust and no star, only a way of seeing who was greeted in person, who was kissed and how, who was a power and who might not be. Senators entered first, then the richer men of business, the *equites*, then sometimes some from the *populus*, the city mass who had luck and the time. The *amici*, the emperor's friends, were there all the time.

Already jostling for position, enduring the daily acceptance of an autocrat's right to rule, were the sons of the elderly Publius Vitellius, Publius and Lucius to the fore, Quintus and Aulus a bit behind. A curious enquirer into who mattered (or might matter) in the first year of Tiberius's reign heard names in a shifting list – the emperor's Claudian cousins, Julian nephews, slaves, ex-slaves, Greek prophets, gentlemen soldiers and lawyers.

Most were present in Rome, but not all. Germanicus was the most potent name, the newly designated heir, deemed suitable but not quite yet, a man with plans, but ones best kept for a future time. Tiberius's brother's son, aged twenty-nine, was away taxing Gaul when Augustus died at Nola. An immediate return seemed unlikely.

There was Germanicus's wife Agrippina, a power in herself, new mother of a daughter, named after herself and born in an army camp beside the Rhine; there was Julia's daughter, Julia, Augustus's granddaughter; and their many younger children in the imperial bloodline. Most of these were daughters too. The very model of government by a household meant maybe bigger roles for women.

As well as the young Agrippina there was a boy, Gaius, called Caligula in his father's camps because of his little *caligae*, the Roman soldier's standard-issue boot. There was the emperor's own son, named Drusus after Tiberius's dead brother, aged twenty-eight, wilful and insecure. In the next generation there was Tiberius's grandson and namesake, Tiberius Gemellus, the single survivor of the younger Drusus's twin sons, also Gemellus's sister, the sunny-tempered Julia, whose health had so concerned Augustus on his deathbed. All these and more had homes, slaves and ex-slaves on the Palatine.

6

PUBLIUS AMONG THE FISHES

A year after Augustus's death, while the courtly Lucius Vitellius was at the slow-shifting centre of the empire, his bluff elder brother, Publius, was at its northernmost edge facing a clearer and more present danger. Lucius was in Rome with his wife and their son, Aulus, who the augurs had said should never be in charge of an army. Publius, whose birth auguries were unrecorded, was in Germany proving that the family prophets might have barred the wrong man from army service. In temporary command of two legions for Germanicus, he was leading an unnecessary march that had become a mass drowning.

Indistinguishable from his men, the military standard-bearer for the Vitellii was stumbling through salt ponds that were with every minute less distinguishable from the great grey surrounding sea and sky. Winds filled with rain were roaring over banks of sand that had been land only an hour before. With every cloud of freezing air or fleeing birds came whips of grass like leather, shards of razor shells, goggle-eyed fish, lurid, orange, purple and alive, blood-red parts of what may once have been fish, prawns as clear as water, spiked fins and gills hardened and heading for the few rocks that anyone could see.

All around him was chaos that had so recently been order. Men were swept away by the waves or sucked under as though by unseen mouths. The air was a roar. Only under water was there silence. Horses, oxen, baggage, lifeless bodies floated about and blocked the soldiers' way. Separate marching groups became confused, their orders confused, struggling sometimes with their heads only above water, losing their footing, their comrades and their lives. Cries of encouragement to one another died against the North Sea sky. Nothing distinguished the brave from the coward, the careful from the careless, forethought from chance. The same grey power swept everything before it.

Publius began his day on a dry shore where the waves were coming in gently, not as warm as in the Mediterranean but as calm as marble, grey-blue lightened by curls of foam. His orders were directly from Germanicus himself, who wanted two of his legions to be marched back to their camp along the shore rather than overloading his ships. It seemed a simple enough command, one that his young courtier-in-arms, Publius Vitellius, could follow with ease.

Germanicus was a soldier-scholar who knew some of the principles of weather. He made his own translations from the Greek meteorological poet, Aratus. But Aratus, writer of the *Phaenomena*, observer of Macedonia and the eastern Mediterranean, had never seen the German sea. Nor had Publius. The Vitellii were not known for literary interests at all.

Publius was part of a raiding party sent by Germanicus eastwards across the Rhine, not an invasion force marching to conquer new territory (that would have been in contravention of Augustus's still-active will) but far enough to slaughter, humiliate and avenge losses of the past. It was a carefully calibrated exercise in propaganda, through the territory of friendly tribes.

Then came the first signs of the north wind in the high tide season, a flowing together of nature which, across the sea in Britain, once destroyed the fleet of even so meticulous a planner as Julius Caesar. Germanicus was no Caesar, not on the beaches or battlefield, even if he could claim the heritage at Rome. His name suggested a knowledge of Germany that he did not have.

Publius's 10,000 soldiers knew no more than their commanders. They did not smell the tides before they came, before the flat marble waters became a surging limestone white. The sea swelled. The sky fell. Daggers of ice flew as though thrown from miles away or hauled from hundreds of feet below. Publius's whole force – the first time that one of the Vitellii had held command – was pushed back on to quicksand indistinguishable from solid ground, shallows that became the sudden deep.

Previously Publius was happy to be strengthening his position in the entourage of the heir to the empire. Presently he was facing mass loss of life, the kind of disaster that in Rome would be political death even if he did not commit suicide first. The last commander to lose whole legions in Germany, just a short distance to the south and only a few years before, killed himself to save the honour of his family. The Vitellii might expect nothing less of Publius. All around him men breathed in the roaring air or found the silence of drowning.

Eventually the horror ended. After uncountable hours, in a world where counting had died with every other sign of order, Publius was among the survivors, struggling from the grey on to the few patches of ground that were still black. Around them was the seasonal harvest of that night-fishing in the day, nothing but dead parts of creatures that none of them had ever seen before, still less eaten, and ghostly, green-boned eels that were somehow still alive, able to live in air as well as water.

The rocks were a parody of a dining table at Rome. The vomit from the deep was like that from the stomachs of gluttons who puked where they ate. It was no more use to the hungry than the floor when the palace banqueters had left, shells without oysters, prawns still raw, serrated razors soaked in salt and sand.

Those who lived had lost their weapons and armour, emerging with bare or bruised limbs, conscious that they would rather have been attacked by Germans, with an opportunity at least of battle honours, than assaulted by such forces of nature. But when dawn came, they pushed their way to the meeting place where Germanicus had arrived with the fleet, silencing the rumour that all were drowned instead of, as was embarrassingly clear, merely so many of them.

7

BETWEEN THE EMPEROR
AND HIS HEIR

Back in Rome, when the elder Publius Vitellius, Augustus's veteran procurator, assessed the most successful of his sons for the new age, they were shaping into ever more contrasted pairs. His elder and namesake, survivor of a near-catastrophe, was a traditional politician of the army, his younger, Lucius, a subtle courtier of the new administration.

Publius had linked himself closely to Germanicus. He was looking to the future. It was common in eastern courts for ambitious courtiers to look far ahead, sometimes too far, to back the next leader while the current leader was still alive. The danger came from seeing inevitability where the incumbent saw a threat, but few in Rome had studied examples from Alexandria or Babylon such as those. Publius may not have had much choice in 15 CE than to join the new heir to the throne in the northernmost part of the empire. Or he may have seen the move as his main chance. It had quickly almost cost him his life before his life in politics could even begin – a near-death not just by drowning but by failure too.

When Germanicus was away from the court and his mother Antonia, during Augustus's last week in Nola, he was organising a census for taxing Gaul. He had then moved through the German forest on an exercise of propaganda and expiation, the kind of military manoeuvre valued most in the new era in which the empire was neither expanding nor contracting but consolidating what Julius Caesar and Augustus had won.

His chief destination was the long, thin battleground where the army of Quinctilius Varus, friend of Tiberius and fellow consul with him, had six years before suffered the most humiliating possible destruction, the loss of five legions, some 30,000 men, ambushed and extinguished on a rain-soaked road. His target, after burying any dead that still remained, was to punish any of the guilty victors he could find or pretend to have found.

Germanicus's father, Drusus, Antonia's husband and Tiberius's younger brother, was remembered as a ruthless hammer of the Germans. His son carried both his added name and the expectation that went with it. Publius Vitellius was not alone in wanting to march alongside Germanicus. Youth, vigour, learning in Greek and Latin, the translator of a prophetic (if unhelpful) weather poem all fitted admirers' idea of what an emperor should be.

Germanicus was thirty years old. Augustus had been nineteen when he began his vengeance against Julius Caesar's assassins, only a little older than Germanicus when he took sole power at Rome. Tiberius was almost twice as old, and his best days under arms were at least a decade before. It seemed reasonable, even prudent, for an ambitious man like Publius to look forward.

The new emperor seemed at first content with a burnished image of Germanicus, a prince of both the Julians and the Claudians and a useful link between them. Tiberius and Drusus, who was only twenty-nine when he died, had been friends as well as brothers. But even if there had been no sibling sentiment, predictability for the future promoted stability for the present, a stability on which Tiberius by himself could not rely. A celebrity heir cast stardust on the emperor. Flattery of Germanicus as the 'new Alexander' was welcome to Tiberius as long as there were no new acts of conquest to make the name more than a badge.

Even in faraway Tomis, by the Black Sea, hardly less cold than the German Sea, Ovid cast his pleas to be allowed home to Rome in language laudatory of Germanicus. After Augustus's death he changed the dedication of his poem celebrating Rome's religious calendar, the *Fasti*, to Germanicus. This was a suitable gift for a scholar heir, but one not driven by literary taste alone. Germanicus was an asset to Tiberius and a poet's flattery of the young prince, as long as it stayed within bounds, was useful to Tiberius too.

The right flattery of Germanicus could be a benefit for the ruling family as a whole. Germanicus was the first priest, the *flamen*, of Augustus. He had a new daughter, Agrippina, born in his German headquarters, as well as Caligula, his already swaggering son. When a legionary on the Rhine frontier studied the sheath of his sword, he saw Germanicus offering a statue of the goddess Victory to Tiberius while Augustus protected the good fortune of them both.

When Publius Vitellius left Rome for Germany, the aim to cement the heir's status without rousing the insecurity of Tiberius was not hard to understand. But the balance was already uneasy. The emperor sometimes seemed to be favouring the succession of his own son Drusus, from his first marriage, who was only a year younger than Germanicus.

Petulant and conscious of his status, Drusus held the title of consul and seemed to be being marked as the more legitimate alternative, particularly if Tiberius were to live long enough for Augustus's instructions to fade and his bloodline be forgotten. There were, and never would be, any rules about whether Augustus's natural heirs had primacy over the children of an incumbent emperor. A courtier, even one who preferred military tradition to the domestic arts of the palace, had to judge with care.

Some 1,000 miles from the Palatine, the Rhine was the border between the lands which, thanks to Julius Caesar, were seen as already on their way to Roman civilisation and those which were not. For Tiberius the tribes of Gaul were chiefly a challenge for tax-collectors. Those called Germans were different and still needed pacification. The distinction between the two groups was not as clear in the cold swamps and forests as it sometimes looked in Rome, but Tiberius knew the terrain – of both politics and geography – as well as anyone. He did not need his courtiers for that. Men were what they ate. German food of fresh fruit, forest meat and cheese, as well as their fighting spirit, came from a more primitive age. Dangerous, and dangerously admirable, the German tribes still needed the kind of hammer blows delivered by Tiberius's brother, Drusus, Germanicus's father, also the hammer of Germanicus himself.

Rome could not afford to extend its borders. That was Augustus's last statement of truth. Tiberius could not afford an heir who was too successful in his soldiers' eyes. Augustus would have understood that, even though it was not a problem he himself had had. Trips to seize money and ceremonial visits to rescue standards, bury bodies and expunge the shame of Augustus's greatest military disaster were different from conquest. Publius Vitellius was part of a new kind of imperial mission.

What he found within the Rhine army was a defensive force with little glory ahead and the job of looking backwards to its worst past. The massacre in the Teutoburg forest in 9 CE cost a fifth of Rome's military strength and threatened the invincibility of the empire. It came closer than any setback to shattering Augustus's image of calm. He was reported as tramping the palace floors at night and shouting *Quinctili Vare, redde legiones*, 'Varus, give me back my legions'. But six years later, with tax-collectors and tame reporters in the entourage, Germanicus could begin to right the wrong.

Publius arrived several months into the mission, but Germanicus's legions were still scarred by what they had found in the waterlogged Teutoburg forest. Here were the scattered remains of men whose commander, five years before, had led them into a trap. Human and animal bones lay in the same shallow pits beside rotting goat-skin shields and tents. There were skeletons in armour, bells stuffed with grass, designed vainly to muffle the sound of pack-mules, coins of bronze, the remains of a last imperial pay day that the Germans had not even bothered to recover. This was a disaster that required continuing revenge – and also explanation.

To the troops of Germanicus it was Varus's own responsibility that was clearest, the failure of a bureaucrat, not a fighter, an impoverished aristocrat whose father had killed himself after the defeat of Julius Caesar's assassins, a tax-collector whose travelling treasury had been his top priority in the forest mud. Germany was not ready for lawyers and office men.

The Germans were savages whose rules, in as much as they had rules, were not yet ready to be refined into those from Rome. The German conqueror of Varus was a treacherous Roman ally, educated and trusted, who gave Roman banquets for his enemy and made fake requests for the judgment of Roman law. The barbarians' torture pits, the cages in which they had burnt their prisoners, the trees to which they had nailed Roman skulls, all became a lesson in the difference between Palatine conflicts and the real thing.

Varus was a favourite of Augustus, a valued fellow consul of Tiberius, but the wrong sort of favourite friend. He was too courtly for Germans. Before even the last act of what was quickly called Varus's catastrophe, the *clades Variana*, Varus took his own life. Publius Vitellius, one of Varus's avengers, was lucky not to die as a lesser Varus himself. Two lost legions in a time without war would have been a massive loss.

Publius hardly contributed much to Rome's limited aims – or to any other advance for his family. Instead he led a march which only narrowly avoided being a *clades Vitelliana*, a mass drowning rather than a mass slaughter, but a potential catastrophe nonetheless. On this occasion his political luck was good. It did not suit Tiberius to damage Germanicus any more so early in his reign. Germanicus stood by his friend while focusing Publius's future efforts on tax collection, a family skill of his namesake father and of Lucius Vitellius, his already very useful younger brother.

8

FLATTERY AND FEAR

The courtiers of Tiberius's house had a strong interest in the ruling house being that of the Julio-Claudian family rather than any other. After fifty years few Romans wanted the instability of the old republic. But that did not mean to everyone in every other house that the emperor should forever be a descendant of Julius Caesar.

In his final years, Augustus had been clearly frustrated – clearly at least to those who were close – that neither his own family nor that of his wife could provide a suitable candidate to succeed. There was much reasonable ambition in grand men's minds. The aristocrats Marcus Lepidus, Gnaeus Piso and other family heads with heirs to come might all see their own claims to command Rome's armies, control provinces and be the final judge of the law for Romans and the world. Those closest to Tiberius found quickly that they could both flatter him with his natural right to rule and play upon his fears of rival claimants.

When Tiberius took the throne, he did not pretend to be a new Augustus. His continuing argument – in words and signs – was that the old Augustus was still present in all their lives. His aim was that rule by a single Caesar was instead to be as ordinary as all the previous conventions of the past, no more requiring a man of god-like status than the consulship had. Just as it was a matter of routine for there to be a Roman Empire, a fact of geography long preceding any act of Augustus, so too the rule of the Caesars would be made routine.

But what was routine behaviour around an autocrat? Tiberius's accession raised ever more starkly the question of what an emperor really did once there was no more expansion of the empire. The answer was that he responded to thousands of requests from all across the Roman world. His responses rarely required the enactment of a principle: mostly they required knowledge of individual people and places, taxes and exemptions, subjects on which any single man would need specific advice.

Tiberius affected to believe that the senate should provide this wisdom of experience, as it had in the best years of the past. He tried to present himself to the elite as one of their own, merely the grandest Claudian of his father's family, no radical, no populist. He vigorously encouraged senators to seize their responsibilities last shown before the era of Julius Caesar.

This was quickly a failure. Tiberius flattered the senate as a whole, but individual senators were reluctant to believe him and frightened to take what he seemed to offer. Like Augustus he rebuked any member of the senate who called him *dominus*, a word too flagrantly signalling a relationship of master over slaves. But even at the beginning, softer language only partially concealed hard facts. An imperial smile from Tiberius hid many realities, some imagined, others all too real, thoughts and visions of an uncertain future. For those slow to adapt it was easy to fail and fall.

Ambassadors, supplicants and allied kings alike needed guidance they could trust. They found that personal aides, *liberti* (freedmen who had once been slaves), army friends and old imperial servants had the best claim to know the emperor's true mind. And if Tiberius had no view on an issue (which inevitably was very often), they needed advice on how to flatter him into believing that, from his own wise mind, he had come to favour the cause that was their own.

There was almost no systematic government or policy formation. Making the arbitrary slightly more predictable was worth fortunes to petitioners from Rome and across the empire. It also made the whole system work. It was useful to know when the emperor was drunk and when he might be sober. The emperor's routine exercise of power was by legal business. But there were no timetables or state lawyers to organise the courts. There were virtually no state functionaries of any kind.

In the remaining Greek monarchies of the east, those from the age of Alexander the Great that had not been brought under Roman control, there was a simpler model of rule. The kings there had no surviving sources of power that they had supplanted or wanted to supplant. They were the sole power. Augustus had kept the traditional republican institutions of Rome on a form of political life-support, flattering the senators and magistrates that they still mattered, accepting their flattery in return. This was an act – and a hard act to follow.

The 'dictator's dilemma', already a dimly expressed problem of government, became more acute. How could the emperor spread responsibility without losing control? How could he know that the courtier was being frank in his opinion? How could the courtier know that the emperor would do what he promised? Neither side could know. Only the most intimate could even pretend to know. Power shifted to friends, family members and personal servants who began to be public servants. The dining table became the desk. Flattery and gluttony began to be arts of survival as well as government.

Some of the ingratiating and greedy became famous – and then infamous. Many more survived quietly for decades, unknown or almost unknown. There were courts within courts, one of them headed by Germanicus's mother, Antonia, a daughter of Augustus's sister. Unusually, Antonia had the independence to remain unmarried after the death of her husband, Tiberius's brother Drusus, in 9 BCE. Lucius Vitellius owed much to this *grande dame* of Rome. Influential slaves in Antonia's house included Pallas, a teenage Greek accountant, and Caenis, a slave who claimed to carry in her mind 'everything that you have written and anything else you tell me'. In a court of wax tablets, a memory that no one could erase was both a useful and a dangerous asset.

There were also men whom Tiberius found good company, respectful and not too ambitious, whom he had taken on his military campaigns. Typical among these was Gaius Rubellius Blandus, whose family had never boasted a senator and whose house was in Tibur, Rome's nearest pleasure resort. Blandus's name stood for smooth-talking flatterer, an example to all.

Pre-eminent on the Palatine was Lucius Aelius Sejanus, the chief of the palace guard and, just as importantly, a man whom Tiberius could trust with almost any task that he had no appetite for himself. Sejanus was the master of what was not quite yet an imperial private office, also of its banqueting tables. In a very visible Palatine house, decorated as though for a party, was Piso, a grandee close to the Claudians who thought he was already their equal. In their different ways, both of these men – and others too – thought that the house of the Caesars needed new management, maybe without any Caesars. Lucius Vitellius moved between all sides.

9

WORDS FOR A PALACE

As the courtiers of Tiberius adjusted to his power, outside the gates of the *domus Caesaris*, guarding the path down to the Forum, were ever more parades of gifts to him from abroad. A wise diplomat kept his flattery short and his offerings effusive. The mass of the Roman people appreciated the respect shown to their emperor by exotic slaves and animals, a man who was nine feet tall, a hunchback, a dwarf, a giraffe or a giant fish.

Monsters massaged the egos of those citizens who, if not wealthy or well fed, could at least feel comfortingly normal. In the absence of regular gladiatorial games, generous feasts and other necessities of electoral politics, this was flattery to the whole city population. Dead monsters were popular too, massive bones and tusks which, in an age long before the knowledge of dinosaurs, might be relics of beasts dispatched by Hercules. Gifts of more tradable value, gold crowns and silver tableware, were kept in the emperor's personal treasury or in the official treasury, the distinction between the two being fuzzy under Augustus and set to be fuzzier as time went on.

Along with the leadership of its greatest household, the Palatine was changing. It was becoming ever more like an imperial palace. It had ever fewer neighbours. More great houses of the old elite were mere palace annexes, linked by covered lanes, the corridors of the new power. Tiberius himself took a massive site, facing away from the Forum towards the stadium known as the *Circus Maximus*. There he ordered the house that would hold the courtiers and cooks, the enslaved and the free, who were closest to him.

The scale of this was new. Augustus had taken over a few houses of his father's assassins to provide public space and the great temple to Apollo, its pediment floating on only four columns, one of the wonders of his Rome. When he moved to the Palatine it was not even into one of the grandest houses. Augustus did not like to be associated with personal extravagance. He was happy to live and work on the site of Romulus's hut, to look down from his study and see the rooms where his nephews were learning the history of great men that he and his writers were busy constructing.

The exiled Ovid was the first writer to note how Augustus had created a place from which to rule which would soon define ruling itself. The civic crown of oak leaves, a soldier's decoration for saving Roman life, stood above the main entrance flanked by laurels of victory. Yellow marbled walls supported red-tiled roofs. Colonnades stood against the stare of the sun, nut trees among vines, bronze birds next to beasts spewing water into bowls. Tubs of oil scented the principal hallways. Tubs of urine awaited the wool-fullers who needed the acid for their work. Palatine games, theatre and gladiatorial shows, celebrated Rome's founding emperor inside his own home.

Palatine and palace: it was a metaphor that never died. Ovid, in Rome and with a guarded irony, compared it to the home of the gods. Then, in exile, he imagined more of what had not quite arrived in the age of Augustus but was rapidly on its way. The new architecture – of place and mind – came from the needs of autocracy and from the east, where autocracy was the only way to rule. Apollo's prophets looked out eastwards. When ambassadors from Judaea met advisers of Augustus to partition the kingdom of Herod the Great, the easterners must have felt much more at home in Apollo's temple, architecturally and politically, than were the hosts. The public space in front of the palace had room for some 8,000 Jews opposing Herod's complex plan of succession.

Much of what later became familiar as Roman architecture was then wholly new in Rome. The marble oxen on Apollo's walls were as though alive. It was beautiful but treacherous political terrain. Good government required guides. Even Tiberius's mother said she never understood her son's jokes. There were no guides paid at public expense. In 17 CE one of Lucius's less successful brothers, Quintus, lost his status as a senator in a purge of those too poor for their place. Another, Aulus, survived quietly and gained the status of a minor gourmet. Under the republic the succession to the consuls who ran Rome, however corruptly conducted, was clear and by election. Under the Emperor Tiberius, success and failure came from a cloud of imperial will and routine, a haze that the Vitellii had to see through or die.

PART TWO

High in a high tree, safe at ease,
A happy Crow held stolen cheese,
Till on the ground a flattering Fox
Knew just the way to fill his lunch box.
'Darling, how fine are your feathers of black,
How divine your face and your shining back.
If only just a little you could sing,
You'd have no rival on the wing.'
Then she, too eager to display
Her beauty in the vocal way,
Let go the cheese of luscious taste,
Which Foxy seized with glutton's haste.

Phaedrus (first century CE)

10

THE FOX AND THE CROW

While the Vitellii and their rivals manoeuvred their way around the Palatine, surviving present dangers and thinking how to survive the future, there was one man keeping a written record. It was not a direct history of this time. It was instead a rejection of the reality of that, even its possibility. The fables by a writer who called himself Phaedrus were guides to the problems of court life. They looked as though they were for children, certainly to later readers and probably at the time. They starred animals and servants. They were seemingly simple stories about dogs and underdogs in the voice of an underdog, slave stories maybe written by a slave but maybe someone aping that role. No one was ever quite sure.

Phaedrus adapted Greek stories, the already famous fables of Aesop, and invented his own. He translated Greek, but like all the great poets of Rome he made them Roman as well as mere translations. His characters ranged from dogs to frogs, mice to lions, and from courtiers to the emperor himself. The settings were in both town and country. Food and flattery were their persistent themes, the way that they were intertwined and how they explained the world.

Aesop had been his own man of mystery, a captured slave from a golden age of writing some 500 years before, contemporary with the best-known philosophers and playwrights but given only the barest outlines of a character himself. He was said to have been a very ugly member of a great Greek household, a stutterer and clown who won his freedom by his art.

Perhaps he was. Comedy from the weak, both mocking and flattering the powerful, has a persistent history. The story of Aesop's road to freedom may have been in itself a fable. His origins as a slave, if true, would have allowed his life story to be fabricated by anyone in as much as anyone might care to tell it at all. Aesop was either an imaginative man or an imagined man, an inventive genius or a gatherer of tales by others. It was a long time since anyone had known.

Phaedrus was more imaginative than imagined. His identity was concealed, but he existed somewhere in or around the court of Tiberius. He understood the ways of survival for the weak among the strong, some of the weapons which the weak have and which the strong lack. He may not have known much more about Aesop's life than Aristotle did. What he did know, much more importantly than any facts of biography, was that Aesop's work had been successful. It told neglected truths. Just as Roman poets had adapted the sexual torments of Sappho for the age of Julius Caesar and the heroism of Homer for Augustus, Phaedrus adapted Aesop for the reign of Tiberius.

One of the best-known of all Aesop's fables was *The Fox and the Crow*. A hungry fox is at the bottom of a tree looking at a crow on one of the highest branches with some stolen cheese in its beak. The fox is not a climber. He will never reach the top of the tree. Instead he flatters the crow, calling it glossy and glamorous, worthy to be king of all the birds if its voice were as sweet as its looks. When the thieving bird lets out a caw to prove its perfection, the cheese falls to be eaten by the fox.

Various lessons could be learnt from this – about the credulity, stupidity and insecurity of those at the tops of trees, about the necessary cunning of those at the bottom. A piece of flattery, skilfully delivered, was certainly a useful way for a flatterer to be fed. No real harm was done. The fox was hungry, the crow one of the least musical of birds. The cheese was stolen anyway. It was a gentle story of ordinary life.

Aesop's fables of very human beasts – the *Frogs Who Wanted a King* and *Why Dogs Lick Their Arses* – preached good sense and proportion while pricking the pride of the pompous. *The Goose who Laid the Golden Egg* was a warning to the reader to recognise when he was lucky. A Greek philosopher of Tiberius's time both praised Aesop's power and likened it to the art of simple food: 'Like those who eat well off the plainest dishes, he used humble events to teach great truths, and after serving up a fable he adds to it the advice to do a thing or not to do it.'

'Aesop', the philosopher went on, 'was really more attached to truth than the poets are; for the latter do violence to their own stories in order to make them probable; but he, by announcing a story which everyone knew not to be true, told the truth by the very fact that he did not claim to be relating real events.' In the new age of emperors, these fantasy characters in fables delivered their messages about real life not in the Greek of slaves and the elite but in the Latin of the Romans in the street.

Phaedrus, like Aesop, was said himself to be a former slave, freed by Augustus and probably around thirty years old at Augustus's death. That was all. Whether in Greek or Latin, there was no more need for a writer to record the life of a fabulist than the life of a cook. Whoever he was, his work presented an accomplished variety of different faces: poet, reporter, preacher, accomplished ironist. In five books of fables he warned against listening too much to fabulists, including too much to the tale-teller known as Phaedrus. He prefaced his Latin version of *The Fox and the Crow* with the warning against flattery for both its subject and object, the human fox as much as the human crow. As a writer of his age he was a realist. He focused on what went on.

Horace, the poet whom Augustus had wanted in his court as a personal secretary, also knew the story. He used it to warn against both the smooth-talking and the open-mouthed, the vain and the over-reaching. But Horace, writing from his rural retreat, was read only by the elite; Phaedrus, whoever he really was, was for everyone.

11

WHO KILLED THE PRINCE?

Four years after the near-catastrophe on the northern German shore, Publius was a lucky man with a career still on the rise. He was back in Rome and in the service of Germanicus again. The difference this time was that Germanicus was dead, last seen on duty in distant Antioch, and Publius was prosecuting the man accused as his killer. To have won the brief was already a sign of his status; it was an honour to champion the heir who, even more so after his mysterious end, was a popular hero. It was also an assignment that could be the ruin of himself, and maybe his family too, as surely as if he had lost his legions in the sea.

The accused was Gnaeus Calpurnius Piso, a close friend of Tiberius, one of those whom Augustus was once rumoured to have seen as his best successor. The law court was in the senate house, the *curia*, at the foot of the Capitol hill. Behind it was the *carcer*, the prison, where the condemned might be strangled if the prosecutor won a guilty verdict. Above them both wound the notorious Groaning Steps from the summit, a mythical place of public humiliation for the damned. The people of Rome were already showing their interest in the case. There were crowds on the plateau at the top of the hill from where the body of the convicted man might be pushed and pulled, tumbling down these steps before being hurled by hook into the Tiber.

The *curia* was intimidating to lawyer and defendant alike, in some parts like a bare cell, in others like a temple and a luxurious dining room. Beneath Publius's feet were bright mosaics, roses, sheaves of corn and horns of plenty. At the end of the rectangular room, eighty feet away, was a statue of Victory standing on a globe, offering a wreath of triumph, representing the result of the sea battle that had brought the Caesars to power fifty years before.

Plain plaster covered the walls above his head. Marble shone on the sections below. On three broad steps, some fifty feet wide, sat several hundred senators of Rome, their togas striped in purple, their slippers red. This was a day on which Tiberius was affecting the role of just another one of his peers, one judge among many. Publius was dressed in the same way, as a civilian not a soldier, arguing for his future, not fighting for it, navigating a political terrain that was no less perilous than that distant sea.

The brief was not simple. It comprised both the facts surrounding Germanicus's death in October, 19 CE, few of them clear, and what Tiberius wanted the facts to show, a fact that was even less clear. Tiberius could have taken the case for judgment inside the *domus Caesaris*, but he had not. Publius would have preferred to know the emperor's preferred verdict before he began, but he did not. He was in the kind of trap that was becoming ever more dangerous in court politics. He had to present the illusion of being free, the appearance of being in a traditional trial when only the appearance was left.

Was Tiberius pleased that Germanicus was no longer a rival? Had he perhaps even ordered Germanicus's poisoning in distant Antioch? Or was he displeased that he had lost a popular heir since now he had to organise a succession to himself without the prop of Augustus behind him?

The jury on the marble benches was like a painting designed to trick the eye, like the mosaic floor whose corn and fruit seemed solid, almost real. He could see all the senators, but only one of them stood out. The only mind that mattered was the mind that was hardest to read.

If Tiberius was pleased at Germanicus's death, did he want to appear so? Probably not. If he was displeased, did he want to appear vengeful against the assassin? Possibly. Publius's task was to steer through quicksands that made the seas of Germany seem kind. It would have tested the skills of Rome's greatest advocates and flatterers of juries from the past. And Publius was no such man.

Everything about the trial showed how much had changed in the five years since Augustus's death. When Publius had served in

Germany with Germanicus, he had been there as one of the new heir's supporters and friends. But when Germanicus had moved on to govern the entire east of the empire, Tiberius had provided his own choice of helper, a friend, a rival according to some, a man who was also a minder.

The company of Piso had not been welcome to Germanicus. Piso and his wife, Plancina, were supremely grand and self-confident, a vivid reminder of the years of aristocratic independence that Augustus had steered towards its end. Tiberius had promoted him both to share his heir's administrative responsibilities and to keep a close eye on his plans, anxious to ensure that Germanicus and Agrippina, Augustus's direct descendants, including their eight-year-old-son Caligula, did not find further ambition within themselves while their emperor was alive.

It had been a perilous pairing from the start. Piso, as Tiberius well knew, was ambitious for himself. Plancina was a close friend of Livia, the matriarch of the Julio-Claudians but a Claudian first. Piso's elder son held the rank of Tiberius's personal quaestor, a junior position which bound the holder in loyalty for life. Piso's family was filled with long-standing supporters of the Claudians, of Livia, her son Tiberius, and Tiberius's son Drusus. Even after Germanicus's death, Piso had exuded confidence, sailing slowly back to Rome as though on a holiday cruise, holding a great feast for his friends in 20 CE on his return.

As he climbed the steps to the *curia* Publius could have been forgiven for his fear. He was about to prosecute Piso, one of the highest representatives of the respectability to which his own family aspired, a man whom Tiberius might have deliberately used to solve his own family problem. The Vitellii, like others senior to them in the court, needed to recognise force, counter-force and rapid change. So too did Blandus, who had reached the consulship in the previous year, not as grand as Piso or even the Vitellii, but advancing in his own courtly way. Tiberius's mother, Livia, was still a power in her own right. The Vitellii owed their allegiance to her as much as to him. That was one of the simpler of their divided loyalties.

*

Publius had swum for five years in these shifting political currents. Barely had he returned from Germany before the household was filled with rumours that Germanicus was eyeing an early succession, or that his friends were plotting on his behalf, or that the emperor feared that they were. Germanicus left again for Egypt and was acclaimed in worshipful terms as a saviour of the human race by the people of Alexandria. His rejection of the honour was not firm enough for Tiberius, who soon wanted Germanicus further out of his sight, though not beyond his oversight. Piso had been part of his solution, or so it was believed by many.

Then suddenly, and in faraway Syria amid one of many quarrels with Piso, Germanicus was gone. The distant death, its news delayed, confused and lurid, convulsed the court, the senate and the army. There was silence in the streets, a cessation of business, pleasure and all the buzz and hum of the city. The heir was lost, but it was as though a great battle had been lost, legions sacrificed and poison were passing through every house. Agrippina brought back her husband's ashes in an elaborate ceremony. There was even a rare public appearance by Germanicus's brother, Claudius, a stumbling, shambling figure but still a presence to remind watchers of their mother, Antonia, the bloodline of Augustus.

Tiberius did not react immediately. He did not have Piso arrested, or brought back by palace guardsmen. The guard captain, Sejanus, was himself thought to be involved but no one knew exactly how. Piso's slow cruise was allowed to continue. When the silence of the people turned to rumblings around the Groaning Steps, a trial seemed a necessary minimum response. But that did not make necessary a guilty verdict.

This was going to be neither a trial before the people nor a secret trial within the *domus Caesaris*. Tiberius had given judicial responsibilities to the senate soon after taking the throne and this was to be a senate trial, announced on the day after Piso's return, the morning after his welcome banquet for himself. The floor of his great dining hall was hardly cleared before Piso knew of the threat, also that the trial would not be hurried, that he had time to prepare his defence, and that there was a good possibility of acquittal before a jury of his peers.

For Publius there was time too for assembling evidence. As a friend of Germanicus he had formed a firm view of what had happened in Syria, but for his role as a prosecutor facts were few. Piso had not been with Germanicus in Antioch on the hot summer day when he died. That did not make him innocent. If he and Plancina had already poisoned him, or previously arranged his poisoning, that would have been merely wise.

Piso had certainly celebrated when he heard the news of the death, garlanding his ships and holding days of on-board banquets for his friends. But it was well known that each man would have been happy at the death of the other. Antioch was a diseased and dangerous place.

There was no doubt that Piso was a proud and ambitious man, one of those who both fully recognised the legitimacy of the emperor and did not accept that a successor had forever to be a Julio-Claudian. This would be perilous territory to cover in open court. Even in the quietest corridors of the palace it was best put in code.

Everyone who mattered knew that Piso had quarrelled with Germanicus about power and precedence, about relations with local kingdoms and who was responsible for them. He had mocked when Germanicus and Agrippina flattered the Athenian crowd and accepted heavy gold crowns from the king of Parthia. He had disagreed even about kingdoms whose existence was unknown to most in Rome, exotic names like Commagene, which had become part of Roman Syria, and Armenia, which had not. Any border on a map or banquet in a tent had the potential to enrage.

The charges covered not just the death of Germanicus but the disrespect to Germanicus's authority and division of their army into rival factions. Publius could persuasively charge that Piso had relaxed military discipline to win the loyalty of the local legions, paying imperial bonuses under his own name, encouraging Pisoniani to spar with Caesariani. These were serious accusations. Plancina was personally imperious and vicious, a mistress of magic arts. Whether Piso was a murderer was harder to turn into a charge.

But whether he was a murderer mattered much less than what Tiberius, whose seat in the senate was as visible as his motives were opaque, most wanted him to be.

Popular anger against Piso and Plancina was already intense, enflamed by long and loyal support for Germanicus and new sympathy for Agrippina. Piso's ornate Palatine house, impossible to hide, was an added incitement to the resentful. Many still thought that the accused would escape. Tiberius had allowed Piso every possible legal help, a signal that he was seeking an acquittal.

The emperor seemed more confident with his heir gone. He gave a generous reward to the poet Clutorius Priscus for a panegyric safely praising Germanicus's posthumous virtues. Observers of Tiberius's moods, schooled by six years in which this was the currency of their lives, noted his pleasure at the birth of his twin grandsons to Drusus and his wife, brothers to the teenage Julia whom Augustus had asked of as he died. Their arrival in the world had come on the same day as Germanicus's departure.

12

THE ONLY VERDICT THAT MATTERED

Publius Vitellius was about to speak to a brief for which life had prepared him well. He had spent time with Germanicus in Syria, as he had in Germany. He had shared the easy familiarity of military life. For three months he had been collecting evidence against Piso and Plancina and preparing an indictment. He could say that he himself had seen signs of poison on Germanicus's body and had arranged to send to Rome a local poisoner as a potential witness, Martina, a close friend of Plancina.

All this he was preparing to argue to Piso's fellow senators. Among the people of Rome this was a popular cause in support of the prince whose troops he had led to near-disaster on the German beaches; on the Palatine it was a perilous risk. It was possible that Tiberius wanted not only Germanicus dead but Piso saved. No one could be sure. Publius's risk was a risk too for all the Vitellii. One brother, Quintus, was disgraced by extravagance. Another, Aulus, was beginning to earn the glutton's reputation that would later stick to his nephew – and then to the whole family. Only Lucius was quietly climbing the household ladder.

Piso's defence, due to be made a week after the case for the prosecution, was to be led by serious figures, the kind whom Augustus, when he had been thinking of a successor from outside his family, had considered for the throne itself. Piso's supporters were a powerful alliance of the senatorial old guard, even though many of his most distinguished friends had refused to join. On the question of the poisoning, the case for Piso was strong. Although Agrippina believed that her husband had been murdered and Germanicus, she said, had believed so himself, evidence was slight, the accounts of the killing implausible and divergent.

Publius's speech for the prosecution would be the last of three, the summation of the charges at the end of two days of evidence. Though an eloquent climax, he hoped, it was never going to be impregnable. There was barely a dispute about Piso's contempt for Germanicus, his encouragement of divisions between Pisoniani and Caesariani, the promotion of the worst soldiers, who called him 'father of the legions', and punishment of the best, particularly Germanicus's friends. But while serious for a charge of sedition, it did not prove murder.

Nor did celebratory banquets prove Piso's guilt, still less the stories that he had opened up temples to allow others to celebrate. Much of the evidence from the first two prosecutors had been of extortion in Spain, common enough in a Roman trial to denigrate a man's character but of no relevance to the case. Unless Piso was a master revolutionary, aiming to bring down the whole system of rule by the Caesars, the principal advantage from a crime of murder would come to Tiberius's own son and grandchildren. Piso might have had his dreams of a new imperial house, headed by himself and continuing for his own heirs, but none of these points of succession were ones that could be discussed in the open.

Publius could not prove the poisoning. He had no last-minute evidence. His star witness, Plancina's friend Martina, had not survived the journey, poisoned either by her own hand or that of another whose identity was unknown. He could put before the senators only the discovery of body parts, the name Germanicus on charms pierced by nails and the paraphernalia of witchcraft by his bed.

As he began his speech, as the senators listened with due concentration, Publius did not advance anyone's understanding of the facts. As he stared down at the mosaic floor, turned sideways to the bare walls, gesturing with his hands in the way that orators were taught, he changed nothing. Gradually, however, watching not too obviously for Tiberius to indicate whether he would stand by his friend or let him fall, Publius saw that he was on the right side.

Piso watched Tiberius too. Tiberius sat still. He was as silent as the streets had been when the news of Germanicus's death reached Rome. Piso read the same signs as his prosecutor and saw that he was abandoned. The people outside the senate had already decided – and for once they would have their way. Lest Tiberius should be in any doubt of their view, the rumbling band of demonstrators had dragged a statue of Piso up to the Capitol, ready to be smashed, dismembered and hurled down the Groaning Steps.

On the morning after Publius's closing statement, Piso was found with his throat cut and a sword beside his body. The last person to have seen him alive was his wife, unless someone else had entered his room to create the appearance of a suicide. A sword, it could be thought, was an unwieldy weapon with which to slit one's own throat, but a judgment of suicide brought the justice that was required. It proved his guilty conscience and helped his family's inheritance of his property. Tiberius's mother successfully pleaded the innocence of her friend Plancina.

After the trial came the phantoms of promotion, property and pretence. A priesthood came to Publius as a mark of the emperor's and the public's approval. He had done a good job. He had been as eloquent as was desirable in the Rome of the emperors, where minds did not need to be moved. The Vitellii had a new honour for their rising family, one of the old honours that still had a purpose under the rule of the Palatine.

The dead Piso was condemned for treason. The public popularity of Germanicus, the enthusiasm of the crowd at the Groaning Steps, made that a popular move. Tiberius did not want to encourage the exercise of the popular will but would enjoy it when it suited him. Piso's family was spared the forfeiture of assets and guilt by association that might have come to them. The men called Piso did not fall far.

The principal problem for the *domus Caesaris* was how to present for the future a legal case which, unlike most of the dramas within the household, had been a play on the stage of the whole Roman Empire. The legions and the provincial leaders were still restless about the fate of Germanicus and what it might mean for themselves.

The result was the most sacred and permanent trial record that Roman craftsmen could produce. Words that had once been sounds in the Palatine air became engravings on tablets of bronze. Every big city in the empire and every camp where the legions spent their winters was to have a detailed account of Piso's trial, the case brought by Publius Vitellius, the virtue shown by Tiberius, the gratitude due to him and his own heirs now that Germanicus and the iniquitous Piso were dead. The rule of Caesar's house for the future, and the principle of heredity within it, was set out not in nods and nudges but in letters of tin fused with copper, the traditional formula for the permanence of law.

On bright-polished tablets more than a metre wide, placed where parts would survive for 2,000 years, was a new version of both a past and an eternity. First, the name of Tiberius was joined with that of Augustus in public gratitude for ending civil war, a role in which Tiberius himself had played no part bar the suppression of some legionary revolts over pay. Secondly, Tiberius was hailed as the paragon of old Roman virtue, of justice, clemency and greatness of spirit, *magnitudo animi*. Germanicus became a hero of all time. An arch would stand in his honour in Germany, the land whose River Rhine he had defended for Rome and whose Roman victims he had avenged. Thirdly, Tiberius's descendants were to stand in line to succeed. Tiberius was not merely emperor, but the father and grandfather of emperors. His son Drusus, an infamous drunk, stood newly and clearly next in line. After him would come his grandsons, twins, Tiberius and Tiberius Gemellus, born on the day of Germanicus's death.

This *Senatus consultum de Pisone*, the decision of the senate in the case of Piso, was Tiberius's answer, brazen in every sense, to the lists of 'What I achieved in my life' outside Augustus's mausoleum. It said who would continue the work which the son of Julius Caesar had begun. Bronze stood for what was genuine, true and needing to be obeyed. As Ovid had observed (he had died in exile three years before), bronze was a medium of threat as well as information.

Not everyone would read the tablet's words, tightly inscribed as in a dedication to a deity. Many soldiers and citizens could read nothing. But they could hear and they could know. They could know what had happened in the recent past and how they should think and speak about their emperor in the eternal future.

The last words of the announcement noted that one of its authors was the son of Lucius's sister Vitellia, Aulus Plautius, who was a personal quaestor for Tiberius alongside the forgiven son of the reviled Piso. Lucius needed a careful response to his brother's role in Piso's trial.

He had to adjust his balance. He had long watched over Germanicus's interests at Rome while assuring Tiberius that any succession by Augustus's choice of heir would be both far off and part of the natural order of the house. Tiberius's personal soothsayer had helpfully agreed. Germanicus's death had brought an end to this order.

But for Lucius the adjustment of balance did not mean precipitately changing sides. The message of the tablets was clear, but a story was still just a story. He did not abandon the family of Germanicus, the prospects of Agrippina and the battered – but still surviving – hopes of her children to inherit in the future.

Publius was more impatient. The loss of Germanicus left a personal gap in his life. He sought a new standard-bearer to replace the one he had lost. Sejanus was the prime candidate, and not for Publius Vitellius alone.

13

TIBERIUS, TIBER AND TIBUR

On the Palatine no courtier would likely be hungry. The fox's cheese or the meat of a dog stood for what might be gained by flattery, a metaphor more than a meal. Not far away, however, it was a different story. Empty stomachs were a mass misery. Rome's food supply was frail. Whatever the boosters of Italy might write, or even think, its land was not able to feed and water its cities.

Essential food came from abroad. There was no alternative at a time of rising populations and unproductive farms. Water needed aqueducts if the fresh streams high above Rome were not to become useless mud before they reached the city. The provision of both required economic and political instincts that Tiberius lacked.

Transport by sea was much cheaper than by land. But when corn came by ship from Sicily and Africa, supply was vulnerable to weather in distant fields and stormy seas. Augustus knew how grain shortages threatened hunger and unrest. He twice faced famine in his reign, worst in 6 CE, when he had publicly had to send his slaves into the countryside, order the senate into indefinite recess and double the grain rations for the starving who stayed in the city.

Augustus encouraged the freeing of slaves for loyal service and exceptional talent, promoting small businesses and farms. He stimulated the circulation of cash throughout the country by building roads and aqueducts as well as temples. On succeeding to be the head of a household that was also a government, Tiberius's first policy was massively to cut expenditure, winning praise from conservatives in the senate who took a similar approach on their own estates. A follower of Augustus's will abroad, he did the opposite at home. The result for Rome was a reduction in paid employment and opportunities for commerce with no gain in the security of food and water.

The death of Germanicus opened a window on to what was happening both near and far beyond the court. In Rome the people began protesting, not just about the fate of their hero but against sharp rises in the price of corn. Tiberius was content, when it suited him, to flatter the men and women of the Forum that he cared about their views on the guilt of Piso. He was compelled, whether he liked it or not, to keep the citizens fed.

The Romans around the Groaning Steps, pushing Piso's marble head and hands, were hungry as well as angry. This was a dangerous combination, the hunger a ready fuse for rage. The Vitellii and their rivals needed to understand that, to balance flattery of Tiberius for their own survival against telling truth to power. The closer the courtiers stood to the object of their obsession, the less close they were to what was happening outside. No one had to travel far to see the problem, but it was safer for most to keep their eyes on Tiberius than on the people he ruled.

Gaius Rubellius Blandus was a slightly different kind of courtier, a man from just outside Rome whose final name meant smooth and obsequious, a good start for his journey through life. Even more useful was the place where he lived, Tibur, the future Tivoli, fifteen miles to the north-east of the Palatine, a place for luxury but also for reflection, with a spa, a marketplace and a university.

The success of the Vitellii was already part of a pattern. Other provincial families were following the same route by which wealthy fathers secured seats in the senate for their sons, and the sons picked their way through the dangers of Rome. Blandus's family had never been able to boast a consulship but, as a smooth-talking companion, a rare friend whom Tiberius liked and trusted, he had become a consul of the previous year. He had a base sufficiently close to Rome to do his job, but sufficiently far away to see something of the countryside.

Tibur was the city's resort for the rich, closer than Nola and the towns around Vesuvius where Augustus had ended his life. Just as the Palatine gave its name to future palaces, so did Tivoli become a label for future gardens of entertainment. Romans with homes in Tibur boasted of a paradise, a place for extracting Italy's finest water, as well as its fashionable limestone, Tiburtine, which, under the name Travertine, became sought after across the empire.

Before marble floors and walls were common in Rome they were the glory of Tibur. There was local food and wine as well as water, welcoming relief from city sounds, smells and responsibilities. Mosaic floors in the Greek style looked like the remains of a banquet, bones scattered among scales and claws. Men dined to the illusion of walking among prawn shells, broken fins and backbones.

Tibur's greatest glory was the river on which it stood. The Anio's bright streams fed apple trees on the heights, falling spectacularly for some eighty feet before crashing through pools to the figs and plums below. Its drinking water was famed and smelt of orchards. At the bridge below Tibur the Anio waters were fresh and bitter, astringent to the skin of those who bathed in it, settling to the stomachs of those who drank.

Tibur's water was as much needed at Rome as the food from its markets and fields. As Blandus, or any traveller, could see, that same water became useless as slowly it turned towards the sewers that led to the sea. Rome's demands were growing fast. Even in good times there was never enough and, even on the Palatine itself, Rome lacked all the water that it needed as it grew. The bitter, clear clouds that cascaded in Tibur were wasted into the sweet, brown Tiber before they could reach the baths, still less the luxurious dining rooms and cramped kitchens, of the capital of the empire.

Aqueducts were not yet a symbol of Rome, were too few and, for the taste of Tiberius, too high in cost. In the interests of the city, a mountain spring needed to flow into a basin with other springs, then flow on not as a torrent but gently, metre by metre, down slow inclines, raised on high arches or buried in tunnels. Rome's first aqueduct, the *Appia*, built by the man who constructed its first road, had carried water from springs south-east of Tibur for 300 years. Six others followed, financed by conquest, but failing to match the demand.

Tibur, Tiber and Tiberius were joined by more than their names in the murky history of Latin. They were linked in a chain of poor information and difficult decisions. The assessors of the Palatine had to balance the water-needs of city people and country farmers, taxing the producers' profits, securing grain at reasonable cost for the Roman poor and the army when imports were impeded. It was a very modern challenge with no modern tools. Grants, licences and regulations struggled against water-theft and all the tricks of grain producers who hoarded in times of scarcity.

In the year of Germanicus's death, and Publius Vitellius's survival in the courts, a journey to Tibur was a better chance to learn about politics than a walk across the Forum. In fields to the east stood hot blue bathing pools where sulphur belched from the sand. To its west the rocks were dry except in winter. On either side of the road to Rome stood a story of struggle very different from that seen in the senate or on Capitol hill. The harvest had failed. Where there was food, there was not enough and the price was too high. Gaius Rubellius Blandus had a view less easily seen by Publius and Lucius Vitellius, men inside the household and looking ever further in.

In good times Tibur's markets amid its temples and villas were packed, its long hillside loved by leisure-seekers for its air and water-falls, but also by farmers for its access to Rome. It was the crowded gateway from the Apennine mountains to the capital's countryside. Its presiding god was Hercules, not in his role as clubber of monsters but as guardian of the herdsmen who moved their flocks, as regular as the seasons, between the low ground and the high.

Lambs and goats moved through Tibur in rich flocks. In Tibur the sellers sold grain from everywhere. Fruit and vegetables were the local crop, from salad gardens whose produce needed buyers while it was fresh, small fields whose owners made big profits and whose customers were well fed. When food and money flowed freely over Tibur's trading floor, coins with the heads of Augustus and his family preached the necessity of the *domus Caesaris* for the safety to eat, drink and spend. A shopper's bag of denarii commemorated the worship of *Divus Augustus*, emphasising the importance not just of a palace but of a holy house, the *domus divina* of the Palatine. The security of the *res publica* was inextricably enmeshed with the security of the *domus divina*. But when food and money did not flow, nothing was secure.

14

HERCULES THE HERDSMAN

In his youth in his home town, before any journey down on to the Palatine, Blandus knew where to find out what the court needed to know. The market in Tibur stretched down, stall by stall, over winding paths past the country houses of some of the greatest men of Rome. A patient traveller, one like Blandus who was known to all, would know ever more as he descended.

At the highest point was the broadest terrace with the best views, not the finest house in the town but probably the largest, fifteen flat acres from which to look down on the capital. It belonged to the family of Quinctilius Varus, pioneer courtier of Augustus and successful looter of Syria who would be forever known for losing his legions in the Teutoburg forest. Publius Vitellius had almost lost his life and reputation thanks to Quinctilius Varus. The Quinctilii Vari still had their clients and their farms, sources of vegetables and fruit regardless of any standing, or lack of it, at court. Varus's son was a rival of Blandus and the Vitellii, part of the club of young men making their way but not one who caused much disquiet.

Further down there were shrines to Faunus and to the fire goddess, Vesta, both divinities traditionally entwined with Rome. On the next levels sat a temple to the water nymphs, friezes of bulls' heads and flowers, hibiscus and fruit, the market office itself, tables of measures and weights, marble bowls for corn and oil. Traders bought and sold under the still, stern gaze of Augustus, seated as if in a chapel of his personal divinity. The richest of them had built a market temple to mark their emperor's return from a trip on which they feared he might die. One of them ensured that his name be carved where the corn was weighed.

Gaius Rubellius Blandus knew the great and the lesser of Tibur, the titans of the Capitol as well as the traders in carrots and corn and the priests who predicted the future. He was a modest man with a family interest in the local temples and antiquities. His grandfather had taught rhetoric to politicians, but had not used his arts on his own behalf. His father had briefly governed Crete, one of the lowest posts in the imperial service.

The proudest concern of the Rubellii sprawled over the next level on the downward path, the restored local temple which Hercules, protector of herdsmen, killer of animal giants, half man and half god, had dedicated during his labours on earth. This Hercules ensured the provision of milk, cheese and yoghurt, as well as the commemoration of his famous labours. Through every known age, stretched across the landscape, it had stared down on visitors from Rome, the first to greet them and accept their favours, the last to bid them goodbye.

Augustus once pillaged its treasury to pay his troops. But that, like so much strife, was safely buried in the recent past. Augustus had become a Hercules, demi-god of trade and prosperity brought by peace. For the Rubellii the temple was the pride of Tibur, his family's restoration its own greatest pride.

Gaius Rubellius Blandus was not an exceptional man. He began his courtly career as a reliable friend at Tibur, additionally rich from family land beside a very different river in the province of Africa, a good companion, lightly flattering as befitted his family name, *blandus* being a favourite word of the love poets, and used by Ovid for flattery to the goddess of love herself. As a consul he held an office more of honour than power. As an orator he was more smooth than forceful. As an historian he was no more than an antiquary.

The local came first. The Rubellii were leaders among the old Tibur families, provincial in the eyes of the Roman aristocracy but proud that Tibur had been a town with its own ancient sibyl, prophesying to kings when Rome was mere mud, an enemy of Rome when Rome was struggling to survive. The Rubellii were grander than the Vitellii in their provincial origins but milder in their ambitions. All of the senior members had the additional name, Blandus, not a description of which to be ashamed in the new age.

Blandus was a regular traveller on the routes to the capital. Beyond the temple the road ran straight towards the single bridge across the Anio, then south and west to Rome, the start of a journey which, while suburban, was notoriously wild even at a time without famine. The poet Propertius, dead for thirty years, once a careful critic of Augustus but, like so many a convert to flattery, famously weighed its delights and dangers. On the one hand there was the anticipation of sex with his mistress; on the other a landscape of lost paths, muggers and wild dogs. Propertius in his poem travelled to Tibur from Rome for sex; when Blandus travelled the other way, from Tibur to Rome, he was answering the calls of power, service for a year in a minor office in the imperial mint and as one of the public magistrates allocated to the *domus Caesaris*. That was how he came to know Tiberius, who found him agreeable and invited him as a companion on military manoeuvres.

Walkers descended either past the lakes and quarries already abandoned as a lost antiquity, or more steeply and directly through the stinking sulphur ponds either side of the main road. Those who were more relaxed might take the more gradual decline through fields and small farms which, when the city was smaller, had produced its food. Like most of the rest of Italy, ruled from the resorts around Naples and Rome, the farmers along the way had little in common with the luxury of Nola, Nuceria or Tibur.

For 400 years, food and politics had been indissoluble at Rome, in bribes and on stage, in farce and as brutal force. The Forum was a food market before it was a centre for politics. There were many early *fora*, for meat and fish and vegetables as well as rhetoric. *Fora* for wine and luxuries followed quickly on.

Starvation was a weapon and feasting a still-remembered political reward. The earliest feasts, at Tibur as elsewhere, were visible to the many, created and consumed in the open. They were political. They displayed power – over peoples near and far. Ambitious politicians, their coffers filled from eastern conquest, saw the benefit of banquets for votes at home.

The collapse of the states created by Alexander the Great brought into Rome for the first time bronze couches, tapestries in purple and gold and tables on pedestals of marble. Greek slaves revolutionised Roman banquets. Guests came to expect more elaborate meals prepared by skilled chefs, served by elegant waiters, and accompanied by girls who played the harp. Cooking used to be done in Rome by the lowest orders of a great house, but now it came to be looked upon as art, divided among specialists who saw themselves as proudly distinctive, one from another, as members of an orchestra: the man who made the white bread would no more make the brown than a flautist would play the drums.

These changes happened very quickly. Within a generation, the flow of money and slaves generated by Rome's wars changed Roman political competition. Established politicians who were too old to take command in one of these lucrative campaigns had no hope of matching the glory, wealth and popularity of successful younger men. The losers could only contrast their supposed fidelity to traditional Roman virtues with the love of luxury that these young warlords displayed.

For the winners liberality became a signature virtue, a proof of power. Julius Caesar, characteristically, made his own personal impact. His public banquet to mark one of his earliest offices, in 65 BCE, ensured that no one remembered again the efforts of his predecessors. At the feast to mark his third consulship in 46 BCE, two years before his assassination, he for the first time presented four different wines at every table. More than 100,000 dined on lampreys, eel-like delicacies gathered by supporters for whom catering became a critical political art. Whether the food was fish or fowl, it was important that the sudden demands for banqueting did not create shortages and higher prices in other parts of the market.

Caesar himself, who presided wearing bright costume and garlands of flowers, left a legacy of feasting which his successors had to match and adapt and sometimes curb if the custom risked public disorder. Tiberius, to celebrate a military victory in almost his final act as heir to the throne, gave a public banquet on 1,000 tables.

Curbs on public largesse were never popular. By the time that Tiberius was emperor, 'The Inspector of Morals' was the title of a play for holidays. Its central character was one to be mocked. No one liked the feast-inspector. Any banquet was a modest economic redistribution, and the people did not appreciate official curtailment of the menu in the cause of improving their characters.

Food had to be the first demand of politics. Flattery was a way to being fed. Cooks consolidated their status as artists. Companies of cooks made their owners as rich as any men in Rome. A man called Cestius, a member of the priesthood that oversaw public banquets, built himself a pyramid fit for a minor pharaoh. Eurysaces the baker had a tomb that elaborated every part of his trade as though he were a conqueror.

The poor took whatever they could get. It was a responsibility of the emperor to ensure that the voters of Rome should at least have bread. At any time, dangerous hunger might be only a few days of failure away. The wisest of the court kept that truth close to the top of their minds. Some knew when choice between cheeses was possible, when it was too costly and when shortages of everything, even starvation, loomed. Others were more concerned with how banqueting advanced their own interests, others still with how their behaviour might look to those who were hungry. The loaded plates, like every other part of politics, began to disappear indoors, joining the pleasures of those very many, not to be forgotten, who always preferred to live out of the public gaze. Notorious among the conquerors content without politics was Lucius Licinius Lucullus, pillager of Pontus in 70 BCE, who became an early Roman to gain a bad Vitellian reputation for fine dining, finally falling into a fatal insanity and leaving as his legacy his gardens of eastern cherries.

15

CARE FOR CUCUMBERS

The gastronomic rules of the court were unpredictable. It was pious to praise the people of Italy for living modestly on corn and vegetables even when these were soon to become merely a banquet's 'first course'. It was prudent to eat the second and third courses if the emperor was doing the same.

As the heir to the throne, Tiberius had feasted the people but also curbed what he saw as excess in his dining rooms. His cooks served leftovers to those who had previously plotted over camel heels and roasted ostrich. He served only one side of a wild boar, saying that it contained every variety of meat that the other side did. As emperor he would have legislated to ban excess at banquets if he had not feared derision and a general ignoring of the law. He did, however, forbid the selling of pastries in the street.

One man's excess was another's proof of power. To be known as a gourmand at court might be a good thing. It showed discernment. A gourmand was one who asked the gods to give him a crane's neck so that he could savour delicacies the longest. Or so Aristotle had said, and Aristotle was much to be trusted. A glutton simply wanted to stay the longest at table. That was a crime even if its boundaries were hardly clear.

A man might have a good reputation for judging wine. Tiberius supported the principle of good vintages and bad, the discrimination that Caesar had introduced to the public with his four different flasks per table. He was not pleased when his soldiers on the Rhine had called him Biberius the imbiber. A reputation as a drunk meant more about a man than mere drink.

Tiberius's official favourite vegetable, as passed down by later writers, was the humble cucumber. His imperial luxury was to have it on his table at all seasons. His slaves used frames on wheels to catch the sun's heat at every time of day, moving the vegetable beds like patients in a care home, with sheets of sparkling mica, *lapis specularis*, as reflectors, thick mirror stones as blankets for the winter.

Augustus had had his little figs. Tiberius had his little cucumbers. Larger gourds were less attractive. Stuffed marrows signalled luxury, pumpkins an empty head and obsession with sex. Tiberius sensed the truth that the charge of gluttony was about more than food, that like sexual slurs it was an accusation of weakness and bad character. The glutton fish licked the leftovers tipped into the Tiber. A *tripatinium* of bass, lampreys and mixed fish was the height of sophistication. Lines of distinction were fine.

The language of eating was closely linked to sex in the Latin of the streets – and in grander literature too. A slow chewer was a slow sucker; a pot or ladle used by women in the kitchen was a ready metaphor for a vagina; butchery shared the verbs of buggery. Gluttony was a slur from the same vocabulary. It was always different from being a gourmand, an art only for the rich, or greediness, which everyone might like to enjoy. Gourmands could be addicts, obsessed with a rare fish or thrush to the exclusion of all else. But gluttony was a definition that extended beyond the table. It was a character flaw, a permanent part of a man.

The hungry were not always hungry. The fox in Phaedrus's fable saw a single chance. The crow deceived by flattery made a single mistake. But the glutton was always a glutton. Gluttony was persistent, shameful and a private vice shared only with other gluttons. To typify someone as a glutton was to accuse him of lacking a cool head and the sense of proportion and priority necessary for leadership. It meant laziness and thoughtlessness for the future.

Excess at the table was a charge that stood easily for other crimes but, most importantly, it would come to stand for the crime of political failure. Losing power was a far bigger fall than overeating, but lurid details of guzzling and vomiting would stay longer in later memories. Over the next fifty years the charge of gluttony was ever louder heard against those on the Palatine.

Phaedrus told a fable about a hard-working Hand and Foot who grew tired of being attached to a greedy Stomach. They decided to be slaves no longer. They deprived Stomach of food. Stomach rumbled, grumbled and then starved. Hand and Foot starved. By the time the limbs changed their mind, it was too late and all three were dead.

In Aesop's original version of the story Stomach succeeds in taunting Foot back to work. For Phaedrus, writing in imperial Rome, there was a harsher message about what happened when the greedy and the hungry grew too far apart.

16

VITELLIA'S NIGHT OUT

Vitellia, Aulus Vitellius's aunt, watched the success and failure of her four brothers from the house of her husband, Aulus Plautius, a former consul from a quarter of a century before, the suppressor of a minor slave revolt for Augustus. She was the mother of the son, also called Aulus Plautius, whose name was at the foot of the bronze tablets setting out the future of the empire.

Vitellia had only one name because that was still the style for women at Rome. Rule by the *domus Caesaris* helped some women to extend their household power over the empire, but it no more extended their names than it protected them from being abused in histories for lusting after sex and power. All Roman women, with very rare exceptions, had only one name, and Vitellia was very respectable but no grandee.

The little-recorded sister of Lucius and Publius Vitellius became briefly known only for attending a party in 21 CE. It was a poetry reading, the kind of event that Augustus had encouraged on the Palatine. But the poet on this occasion was not of the calibre of the great survivors of Latin poetry, not an Ovid, a Horace or a Virgil, but a writer of flattery-on-demand.

The man reading aloud his work at the party was the same Clutorius Priscus, lover of luxury food, beautiful eunuchs and profitable praise, who had benefited so well from his poem flattering the dead Germanicus. Vitellia's brother, Publius, had provided the prosecutorial prose against Piso, but Priscus had produced the poem.

Priscus was a star. After his first triumph he paid one of the highest-known prices for a eunuch, a much-desired sexual partner known as Paezon who had been the property of Sejanus. The poet next dreamt of being even closer to the centre of power, the laureate of the new age. With his new poem for Vitellia and her fellow guests Priscus was hoping to repeat his previous success and go further.

His chosen subject was not, however, dead. Nero Claudius Drusus was the son of Tiberius whose succession had been promised to the empire in bronze after the trial and death of Piso. He had been seriously sick but was still alive, and particularly alive to any real or imagined slight. This did not discourage Priscus. Despite his all-too-visible excesses at the dining table, Drusus was much doted upon by his father, and the prince's latest illness had been enough to remind Priscus that some well-prepared praise might be a good investment of his writing time. He needed words for every eventuality. A poem could not be produced at the speed of a poison or an emperor's whim.

Vitellia's party was an opportunity for testing lines and themes. Priscus's portrait of Drusus in words would, of course, be flattering. The young man's well-known drunkenness and ill temper would not have been part of the poem, much more his Homeric bravery in battle and his assured path to the immortals on gilded wings. That was the kind of verse that had won Priscus his first big pay day and might reasonably do so again if the right words were ready for the moment of grief.

If Priscus had restricted himself to preparation, all might have been well. His poem continuing the tradition of the great Greek praise-makers might even itself have survived, likening Drusus to stars and planets and the heroes of epic times. If Drusus had been newly dead, Priscus might have earned an even bigger reward than he had for Germanicus. Instead he read aloud a work in progress, a premature obituary which, however flattering, could never be flattering enough.

Vitellia and her friends were his audience. Everyone knew that Drusus was still among the living, that the poem was only a draft, but its imperfections were perhaps less obvious than its simple existence. Someone in the audience described the entertainment to someone who was outside. Someone outside passed the story on. Palace guards descended to interrogate the guests. Was the poem a proof that someone wanted Drusus dead? Or did such praise of the heir prove that someone wanted the emperor himself dead? The guests gave their answers. The Praetorian guard's prison cells, with their racks, whips and other encouragements, stood ready if they did not. Only Vitellia said she had heard nothing.

Tiberius was away from Rome near Naples at the time. The news reached the Palatine first. It might be another day before a considered version of the night's events was in the hands of the emperor. In the meantime, senior senators did not wish to seem complacent.

To some, a vain and greedy flatterer wanting to impress a party did not seem the worst of offenders. Rubellius Blandus was one of those who thought that exile and a loss of ill-gotten gains would be punishment for Priscus enough. To others, even the possibility of a plot against Tiberius was enough for seeking safety in trial and execution.

Drusus chaired the court. No one knew what Tiberius thought, but without even the slightest delay Priscus was tried, found guilty and strangled in the cells at the foot of the Groaning Steps. The eunuch Paezon needed a new owner.

When Tiberius eventually responded from Naples, he commended the senate for its loyalty but criticised the haste of the execution. Maybe he would have shown clemency, maybe not. He was content that few would ever know. For poets the lasting lesson was the same as that of the fable of the fox and the crow: beware the vanity of testing out your voice.

The servants of the *domus Caesaris* knew of its insecurities, alcoholic excesses, manufactured antiquities and dust-covered lies, even while those outside the house increasingly did not. There were different rules of reality for different places. In faraway northern Gaul, almost as far as Britain, there could be a temple p*ro perpetua salute divinae domus*, to the everlasting health of Caesar's holy house. Nearer to Rome this was a flattery too far. The insiders grew used to games that could not be won, games played in ways that could not be known. Personal judgement, arbitrary judgement being better than none at all, was the essence of understanding an emperor's will.

Loyalty to the house of the Caesars was not easy. Despite the clear sight of the future on the bronze plaques distributed to the empire after Piso's trial, the household knew that no succession was assured. There was Drusus, proud of the praise that had cost Priscus his life, and other younger Claudian heirs of Tiberius, their swaggering entitlement paraded to all. But there were also still the children of Agrippina and their different claim to be the Caesars of the next generation. And there was Sejanus, the man who might now get back his expensive eunuch, the man whom Tiberius seemed increasingly to treat as his deputy. Some even thought that Sejanus might be the first emperor who was not a Caesar.

Vitellia's brother, Publius, survivor of the German beaches and the law courts of Rome, seems to have liked clarity in his strategies for survival. He eased himself into the circle of Sejanus, a group of gourmets, poets and actors as well as guardsmen. Vitellia may thus have known more about the motives of Priscus than her fellow guests, even more than the senators who put him on trial. Her other brother, Lucius, stood back a little from the guard captain. He prized flexibility and would soon become quietly renowned for it. Like Tiberius he preferred ambiguity about what and whom he needed most.

Publius and Lucius both survived and prospered in a house of servants who would be masters, masters forced to be servants, wealthy soldiers, wily children and would-be successors. Publius was the bolder, Lucius the longer-lasting, the master courtier who saw the emperor's need in myriad matters of day-to-day government, satisfied it but did not parade the need that Tiberius had of him. A successful courtier had to walk a slippery stage. Lucius was flexible and forward-thinking. He understood tax and cash reserves. He was a master of both the political and the practical. He was happy to abase himself. With abasement came some, but not all, lessening of responsibility. At the birth of Western bureaucracy, he was useful, the ultimate accolade.

Tiberius was surviving in power as a master of courtly management, an emperor of ambiguity, of seeming neutrality, of concealing a closed mind, obscuring where he stood, of accepting the flattery that he claimed to detest. Tiberius resisted moves to make him 'Father of his Country'. He was menacing towards those who called his concerns for food distribution 'divine'. But none could ever be sure. Proximity was the key to understanding, flattery the currency. Politics was less the manipulation of the many by the few but the one by the few. A successful flatterer required the skill of a man on a razor's edge.

Success might come in many forms. There might be a difference between a flatterer of Tiberius who was ambitious on his own account, on Rome's account, or in fear of the imminent death of his family or himself. It was not easy at the time to see what that difference always was. Motives were hard to discern. The stages were both the law courts where Lucius and Blandus, with the new status of being an ex-consul, worked in different ways, and the couches around low dining tables which no one seeking advancement or survival could avoid.

Tiberius had both to adjudicate like an emperor over free men and to entertain like an emperor. Meanness ruled alongside excess. Unpredictability always ruled. Tiberius once appointed an obscure candidate over one more distinguished because he had watched the first drink a huge flask of wine at a dinner. There was light as well as dark. Without the uncertainties of light and dark, the household would not manage itself, still less a vast world beyond. Lucius was a master of the shades.

17

PEN AND KNIVES

Sejanus's unique source of power was the Praetorian guard, an elite force that he had taken over from his father and hugely enhanced. When Augustus had used the Praetorians for his personal security, they had been mostly out of sight and in billets divided around the city. Sejanus, seeing new dangers in a less secure regime (and maybe new opportunities too), concentrated them in a single, much more visible camp.

His was a role that gave him his own sword and control over the only armed men allowed in the city. It was not an inheritance as grand as that of a Piso, but in the imperial halls of smoke and mirrored marble it was a permanent reminder of reality. Publius took the important role of army paymaster, but the sharpest weapon that he carried was the writing stylus of a bureaucrat. Day by day the sometime soldier scratched notes and orders in a wax-filled wooden box.

Sejanus's power was military but his skills were courtly, not confrontational in the conventional warrior way. He was a soldier trained in household service, more adept than those who burnished their independent pasts, a soldier whose command was not over imperial expansion but over Rome and the *domus Caesaris*. When the emperor said that he hated flatterers, Sejanus was there to be the military man, the type of straight-dealing officer that Tiberius had admired on manoeuvres. When it was time for a banquet of congratulation, Sejanus ruled the tables.

Sejanus's father had been an only moderately distinguished soldier and landowner, remembered best as a pioneer of force-feeding geese for the livers later known as foie gras, adding the flavours when the bird was still alive rather than after its death as satirised by Horace. Food mattered, alongside the force of the knife. Sejanus's enemies said that in his youth he had been the lover of Marcus Gavius Apicius, the most notorious gourmet of the age, master of minced seafood, stuffed dormouse and sow's belly, an influential figure prepared to scour the Mediterranean for the largest prawns. Sejanus's wife was Apicius's daughter, Apicata.

Apicius was an important name in the story of flattery and gluttony at the courts of the Caesars. He was probably linked sexually to Sejanus in order to smear him, but the story may have been true. Food was, as ever, an easy weapon. Many recipes attributed to Apicius survived like the fables of Phaedrus, even if most other details of his life did not. If Apicius deemed cabbage sprouts too common even when the court was dining modestly, they stayed off the menu – and off other menus that lived on long after his death.

Apicius became synonymous with a certain very Roman way of eating and dying. He stood for luxury, complexity and the consequent ease by which goose liver or fine wine could aid the poisoner. Sejanus became notorious for adding death to fine dishes or watching while the condiments, ideally slowly, did their work. The two men's names were in many ways entwined.

The truth of these charges hardly mattered. Paranoia was part of reason. A poisoner might be in the pay of a fellow diner, a potential heir or the emperor himself. Cooks were allowed to be secretive about their more complex recipes. The Sybarites of southern Italy had given their chefs a year's exclusive copyright on a new dish, the first of any known sort of copyright. Knowledge of fish and meats was an ideal education for a kitchen killer.

It was useful to know what one was eating, but not always possible. Conformity was prized. Vegetarians had to beware: hostility to meat might be misunderstood at court as devotion to the cults of Judaea or some other kind of disloyalty or doubt. To eat seated on a chair, rather than reclining on a couch, might recall the vow of Julius Caesar's last civil war enemy, Marcus Porcius Cato, who said he would never lie back comfortably to eat while the tyranny of Caesar survived.

The tyranny of Julius Caesar, if that is what it was, did not survive. It died at the hands of his assassins. The one-man rule of his heirs did more than survive. It prospered. If Cato in defeat were still alive, and had not cut out his intestines with his own knife, he would still have been sitting down to eat.

On any day the dining tables of the Palatine made a stage. If the emperor was there, he was the star. If the emperor was not there, there had to be an understudy, a dangerous role. There were couches for all the players in sets of three, like a crescent moon around its own low table. Each place on the couch had its own name and status, the *summus*, the *imus*, the *medius*, the *consularis*, the top, the bottom, the middle, the consular. The diners ate reclining on their left elbows. There were some conventions on which the emperor might insist and others on which he might not. Anyone might eat and drink enough to blur fears into hopes.

The dishes themselves began with staples of the poor, the bread and wine, the eggs, always something with eggs at the start of a meal, the little vegetables, cucumber, asparagus, sweet carrots, a mullet, something stuffed, a marrow or a sow's udder or both, apples, pears, usually apples. On some days they moved on to more elaborate luxuries, presented as in a theatrical show then taken away to be served in tiny bowls, like Apicius's honey-smeared nightingales, stuffed with prunes, garnished with rose petals and served in a sauce of herbs and grape juice. Sometimes they would discuss the latest dish, sometimes how luxuries were sapping the Roman spirit. Tiberius, stooped, bald, face pale and spotted by dressings, was as unpredictable about food as he was about his favourites.

The most palpable tension was between Drusus and Sejanus, rivals for meeting Tiberius's needs. The prince thought that the courtier had ambitions above his status. The courtier thought that princely status, while probably necessary for succession, was not a necessary condition for giving advice. If Priscus's poem had been better timed to praise Drusus in death, Sejanus would have happily applauded the best lines.

The effort to create a single family of Julio-Claudians continued. Drusus had his already worldly daughter, Julia, aged sixteen, who was married to Nero Caesar, seventeen, the eldest of Agrippina's sons. If Tiberius's Drusus was first in line to succeed to the throne, as the empire had been assured in solid bronze, Agrippina's Nero Caesar might be second. The two young men themselves were quite friendly, a rarity worth noting by those who lived on such indications of truth.

Agrippina would sometimes be at a table herself, with the Vitellii, Lucius ever watchful, Publius more bold, sometimes too the comfortable Rubellius Blandus. Four years after the death of Germanicus and the trial of Piso, Tiberius was still in a barely concealed conflict with Agrippina and her children who, as well as Nero Caesar and Agrippina, her dominant daughter, included Gaius, known still as Caligula.

These young men and women could not simply or safely be murdered. Agrippina could be accused of lusting for power, gagging and gasping for it as though power were food: Latin had a precise word for such abuse, *inhiare*, to gape with open mouth. But the family of Germanicus remained popular with the people of Rome and maybe necessary, in a last resort, if the Julio-Claudians were to keep power. Caligula, tall and awkward as a youth, no longer with his childlike charm, needed constant surveillance. Tiberius required both informers on their plans and an enforcer who could make plausible threats when these clashed with his own.

Agrippina and her allies had to be kept down but not immediately out. They found themselves pursued through the courts, mostly on the evidence of informers associated with Sejanus. Her friend, Claudia Pulchra, a great-niece of Augustus, was condemned for witchcraft and plotting to poison the emperor. She was the widow of Quinctilius Varus, whose suicide in the Teutoburg forest was designed to save her fortune and her life – and had done so from 9 CE until this time of peace that was turbulent in a very different way.

Tiberius was discovered privately worshipping the spirit of Augustus. In 26 CE Agrippina accused him of simultaneously offering sacrifices to Augustus while prosecuting his descendants. She fought back fiercely on behalf of her friends and sons. Like Antonia, she had her own court within the court. There were the warring Caesars and there was Sejanus. The cautious would try not to be too visibly part of parties, whose membership was ever fluid. Drunken words might be useful evidence in the courts – or more likely in Palatine rooms where a quieter verdict could be given.

In the stories of Aesop was a warning to those trying to back both sides. There was once a bat, anxious in an age when the kingdom of the birds was at permanent war with the kingdom of the animals. The battles swung one way and then the other, but the result was never clear. When the birds were on top, the bat joined the birds; when the beasts were winning, the bat was animal. As long as there was open conflict the bat was safe, but when a peace was made its treachery was laid bare, and it was condemned to life in a dark cave for a cell.

18

THE WAY OF THE GUARD CAPTAIN

After a decade of the new reign, the captain of the guard was ahead of all his rivals at court. Tiberius, giving flattery as well as receiving it, referred to him as 'my partner in my toils', raising him through the senatorial ranks as well as those of the Palatine. He would eventually become consul, without having held any previous office, but this was barely more than a bauble beside his swords and psychological sway.

Sejanus held physical power as the Vitellii, the freedmen accountants and other courtiers did not. In the middle years of Tiberius's reign he outdid every competitor for the emperor's trust and attention, combining the arts of the Palatine table with the threat of military force. Beyond the emperor himself Sejanus's base of power was a wide network, threatening, bribing, charming as he chose. He gained the reputation as a poisoner of rivals, both their minds and their bodies, someone with whom it was in every sense dangerous to dine. Whether he ever mixed the atropine with the apples will never be known. His most enduring contribution to the history of the imperial court, and all their many successors, is that he may not have needed to.

The guard captain kept close everyone to whom Tiberius listened. From happier days in retreat in the Greek islands the emperor kept an astronomer, astrologer and prophet called Thrasyllus whose wife, Aka, was a princess from her father's tiny realm of Commagene, south of the Black Sea. Commagene was an absolute monarchy, home to Armenians, Iranians and the subjects of Alexander's generals. Thrasyllus understood the licence and limits of autocracy better than those less experienced. Sejanus stood beside him. All swam in a swirling vortex. For no one was the water calm.

There were flatterers at court who called a man what he was not and the jealous who did not call a man what he was. There were men and women, like Thrasyllus and Aka, whose time Tiberius owned, and those he could merely command. There were scholars and aesthetes, learned buyers of the new art and architecture. There were washers and cleaners, keepers of the many more ancient masks and statues, tasked to brush away the dust and flies between the marble fingers of history, the wrinkles in bronze of powers gone by. Others still yearned for those lost powers.

Prophecy and flattery were closely entwined. Tiberius believed that Thrasyllus had predicted his ascent to the throne – and that his predictions of a long life for the emperor would come true too. There was no more critical fact about the future than the age at which the emperor would die. Phaedrus wrote that if he ruled the world himself, men would be as long-lived as crows, the most venerable as well as most flatterable of birds. This was the issue regularly highest in Tiberius's mind.

Thrasyllus had huge courtly power. Melting down a statue of the emperor to make silver plates should have been a capital crime. Thrasyllus used his authority to save a member of his family accused of that ultimate transformation of flattery to gluttony. Sejanus stood close to Thrasyllus and Publius close to Sejanus. But Sejanus looked outwards into Rome, not just inwards into the palace. He was popular and generous to those who brought him news from the street.

The guard captain earned public praise, and his own gleaming statue in Pompey's Theatre, for controlling a massive fire. A senator who criticised this statue for ruining the legacy of Pompey more than the fire ever could have done found it soon politic to starve himself to death. Sejanus was decisive when he needed to be, skilled at using others to execute his decisions, a rising master of the court, able to hold Tiberius's limited affection as, for a while, none other could.

The rivalry between Drusus and Sejanus took a more dangerous turn. Whether for Tiberius's sake or his own, Sejanus fanned further the emperor's fears of his own family's popularity. Drusus, drunk after dinner, struck Sejanus with his fist and accused him of failing to show appropriate respect. Sejanus did not forget. The vortex tightened its grip. He was adept at poisoning Tiberius's mind even if he was innocent of poisoning the bodies of his fellow diners: his message was that the young son always wants the father gone, that the younger generation was a permanent threat to the old. That was the way of some of the great myths of Rome, the history adopted by the Caesars and their poets.

In intrigues that must have tested the tactics of any courtier – and have tested historians since – Sejanus risked trying to join his own family to the Caesars. He planned an imperial marriage for his four-year-old daughter. The unknowing girl was briefly set for a life with the son of Germanicus's brother, Claudius, when her future husband died by choking on a pear in a game of catch. Only then did Sejanus, it was said, turn his attention towards eliminating Drusus, seducing his wife and, with her help, and that of his favourite eunuch Lygdus, slowly poisoning the bibulous heir until he died. Drusus's wife, advised by Thrasyllus, may herself have been active in promoting the same plan.

Or there may have been no plan. Drusus's notable gluttony might have been enough. At the time there was no suspicion. Lygdus was not tortured for a confession of whether he was a rival in bed or accessory to murder. Drusus was loaded with honours at his funeral, the same processions and statues that had been given to Germanicus, flattery being by this time a currency, subject to inflation and needing to be shared equally in public sight. Only Priscus's poem was missing from the wake.

Sejanus then made a second attempt to join the family by marrying Drusus's widow himself. Tiberius forestalled this in a restatement of the claims of Julio-Claudian blood. Sejanus was still a provincial seducer in the eyes of the grandees, useful but not to be allowed beyond due bounds.

Phaedrus skirted around the drama. He mocked another crow, not a prey to trickery by a fox but one who dressed in peacock feathers, a more deliberate form of vanity. He wrote of the frogs who, fearful of drying ponds, wanted Jupiter to stop the marriage of the Sun and any chance of new suns. The frogs were the Roman people, Jupiter was Tiberius and Sejanus the sun.

The jilted bridegroom responded by fuelling further Tiberius's paranoia against potential successors both in and out of the family. In 23 CE Tiberius's sixteen-year-old granddaughter Julia, whose childhood health had worried Augustus on his deathbed, married seventeen-year-old Nero Caesar, son of Agrippina. This was another bid for stability which failed in its purpose. Julia told all Nero's secrets and more to her mother, who passed them to Thrasyllus and Sejanus. The Roman guard captain, quietly backed by the Greek prophet, responded by persuading Tiberius to leave Rome for his own calm and safety and to settle finally, aged sixty-eight and even more jaded than he had been at his succession, on the island of Capri.

The official reason for the departure had been to consecrate a shrine to Augustus at Nola over the house where he had died. The room in which he had asked for an actor's applause and warned of his successor's slow-chewing jaws was to be erased by a temple. Along the route Tiberius received none of the direct petitions from local worthies that Augustus had accepted as he moved through Italy. There was no public feasting. Few people saw Tiberius at all.

On the way south he enjoyed a private dinner in a lavishly reconstructed grotto, a place where the real blended into the fantastical and life was art. Statues there depicted one of Greek literature's great cave stories, the blinding of the Cyclops, Polyphemus, by Odysseus. Homer's account was one of the most disturbing dinner party stories, with the host as gaoler, the guest as assassin and wine drunk to deadly excess. Between the grotto and the sea were artificial ponds for fish and eels. There was a marble Scylla, looming out as though to snatch unwary passers-by. The *Odyssey* was alive – and with Tiberius as its star.

On this occasion the cooks and artists had too big a role in the show, the engineers too little. A rock-fall over the couches gave Sejanus a lucky opportunity to hurl his body over his master's and save Tiberius's life. He also had the means to make his service known. Sejanus's ability to control the household was at its height. Through his guards, he managed almost all the news that passed between Tiberius and the Palatine.

Sejanus let Tiberius hear what would keep him calm. The emperor's successor on the Rhine, Lucius Domitius Ahenobarbus, died at this time at a great age, the grandfather of Agrippina's little son, Nero. Ahenobarbus's long-ago marriage to Antonia's elder sister had been a grand event. His memories stretched back far before the *domus Caesaris* began its rule. Ahenobarbus had succeeded Tiberius in his German commands. He had put married women on stage in his farces. His feasts for supporters were some of the most excessive before the definition of excess had changed. This was the kind of news, helping to tell the story of Tiberius's life, that an emperor could safely hear.

Other news – the petitions, letters, tax exemptions, the routine reality of imperial rule – became more sporadic. The organisation of the Roman Empire meant that this did not matter much. Governors, once appointed in the Palatine intrigues, governed until they were recalled. Tax-collectors collected. Soldiers patrolled distant villages, married those whom they were patrolling, and rarely thought of the city of Rome at all. They themselves were Rome – and in an age of rare peace for those outside the court.

19

WATER ON DUST

On the road to Capri stood the imperial villa on Cape Misenum, headquarters of the Roman fleet, just a few miles from where Augustus died at Nola. This was the setting for twenty-five lines by Phaedrus starring Tiberius in person, relaxed, conversational, verses which the emperor himself might have enjoyed.

This fifth poem in Phaedrus's second book begins with a protest against a scene familiar in every court – and in every business office that came later – the sight of people busy doing nothing.

> *There is a breed of rush-abouts at Rome,*
> *Hurrying to meetings, occupied in idleness,*
> *Pointlessly puffing, lots to do and little done,*
> *Harming themselves, hated by everyone else.*
> *These are the ones I want to put right,*
> *With a true story, if I'm up to the task.*

The hero of the task comes in the very first line, Caesar Tiberius, on his way down from Rome to Naples. It is a hot day. He stops at his villa on Cape Misenum. One of the house slaves, a top man in this country court, fashionably and somewhat effeminately dressed, makes a huge fuss of dampening down the dust for his master's walk. It is as though he were flicking dead flies from ancestral furniture inside the house not outside, flaunting his wooden ladles of water. This is a peculiarly pointless effort. Tiberius laughs at it. The garden is not a state room and the dust is hardly an intruder.

The slave is not deterred. Suddenly he is out of sight. He has slipped ahead through a gap in the maze of garden paths to make another opportunity to impress, to show off his bared shoulders and the dangling tassels below his tunic, continuing to sprinkle in the hope of winning favour, reward or even a slap around the head, the traditional gesture for giving freedom.

Tiberius stops and calls, '*Heus*', 'Hey you!'. Surely there will be a tip at least. But no. The slave is told sternly that all his scurrying about is for nothing. He is taking liberties, not winning them. A man who wants his life back from this emperor will have to pay a much higher price than wiggling a water bucket.

> *You've done nothing, your effort is withering.*
> *You'll need to pay much more*
> *For a box around the ears from me*

The end of this miniature story is not much of a punchline in any sense. But then Tiberius was never known for the sharpness of his wit. He was better known for his reluctance to give slaves the freedom which they might earn from many other Roman owners. The prophetic Thrasyllus, whose new freedman name was Tiberius Claudius Thrasyllus, was a noted exception. Phaedrus was maybe telling a true story, embroidering a piece of gossip, or writing a fiction which fitted his readers' known facts.

Whatever the case, this was a fable, with characters and a miniature plot more Roman than Greek. This was not a translation from Aesop, or even an adaptation, but a Latin poem in Aesop's style. Phaedrus's target was not the emperor but the courtier watering the dust. Perhaps the emperor even smiled when he heard it. Any nearby flatterers might have laughed with him, as they normally would, forgetting that they were the butt of Phaedrus's wit and that Tiberius was the poem's hero for seeing through their designs.

Aulus Vitellius, at the beginning of his teenage years, was an early arrival at the court on Capri, entering a world which produced enough gossip for a whole school of fabulists and writers of satire. To those who weren't there he was one of the emperor's playmates for princes, an unpaid companion, an object for sexual pursuit. He was one of many, it was said, no one special, just a part of the party.

The name of Capri was linked (probably falsely) to *caper*, that most dissolute of creatures, the goat. Latin etymology was a favourite Roman hobby among those with private libraries. The local drama of Capri, the *phlyax* play, took its name from a Greek word for gossip. Goats and gossip came to define the court on Capri.

The best known *phlyax* writer, Blaesus, wrote plays which mixed characters from the Olympian gods with human gluttons and fools, recognisable figures with those from the stock. Another described the improvisations on Capri as tragic farce. By the time of Tiberius the art of the local players was merging with the Atellane sketches of the mainland. But the tradition of gossip, the mixing of news, religion and comedy, remained strong. No period of imperial history ever produced the flow of salacious rumour and innuendo that Tiberius's long retirement to the island would bring.

The Palatine was suddenly far away. With Sejanus and Thrasyllus by his side, the emperor set up an island court, inviting the useful, the learned, the amusing and those who might be butts for his amusement and aids to his relaxation. Although Aulus was not from one of the grand senatorial families whose heirs Tiberius liked most to humiliate, he was invited nonetheless, a genial, gangly boy whose family was politically useful if he himself was not.

Lucius Vitellius, a father not to be excluded from his son's preferment and maybe helped by Antonia, bought a house on Capri of his own. As a rising man of palace administration he needed to stay in touch. His brother, Publius, undamaged by neither his near-disaster in the sea marshes of Germany nor his defence work for Agrippina, was close to Sejanus and in charge of finance for the army. Young Aulus, son of a third generation of servants, discouraged from an army career by the auguries at his birth, was deemed ideal to be a *spintria*, a brothel boy for sexual entertainments with large casts.

There were twelve imperial villas on this, the most southerly island in the Bay of Naples, which Augustus had bought towards the end of his life in a part-exchange deal for Ischia, its bigger northern neighbour. The largest villa was the Villa Jovis on the eastern cliffs, which Tiberius intended to be soon on the same scale as the

Palatine. He would retain full imperial power, judging, making appointments, setting and exempting taxes, delivering some, at least, of the daily mass of decisions demanded of him. There was ample room for his guests and travelling staff. Not every request got an answer, but that was not unusual. An emperor anywhere received many more letters than he sent.

This retreat was not, at first, an exceptional decision. Rich and educated Romans had long taken their work to the towns around Vesuvius. Capri was not the most fashionable destination. Young men like Aulus Vitellius might have preferred many others. Aulus was less subtle, stronger in language, clumsier in action than his father, but by proximity to power in his own right he might sometimes be more powerful. Thus the next chapter in the history of the Vitellii began, the rising of the son.

For Tiberius, Capri was secure and close to two strategic centres which protected Rome, Misenum, where the emperor's ships were moored, and Puteoli, where the city's corn supplies arrived from Sicily and Africa. In the Villa Jovis he had peace away from unwanted petitioners, ambassadors, their promises and praise. He could enjoy the museum of heroic giants, boars' tusks and bones which Augustus had created to house gifts from foreign ambassadors. He could watch the stars with Thrasyllus and bathe in sulphur pools, which his doctors believed were good for his scarred and flaking skin. He had libraries where he could indulge his pedantries and oversee the education of his young visitors.

The night sky, for Thrasyllus and his emperor pupil, was an education in itself. The poet Aratus, writing 300 years before, described how Zeus had drawn the constellations as messages to mankind. His *Phaenomena*, both in Greek and in its Latin form translated by Germanicus himself, was an essential text for any library. It showed how the Great Bear and the Seven Sisters, the stars on the shield of Achilles in Homer's *Iliad*, moved through the heavens as a celestial code for learned watchers to read. The verse was the universe. Thrasyllus was its reader. Aulus Vitellius and other fortunate young men might be its beneficiaries.

Capri had few harbours where the hopeful or hostile might land, each of them guarded by Sejanus's men. Unwelcome messengers or unwilling guests were hurled down from high cliffs. A fisherman who evaded security to present the gourmand emperor with a mullet had his face rubbed in it. When he joked that he was pleased not to have given Tiberius the crab from his catch, he had the crab ground into his face too. This was a story, whatever its specific truth, that warded off intruders with each retelling.

The navy provided any food and water for banquets which the locals could not supply. The villa had some dozen ovens, a bakery and a staff schooled in specialised culinary tasks. No imperial villa could ever lack a *pistor candidarius*, a skilled maker of white bread. The corridors were floored in white mosaic, trimmed with black. Smooth marble columns, swirling colours of grey and green like a lizard's skin, supported the roof of the main banqueting room.

The rooms of the most distinguished guests, or those requiring most surveillance, were above a tower of massive cisterns that collected winter rain, with pumps to recycle waste to the kitchens, the dusty gardens and the baths. The latest curator of Rome's own water supply, Cocceius Nerva, was one of Tiberius's first and long-staying companions, an assignment that did little to advance the building of aqueducts for the capital.

The baths of Capri became notorious. The hot mineral pools were not just good for an old man's skin but enjoyed, so the gossips said, by boys and girls who catered to an old man's entitlements. Oral sex was always a good joke for gossips. A mouth used to speak the truth was surely best not polluted. A tongue used for flattery was best not polluted further. This was the wit of the rural stage. Tiberius became the butt of the Atellane farce actors as 'the old goat lapping up the doe'.

In Capri, the sex of tongues went beyond Tiberius taking a reluctant woman to his bedroom. He had boys called little fishes who licked between his legs as he swam. He demanded that breast-feeding babies be brought to suck him. He hung a painting in which the mythical hunters, Meleager and Atalanta, barred by prophecy from risking her virginity, simultaneously suck between each other's legs. He commissioned elaborate scenes of troilism. Aulus was not the only *spintria* required so that life could imitate art.

The painting of the virgin and the hero was by Parrhasius, the classical Greek master of realism. If further technical advice were required, the library of Tiberius extended far beyond Thrasyllus's copies of Aratus's *Phaenomena*. On Capri there were erotic romances and genealogies of the gods, pornography and Plato, mathematics and tragedy, Italian farce and the legacy that Blaesus and the *phlyakes* had left, the local tragic farce.

An easy way to lower a man was to imagine him with sexual submissives and sycophants. Often these tales were more about the unpredictability for those around an emperor than the capricious excesses themselves. But it was the excess which survived the longest. Phaedrus's poem about the pompous slave of Cape Misenum was never as popular as those starring crows, frogs and dogs. Capri was a place where an autocrat could both indulge his full freedom – and be abused for living beyond imagination.

The island purchased by Augustus was more like a court of the Greek east than anything yet in Rome. It had no counterweight institutions, not even weakened ones, which could impede an imperial whim. Thrasyllus's wife, Aka, perhaps understood it best. She had been born a princess of Commagene. Her home was north of Syria on the road to Persia, the last remnant of the empire of Seleucus founded by one of Alexander the Great's successors. She knew the licence and limits of autocracy as her husband knew the stars.

Commagene had a royal shrine, high on a mountain, in which the statue of the founder of her own family dynasty, Antiochus I, stood at five times his size in life, flanked by eagles, lions, local gods and the gods of Greece. Hercules, Hermes and Apollo served in local dress. The death of his no less absolutist successor, Aka's brother, leaving no heir old enough to succeed, left a vacuum. To the delight of the Commagene aristocracy, Tiberius, in his third year on the throne, filled it with direct rule from Rome.

Aka was proud to become Claudia Aka. Thrasyllus's granddaughter, Ennia Thrasylla, married Q. Naevius Sutorious Macro, prefect of the watch and Sejanus's deputy. The common people of the kingdom would have preferred a new young king to none, but their views had easily been ignored. Commagene, like all of the Mediterranean from Spain to Judaea, had to take its orders, if any orders happened to come, from the east coast of Capri.

There was occasional bad news from the mainland that the island court could not ignore. In 27 CE a wooden stadium at Fidenae, a town about five miles north of Rome, collapsed during a public entertainment and tens of thousands of spectators were killed, probably the biggest civil disaster of the age. Tiberius briefly visited the site, ordering help for the wounded and punishment for the builder. He did not return via the Palatine.

The main news for Tiberius from Rome came in the autumn of 29 CE. Fifteen years after overseeing her son's succession, Livia died, leaving much of her personal fortune to an ambitious favourite, Servius Sulpicius Galba. Again Tiberius did not return for the funeral. Neither did he pay Livia's legacy.

Only a few miles further out to sea from Capri was the windy island of Pandateria, where Augustus had once exiled his daughter Julia. Tiberius, his fears fuelled by Sejanus, sent her daughter Agrippina, Germanicus's power-hungry widow, to Ponza, a different island between Naples and Rome, but to the same death as Julia by neglect and starvation.

20

PROFITS FROM PROPINQUITY

What was worrying to the senate, the people and the members of the *domus Caesaris* left behind was not Tiberius's retreat to Capri but the length of his stay there. On the Palatine when the emperor was away, there was an empty space. Tiberius's power was barely visible until it was absent. Without regular sightings of the man from whom authority fell, fewer knew where it was falling or where safety might be. Courtiers needed to show to themselves and to others that they were in the inner circle, or even an outer circle.

The military and legal power of the past had been facts that a man might touch; the new power, proved through an almost theatrical ritual, was not. New men could bend long-standing social structures. Information from even the unknowing staff could win huge rewards from buyers who thought they were paying for knowledge.

If a man was for any reason deemed down and out of favour, there might be only a short step to his prosecution for treason, the simple charge of no longer being the emperor's friend. Prosecutors could gain a quarter of the wealth of those they successfully drove to suicide or execution. The names of the accusers were secret. There was sharing of fear and, alongside it, a massive redistribution of wealth from old power to new, from country landowners to courtiers of the city, the *bona damnatorum*, the goods of the condemned. In his miserable exile, Ovid had been pleased, and lucky, that his property at least survived in his own possession and was not given to flatterers or gluttons or the emperor himself.

The emperor had first claim – and could either add to his wealth or distribute the gains to the public, directly or indirectly, as acts of liberality or freedom from tax. Tiberius was either reluctant – or insufficiently understanding – to spend his public money. Business opportunities for constructors were fewer. The corn supply slowed.

Water shortages increased. New aqueducts were still needed. Anyone close to the emperor could hope to claim and gain a bigger share of such chances for wealth that were available. Flattery and denunciation were arts seen as a curse by those under threat. To newcomers they were the arts of opportunity.

Despite rumblings that he should return, murmurs from within his household and wider family, Tiberius remained away from Rome, making occasional trips with Sejanus only to the coast around Naples to show that he was still alive. Thrasyllus, supported by Sejanus, had the vital role of keeping Tiberius calm, reinforcing his predictions of a long life to ensure the succession of his seven-year-old grandson, Gemellus.

The news from Rome of trials and executions, some but not all of them orchestrated by Sejanus, matched the news from Capri of cruelty and decadence. Both avenues of information were distorted in the interests of the tellers. There were more treason trials when the emperor was away, and those who profited from disorder and redistribution were less constrained. But the total number of successful prosecutions in the whole of Tiberius's long reign was only about twenty-five, and about the same number failed.

Tiberius enjoyed the results but affected at least to disapprove of them. To a degree he did disapprove. He was not anxious for prosecutors to create too much social disorder simply to curry favour with himself and make themselves richer. Lawyers were regular butts of the emperor's mockery. He liked to see them at each other's throats.

Flattery of the emperor at Rome had to lessen when its recipient was away. But it did not cease. Flatterers might even have been less embarrassed when Tiberius was not there to hear them. Court life was frozen. It was like a masque, different to the rumbustious improvisations from Naples and Capri and the sketches of Mr Glutton and Mr Fool. The new plays had an almost formal script. The star stood forever in the wings. The cast wrote subplots in which the same routines happened again and again.

Succession was still the main story. In 31 CE the order came from Capri that Agrippina's youngest son, nineteen-year-old Caligula, should be sent to join the boys in Tiberius's entourage. Thrasyllus joked that the awkward newcomer had as much chance of becoming emperor as of riding on water over the Bay of Naples. But the last male heir to Germanicus stayed alive and in the race. Tiberius indulged the boy's love of theatre in the hope that it would soften any violent side to his nature. Aulus Vitellius became his friend.

Meanwhile Sejanus, the archetype apparatchik, was promoted alongside Tiberius to the consulship. He pulled strings that the Vitellii could not. He controlled swords as well as pens. His supporters saw a rising tide. Sejanus's sister, Aelia Paetina, was already married to Tiberius's uncle, Claudius, the slobbering cripple who was nonetheless a Caesar. The age of the Sejano-Julio-Claudians still seemed a possibility, and maybe not far ahead.

Tiberius ordered the banishment from Rome of the farce actors whom Augustus had aped on his deathbed. They were at the same time 'so indecent and so popular'.

21

DEATH OF THE DAMNED

Two hundred miles to the north in Tibur there was anticipation, excitement and fear. Gaius Rubellius Blandus, long one of the town's leading men in Rome, seemed set to marry Tiberius's granddaughter, Julia, whose sickness as a girl had troubled the dying Augustus. Although many, both rich and poor, were facing economic disaster, this was at least a boost to local pride in troubled times. Any grand wedding meant a feast, meat and wine in the street for all comers, nuts for children to chase as the bride passed by.

Julia, by this time in her mid-twenties, was already the widow of one potential heir to the throne, Nero, son of Germanicus and Agrippina. She was already a veteran of the court in which Sejanus, her own mother's former lover, remained supreme. Maybe Julia herself had been once set to marry Sejanus. That was merely rumour. By marrying Blandus she might be merely the leading lady of Tibur, perhaps a safer place. Even in the hardest days, the Anio still fell there from the mountains to the plain and the ancient temple of Hercules, older than Rome, still stood proud.

The financial shocks of the decade came from old banking rules newly enforced in the courts. A law once designed to favour investment in Italian land simultaneously caused reluctance of lenders to lend and buyers to buy. Food was short. Farmers without land were falling into bankruptcy. Thousands of slaves, without work and with no right to free food from the treasury, were abandoned and ever more visible beside the roads.

It was not many years since freedom for the enslaved was a punishment more than a gift, an expulsion from the only place that would feed and house them. That had begun to change. Freedom for an individual was becoming more clearly a right worth having in itself. But a reduction in the supply of money, happening for reasons that no one well understood, showed how quickly the past might return and the starving free might again envy the enslaved and fed.

While money was plentiful in the personal bank of Tiberius, it had almost ceased to flow through what was not yet known as the economy. Gold and silver continued to leave the country to pay for imported luxuries. Less returned in tribute and tax. There were no new conquests. The richest lost fortunes in the treason courts and, while some of the new owners, informers, freedmen and provincial prosecutors, spent extravagantly, there were not enough of them and not enough money went on roads, aqueducts and ships, on payments to the free who needed work.

Most of the property of the prosecuted, the *bona damnatorum*, went directly to Tiberius. His appetite for public spending was never high. No major building was commissioned from Capri. Cocceius Nerva, the *curator aquarum*, was a successful servant of the emperor in his retreat but no aqueduct had been completed for forty years. The waters of the Anio were still decorative in Tibur, but still ended splashing uselessly into the muddy Tiber before it entered Rome.

The courtiers of Capri reacted more intelligently than their critics later complained, making large loans available and allowing more time for borrowers to adjust their affairs. The shock was still harsh. Among the senatorial elite, those not exclusively beset by their bankers, there was the additional social shock when Rubellius Blandus, a mere provincial knight, was set to marry Julia. It was not necessary to love the Julio-Claudians to think that this was yet another disruption to the established order.

Then suddenly, at the end of 31 CE, there came the kind of news which, more than the marital, the minor judicial or military, the electoral, the social, even more than the monetary, provided a household court, and its historians, with their drama. In a single day Sejanus lost his prime place at Tiberius's side. He fell spectacularly from his great height. He had risen slowly, inexorably as his supporters thought, until his authority collapsed, threatening all who had associated themselves with his cause, Publius Vitellius among them.

The art of the courtiers was always to protect themselves from the buffetings that might come from above. Knowledge was one buffer, caution another. Even when the Palatine play seemed every day the same, openness to the possibility of a changed plot was the greatest protection of all, requiring the subtlety and patience that Lucius showed in almost everything he did and Publius much less so.

Tiberius, it seemed, had gradually made himself less dependent on Sejanus during his seven years on Capri. He had communication lines to Rome of his own. He had used handwritten letters to communicate with the city prefect. His prophet, Thrasyllus, who had grown closer to Caligula since his arrival, had useful links to a likely successor as commander of the Praetorian guard, his own grandson-in-law, Naevius Sutorius Macro. Lucius and Aulus were also beginning to favour Macro. Caligula had his own informant in Rome, a favourite charioteer and former slave, Eutychus, who claimed to have news of a threat to Tiberius's life. Macro took the details to his growing camp of supporters.

Eutychus was hardly a perfect witness. His story first emerged under routine interrogation about a theft of clothes in a changing room at the baths. Even when he was sent in chains to Capri Tiberius was still unconcerned until Pallas, Lucius's ally, succeeded in seeing Tiberius secretly with a letter from Antonia, the mistress of his house.

In Antonia's letter, whose contents Lucius was very likely to have known, were details of Sejanus's alleged role in the murders of Tiberius's son, Drusus, as well as Agrippina's children. Her court still included Caenis, now Antonia Caenis, a freedwoman and her secretary, whose beauty was renowned but whose mind, more importantly, forgot nothing. At what point, Antonia asked, might Sejanus move against the only other obstacle to his ambitions, Tiberius himself?

Tiberius then interrogated Eutychus, who confirmed the story, either because he knew it or because he now knew what would best suit his survival. The emperor suddenly had what he wanted to hear. As long as Sejanus had been threatening would-be successors, he was useful. When the threats had worked he was less so, even maybe a danger. The maybe did not last for long. He was suddenly a clear and present danger.

Sejanus might have seen the signs, but he did not. If there was the same 'smoke for sale' around Naples as in the rumours around the death of Augustus, neither he nor his allies smelt or bought it. As at the banqueting tables, words which at one moment were as clear as glass goblets at another were as cloudy as the wine swilling within. Tiberius tricked Sejanus by the promise of yet higher promotion. At dizzying speed he was recalled to Rome, stripped of his captaincy of the guard, arrested and replaced by Macro.

Tiberius and his court stayed in Capri. The man who had so long flattered Tiberius's judgement, ruled his banquets and manoeuvred as best he could through miasmas of uncertainty died far from his former master's sight. For the last time he passed below the broad eaves of the Capitoline temple to Jupiter, Best and Greatest, beyond its massive colonnades and towards the Groaning Steps to the Forum below. It was an easy execution for the executioner, a slow fall to death. Sejanus's financial fortune, swelled by flattery, usefulness and threat, quickly swelled the emperor's funds. The months after his fall were golden times for treasury receipts. Tiberius took emergency measures to ease the supply of money in circulation for everyone.

This was a much greater jolt for the players on the Palatine than the passing of power to Tiberius from Augustus. Those who had cheered Sejanus for twenty years abused his body for three days. Sejanus's wife, Apicata, incriminated her husband before killing herself. Whether she was a good witness, or even a possible witness, to his alleged seductions and poisonings counted for nothing. The case for the posthumous prosecution was clear.

Sejanus's children followed their father down the Groaning Steps. The female members of his family, once the means for his dynastic dreams, played the most prominent part. According to a law that barred the execution of virgins, his daughter had first to be raped by the executioner. His sister, Aelia Paetina, was divorced before her murder. The name of Sejanus became a byword for a monster, used by Phaedrus, the master of the moral fable, almost as mothers might frighten their children.

In his portrayals on page and stage Sejanus soon paid the price of failure. Hardly a man of virtue, he was merely one of many who were concerned whether the empire would survive, who should be its emperor and how. He played the game, succeeded for more than a decade and lost. By losing he became a seducer of princesses, a pimp and traitor, with a love of fine food too, that common code for monstrous behaviour.

These public executions brought more panic than poison ever had. In Rome it was not only the weakest at court and in the streets who became obedient because they were afraid. The strong obeyed too, and some found added strength for future battles by obeying. The senate was convulsed. Vengeance followed vengeance. Excess pursued excess. With so much in life dependent on the sheerest chance, gluttony was as likely to succeed as watchfulness. Obliteration by drink was as plausible a tactic as verbal obfuscation.

Bodies fell in piles at the foot of the Capitol hill. One prominent victim was Decimus Haterius, an ex-consul known as a somnolent glutton, depraved when awake but too inactive most of the time to be a threat. If this was a tactic, it was successful for Haterius, but only for a while.

Haterius the glutton joined the flattering dead. When a flatterer fell, any who had flattered the flatterer were at high risk of falling too. In a swill of accusations, random more than systematic, none produced new evidence of a plot to seize the throne. Thrasyllus helped to stabilise the court by assuring Tiberius he would survive another ten years. Certain that he would live longer than any plotting against him, he settled back into the routines of Capri. The business of empire had still to go on. The court continued to be run by those who stayed safe and unknown.

At the end of 33 CE, at the height of the financial crisis, Blandus married Julia and joined the imperial household on the Palatine. Just as Tiberius had not returned to Rome for the funeral of his mother, he did not return to celebrate the wedding – or to face those who disapproved. A provincial marrying a princess was still an affront to social standards for some. In the goat island of Capri the reports of sexual licence were like those from the sack of a captured city.

With Sejanus gone, Lucius Vitellius rose again among the ranks of the useful and reliable. Bankers and landowners found common cause. With support from young Aulus, his well-placed son on Capri, he achieved the consulship in 34 CE and the governorship of Syria, a job which did not require his permanent residence in the province. Deciding when to and when not to be in Rome required as much of the flatterer's skill as ambiguity in words. Lucius Vitellius knew how to watch, wait and adjust his loyalties.

Publius Vitellius, successful survivor of his closeness to Germanicus, faced treason charges for having been too close to Sejanus. This time he did not escape. His father, old Publius, was too near death to help behind the scenes. He had support from his quieter gourmet brother, Aulus, famed for his generous feasts, who was respectable enough in the new era to have become consul for half of the year 32 CE. But this was not enough.

Facing the horrors of prison at the foot of the Capitol, Publius attempted suicide with a stylus he requested for his bureaucrat's wax tablet. Blood flowed from his body in a thin stream. Encouraged by friends, he allowed himself to be bandaged and brought back to consciousness but died soon afterwards. His wife, Acutia, would be convicted too. Her failed defender was a young balding libertine, Marcus Salvius Otho, with ambitions of his own.

Lucius and Publius had for a short time been on opposite sides in a struggle for Palatine power. Lucius may or may not have been in a position to warn Publius of the case against Sejanus. What seems certain is that he did not. With neither Publius any longer alive, the future of the Vitellii from this point depended upon Lucius, the forty-year-old consummate flatterer, and his playboy son Aulus, twenty-one and already beginning to match his uncle's reputation at the dining table.

22

LUCIUS VITELLIUS AND THE SON OF GOD

'If you release him, you are no friend of Caesar,' the Jewish crowd taunted Pontius Pilate as he pondered the fate of the man known as 'King of the Jews' and 'Son of God'. Jerusalem was not in Syria, but its peace was the responsibility of the neighbouring governor of Syria. The hecklers were picking at the most vulnerable part of Pilate's armour, his status as the emperor's friend, his source of power. To a man of ambition, away from the latest ebbs and flows within the imperial household, that friendship was evanescent, ever vulnerable to intrigue, also everything that he had. Pilate could confidently tell protesters that there was no legal case against the accused; he could not face the charge that he was 'no friend of Caesar'.

There were always problems facing a Roman ruler of Judaea, year by year many of them the same ones. A claimant to be 'King of the Jews' was nothing new. The prospective crucifixion of a 'Son of God' would be hardly a novelty either, neither the punishment itself, still routine for non-citizens, nor the idea of a god's son on earth (Tiberius was a son of a god just as Augustus had been), nor the accompanying noise. What mattered to Pilate was his status within the court.

For Roman administrators Judaea had for more than 100 years been an incomprehensible nuisance, a place of male sexual mutilation as well as peculiar absolutism about god and seafood. King Herod the Great held Judaea with a firm hand till he died in the middle of Augustus's reign. His divided successors, carefully kept divided by Rome, were allowed to squabble and murder to their mutual content as long as Rome received its tribute and faced no costs.

Pilate, like all servants abroad, needed to follow events in the capital much more closely than his masters ever followed the trials of Jerusalem. The Jews recognised that truth as well as their governor did, not just when the issue was the fate of a self-proclaimed king and 'Son of God'. The various Jewish leaders had cultivated many allies on the Palatine. So had their rivals. A battle beneath Capitol hill produced results; one by the Mount of Olives usually not so much.

The governorship of Roman Judaea came with no legions. Pilate had acquired some military experience with Tiberius and Germanicus on the Rhine, but his job in Jerusalem, like that of Quinctilius Varus in Germany, was as an administrator. He needed calm and taxes, no news of disturbances to reach Capri, no tales told against him by religious leaders or local royalty. If he failed, the army that would have to intervene was controlled by Lucius Vitellius, the governor of Syria from 35 CE, for whom friendship with the emperor was the aim always most paramount.

Syria's previous governor had been a friend of Ovid. He was said to have won the job by joining the emperor in a banquet and drinking session that lasted a night and two days. At the end of the party Tiberius judged his companion 'the most agreeable of friends and at all hours' before appointing him to rule Syria and keep whatever eye was needed on the Jews. This champion eater and drinker had since died and Lucius, weighing the risks and rewards of absence from Rome, was on his way east to replace him.

Syria, as the Romans then defined it, was a narrow coastal zone along the eastern Mediterranean, its capital at Antioch, the base from which Rome managed relationships with various neighbouring kings. Freedoms were forever up for negotiation, liberty for loyalty. For the past sixteen years Syria had included Commagene, the former home of Thrasyllus's wife, Aka. There remained a question mark over whether Commagene might be made independent again if its young heir, Aka's nephew, proved suitable. Thrasyllus's granddaughter, Ennia, was being prostituted by her ambitious husband to Caligula.

Each kingdom had a dynasty of the intermarried. No one troubled by the trials of the Julio-Claudians could fail to note the solution favoured by the heirs of Alexander the Great's generals. Aka's brother, Antiochus III, was married to another of his sisters, Iotapa. Their son, possibly set to become Antiochus IV, was also set to marry his own sister, also called Iotapa. As a check on outsiders' ambitions the custom of intermarriage was ideal.

As an added check on the young children's loyalties several were currently held as Roman hostages. Possible rulers of Commagene were currently living in the house of Lucius's patron, Antonia, permanently spied upon, free to observe the pet eels in the ponds of her house on Cape Misenum but not much more. At many a Palatine banquet the lower couches would be taken by princes and princesses living in luxurious confinement. As long as their parents behaved well back home their sons and daughters could eat the finest prison food that anyone could imagine. The price of any slackening of loyalty to Rome was paid in the permanent threat of poison.

Lucius already knew something of Syria from prisoners and slaves, both highborn and low, also from its place in the death of Germanicus and the trial of Piso. Judaea was always a special fascination to those who cared for strange rules about politics and food. The principle of arcane attention to pigs and prawns, animals' hooves and sea creatures' scales had attractions for gourmands even if the obduracy of the eaters did not.

Although Lucius knew more about the dead Piso than Piso's former province, the promotion was a good opportunity that might not quickly recur. Despite the death toll from informers and prosecutors, in and after the time of Sejanus, profitable public offices did not come up as often as in the past. Tiberius liked to leave men for long periods in post if he could, arguing that Romans abroad were like flies on open wounds and, once gorged and sated by extortion, would do less harm. Pontius Pilate had already served eight years in Judaea.

Lucius Vitellius, longer-sighted than many friends of Caesar, was well prepared for the risk in leaving Rome. Antonia was still his strong supporter. He was one of the consuls for the year 34 CE. He was the principal organiser of the anniversary celebrations for two decades of Tiberius's rule. His son, Lucius, was about to marry Junia Calvina, a descendant of Augustus's daughter Julia, a connection no longer one of disgrace. His close friend Valerius Asiaticus, a wealthy grandee from Gaul, was set to be consul in 35 CE. In Capri Aulus had the responsibility of representing the family interest. The Vitellii were faring fine.

In Capri itself the main news from the east was not the aftermath of a routine crucifixion but a rare sighting of the Phoenix, a bird whose rebirth every few centuries was held to celebrate a royal son's piety towards his father. This was the kind of news that Tiberius liked to hear. If Lucius could maintain the flow of favourable bulletins, alongside stable taxes and the empire's finest dried fruits, he would be a success. News of the decision by a tent-maker from Tarsus that Jesus had not been merely 'King of the Jews', the new king that the Jews quite reasonably had not wanted, but the 'Son of God' awaited by all Jews, had not needed to trouble the imperial household. Saul's re-emergence as Paul on the road to Damascus mattered much less than the new Phoenix, sitting in its nest of fragrant herbs and cinnamon as though scripted by Apicius.

While Lucius and Sextilia were in Syria, Blandus, with Julia, his imperial wife, was governor of Africa. He too was trusted to have a legion under his command. His prime responsibility in 35 CE was to maintain Rome's corn supply. Both men had experience of the court; they were courtiers first and senators second. Both knew how to avoid the emperor's anger, to divide the issues on which it was necessary to consult from those when it would be stupid and dangerous. They had seen closely the mistakes of others. Any scratch in wax on Capri could become a blade of blood in Carthage or Jerusalem, but the wax was only rarely scratched. Tiberius, in what was already the pattern for imperial rule, reacted much more than he initiated.

The prime task for Lucius and Blandus was to avoid trouble. Lucius gained favour with Jewish leaders by restoring some

confiscated robes to their high priests, a costless act. He saw Pilate
as a continuing risk to good order. With courtly skill, Lucius gave
him more than enough freedom to ruin himself, sending him back
to Rome to answer charges over the clumsy crucifixion of some
Samaritan protesters. In being the breaker of Pilate's career he had
linked himself inadvertently, quietly, and somehow very characteristically, to what was not yet the most far-reaching event of his time.

Lucius knew what, by contrast, would be appreciated on Capri.
This had nothing to do with anyone called Jesus Christ. He had
on his staff the refined Spanish food and wine connoisseur Lucius
Junius Columella, an enthusiast for poetry and prose, dogs and natural rarities. Columella was, publicly at least, a critic of the excesses
of his day, praising hard work in the garden over instant gratifica-
tion. He criticised gluttony. His work on wine began with a flattering dedication to Eprius Marcellus, a feared prosecuting lawyer and
professional flatterer of others. He was a useful companion on the
razors' edges of life under Tiberius.

Thanks to Columella, readers throughout the empire also learnt
of the export to Rome of a nine-foot Jewish prodigy for public exhi-
bition on the Palatine. Lucius and Columella knew that Tiberius
had a special interest in the Judaean town of Jamnia and its famed
date palms, which Herod the Great had left to Livia in his will. New
varieties of dates and figs, almost any novelty for a banquet, would
be better received than the latest news of Jewish opinion.

In Antioch Lucius was not only far from his emperor but also
further from his already difficult son. Aulus Vitellius had married
and become quickly estranged from a wealthy woman in his own
extended family. Petronia was the granddaughter of the same Vitellia who had stayed silent before execution of the rash poet Priscus.
They had a son, Petronianus, who was blind in one eye. Showing a
fierce view of her family, Petronia insisted that her estate could pass
to her son only if Aulus was excluded from any part of it.

The future emperor, lacking money to match his lifestyle for
almost all his life, was said to have had his son poisoned to thwart
his wife's wish. The official verdict, not widely believed, was that the
dead boy had intended to poison his father and had killed himself

out of guilt and shame. Aulus's second wife was Galeria Fundana, from a more modest family, who bore him a son and a daughter, the first suffering from such a stammer that he could hardly speak at all. This was perhaps not hard to understand.

Lucius showed that his diplomatic skills could work away from the Palatine. He settled a border dispute between neighbouring Armenia and Parthia. He made a brief military intervention in support of one Parthian king over another. He came close to an invasion into the territory of the Nabataeans around Petra which, in an age of money-saving peace, would have been a rare example of legions marching into the territory of friendly kings. But, to his likely great relief, he was able to halt his offensive plans when all-changing news arrived, not from Capri but from the setting for Phaedrus's fable of the flatterer with the watering can, the mainland villa on Misenum.

Tiberius was dead. Thrasyllus's promises of ever-longer life to postpone the problem of succession had finally failed. A few days earlier his tower on Capri for astronomy, prophecy and for matching Greek verse to the universe had been destroyed in an earthquake. Although Rome's second emperor might not have lived as long as his prophet had promised, he had reached the age of seventy-seven, a long, ancient life. He had ruled for twenty-three years, matching the hopes as well as the fears expressed at the death of Augustus just a few miles away in Nola. It was spring, 37 CE. Gardens were coming to life, a time of heavy-scented flowers for anyone ready to celebrate.

Lucius Vitellius, it was said by his critics, had an uncanny sense of who would be a future despot and how a despot needed to be served. Antioch was as much his place of study as the Palatine. He was not the first Roman to enhance his own kitchens and gardens from hotter, drier lands, nor the first to note the art of bowing down to kiss the ruler's feet. But the timing for his education was good: obeisance might look bad, but it might also be a means of surviving: flattery was as essential an oil of government as any from a palm tree.

Though late to receive the news from Misenum, Lucius ordered immediate celebrations for the succession of his son's friend,

Agrippina and Germanicus's son, the survivor of Capri, Gaius
Caligula. Blandus did the same in Carthage. Everywhere, from the
servants of the *domus Caesaris*, who had their third master, to the
soldiers in Syria, who had another ruler whom they had never seen,
there was enthusiastic welcome.

Pontius Pilate had a particular cause to rejoice. His was a lucky
escape, the avoidance of any appearance in Tiberius's courts and
a disappearance into obscurity. Supporters of the crucified Son of
God began retelling the fables that their master had taught them,
parables as they became known, short lessons on sheep and goats,
wine and banquets, fig trees and fish in a form that Phaedrus would
have readily recognised from his own.

23

GOAT WORSHIP

For the massed courtiers of the Palatine, each individual calculating for the future, every day was a gamble and Caligula's very survival was a triumph over poor odds. The new emperor was not only the son of Germanicus, whose poisoning in Antioch was possibly ordered by Tiberius, and of the elder Agrippina, whom Tiberius had certainly sent to her death. He had also been the only heir in the way of Gemellus, Tiberius's own grandson. Caligula, while on Capri, had had to disguise any ambitions of avenging his parents and anything but his most devoted support for Gemellus. He had done both very well.

In the senate there was brief talk of abandoning the Julio-Claudians. One consul promoted a return to a republic. Others sought the throne for themselves. The Praetorian guard preferred the problems that they knew to those of the long unknown. Caligula had been a favourite of the military since his mother and father had let loose his charm in the marching camps of the Rhine. He had learnt the arts of a court by observing and practising them at the very highest level. An accomplished actor, he continued Tiberius's persecution of actors. He had survived by acting, by shifting roles and rarely playing himself. He would rule in the same way.

Gaius Caligula was not as glamorous as he wanted to seem. He was tall, heavy-bellied, thin-legged, hairier on his body than on his head, a somewhat goatish figure, although to use the word *caper* in his presence was perilous accuracy, one of many new dangers in the third court of the Caesars. Caligula was an emperor whose brief reign, marked by innovative diplomatic and construction projects, acute sensitivity to slights, whimsical mass executions and fantasies of his own divinity, was notoriously hard for those nearby to understand. Tiberius, who had once described Rome as a wolf held by its ears, had likened his successor to a 'viper for the Roman people'.

To understand him and survive, as the Vitellii needed to do, it helped to know how during six years on Capri he had been so extremely adept at surviving. Never, it was said, was there a better servant or a worse master. The maker of that judgement, a wealthy senator, Passienus Crispus, was an autocrat in his own house but adept at always walking humbly in the emperor's train, eating massively or serving at table as required, flattering beyond the rules of normal reason and answering questions with tact.

'Have you had sex with your sister?', Caligula asked Crispus. 'Not yet,' came the careful reply. Crispus saw that Caligula was both keen to boast of incest but maybe not so keen that an ordinary mortal might have committed the same offence. Caligula would dress up in new, god-like clothes for seductions banned by law. A great flatterer learnt to note just how different from the common herd his master needed to be. The Vitellii were well placed to prosper under a head of the *domus Caesaris* whose sense of exceptionalism, sensuality and display was of a different order from that of either of his predecessors.

The young Aulus Vitellius knew how Thrasyllus and Aka had enthralled Tiberius on Capri, reading the stars for communication from the heavens, predicting a long life for their master and the justified postponement of hard choices about who would follow him. Even if the emperor were not a god, he could be made to feel close to the gods. That was a challenge which well repaid those with the wit to understand it. Lucius Vitellius had the experience of his son as well as his own. He became a leading figure on the new Palatine.

Capri had been a laboratory for autocrats, a place to learn how in Commagene a single family had successfully extended what little power the Romans had not taken for themselves. Aulus had ample opportunity to listen and observe – and to watch Caligula doing the same. Although Lucius had been away from Rome at the time of the succession, he brought back from Syria his own practical appreciation of what eastern monarchs expected for themselves and from their people. These, he decided, were not necessarily unreasonable expectations.

Julius Caesar had accepted praise for his 'divine virtue' and personal embodiment of the state. Eighteen months later he was murdered by friends who thought such hubris a threat. The Ides of March turned out to be just a pause in the process of blurring the difference between men and gods. Caligula made up for lost time.

Augustus had been careful. He encouraged historians and poets to flatter his claim of historic right to rule, to say that his house was on the site of Romulus's hut and that his lineage began from the goddess Venus. He began to allow worship of his *genius*, his divine spirit, even in the suburbs of Rome, by those who wanted to be his worshippers. This was particularly popular among the Greek-speakers of Naples.

The concept of divinity at Rome was never as confined as later religions would insist. In the towns around Vesuvius Augustus had allowed shrines to his *genius*, which, while not quite making him a god in Italy, came very close. The Alexandrian sailors who burnt incense for him as he lay dying, and gained new clothes as a reward, were doing only what they might have done at home. Augustus's priest in Pompeii was quickly keen to clarify his status from *sacerdos Augusti* to *sacerdos divi Augusti*, priest of Augustus the god, as soon as the news from nearby Nola allowed.

Writers played their roles. There was a thriving business in stories of descent from ancient demi-gods and glorious victories in Rome's early wars. A Roman general in his triumph had been dressed as a god for a day. Legendary genealogies helped newly ascendant families to elevate their prestige. The Vitellii became one of many beneficiaries of reconstructed history, the elevation to historical status of events that, even if they had ever occurred, were not ones that had ever mattered before.

Tiberius had not needed to manufacture any more ancestry. Being a Claudian and an adopted Julian was enough. He did, however, need to draw his own line between earth and the heavens. Those who wanted to show support for Rome in the east had long worshipped some symbol of the city, sometimes a statue of Augustus and Tiberius, sometimes a more ancient focus of loyalty. Julius Caesar was a somewhat fading divinity. Tiberius needed the benefit of both being divine, which he knew was absurd, and not being divine, which might disappoint would-be worshippers. He could refuse to be venerated as a junior descendant of Venus and yet still stand for Rome, a divine entity of a different kind. The distinction between the two, while important on the Palatine or Capri, was easily blurred by distance.

After the second transfer of power within the first family of the Palatine, the world without emperors was over. Any emperor might readily be a god in places where that was the sort of ruler required. Caligula declared Tiberius unworthy of divine honours, a verdict that Tiberius would have approved, and of unsound mind, which he would not. Only the mint at Lugdunum in Gaul, the future city of Lyons, made the mistake of issuing gold coins showing the newly dead emperor as a god. The judgement that he was mad was, however, one which Tiberius would on many days have made of Caligula.

Later in the same year, 37 CE, a boy called Lucius Domitius Ahenobarbus was born. His mother was Caligula's sister, the Agrippina born in the camp in Germany who would forever be known as the Younger. Waiting to care for the new entrant in the race for power were the nurses who would give him their milk. Both women were former slaves who carried the Claudian name, Claudia Ecloge and Claudia Alexandria, just two specialist members of what was now a ruling household of thousands.

The *domus Caesaris* was the absolute centre of the Roman world. Reasoning about what made good government was still in flux, but the core truth, still uncomfortable to some, was not. The arguments of those who had killed Julius Caesar were studied by the nostalgic. They were no longer of relevance to the Vitellii. The balance of Senatus and Populus in SPQR, the senate and the people, was becoming antiquarian fiction. The balance that mattered much more was between those in the senate and the court who appeased and flattered – and those in the city streets who were appeased, flattered and fed in return.

24

ILL WILL FOR THE TWIN

In serving Caligula, Lucius and Aulus Vitellius had different but complementary points of vantage. Lucius was among the first men of empire. He had never held those older republican certainties that goodness came from Rome and badness from everywhere else, a confidence that had so long applied to wine and fruits as well as constitutions. He was comfortable with words of worship and deeds of abasement, with scenes of absolute power changing the absolutely powerful. Aulus, in the second imperial generation, had already watched Caligula as closely as any man, sharing parties on Capri and chariot racetracks at Rome. Between them they had a fine sense of the new dangers and opportunities.

In the court of the Palatine the terms of Tiberius's will were an early casualty. Like Augustus at Nola, the dying emperor had been suspicious of his successor till close to the end, convinced by Thrasyllus that he would live long enough to pass over Caligula. His preferred choice was his own teenage grandson, Tiberius Gemellus, only surviving twin son of the heavy-drinking Drusus whom Sejanus had manoeuvred to his death.

Gemellus was brother to the young Julia whom Augustus had asked of as he died. His birth had been commemorated on coins. He had his own distinction: no twins had previously been born to the Caesars. The quiet and capable Blandus was Gemellus's brother-in-law and might be his protector. But, when Tiberius's death eventually came, Gemellus was still too young and unsupported within the household.

Tiberius felt able to stipulate instead only that the two young men, Caligula aged twenty-five and Gemellus aged eighteen, should share power. This was a ploy comprehensible within the republican tradition of joint consuls, but not in a government based on the *domus Caesaris*. A Roman household had only one head. For challenging that necessity Tiberius's will was deemed invalid on grounds of his insanity, a regular device at Rome but made ironic by its exercise in favour of a man whose own mind so wavered into imaginary worlds.

Caligula promised to adopt Gemellus instead of sharing power with him, a perilous offer to any recipient. Gemellus, a dark and brooding teenager, became ever more reasonably anxious. He had been born on the day that Germanicus had died, a cause for nervousness among the superstitious. Even when he had only a cough, he suspected worse. He began adding to his diet some daily antidotes to common poisons.

This might have been common sense if the protection were easily available. Cretan carrots and Gallic nard, wild poppy and parsley, myrrh and frankincense, rhubarb and ginger, iris from Illyria were all recommended. For added efficacy there was the blood of a duck that lived on poisonous plants by the Black Sea, served with aniseed, acacia juice, turpentine and malabathrum leaves. But none of these more exotic items would be accessible without risking attention.

Like all cough medicines, they left an odour on the breath. Gemellus took the risk nonetheless. The closeness of the dining couches betrayed him. Caligula sniffed the air. A reasonable precaution was an act of ungrateful distrust, an 'antidote against Caesar'. On the charge of thinking that he would be poisoned at the emperor's dinner table, Gemellus was ordered to kill himself.

The third head of the household of Augustus had long watched and learnt the theatrical arts necessary to survive as an heir and to prosper as an emperor. He had also absorbed lessons that brought benefit to Rome beyond the Palatine. Water had been always precious on Capri, a dry island with few underground springs. It did not need to be so scarce in the capital, a city on a major river surrounded by streams from volcanic hills.

Caligula did not accept that the fountains and waterfalls of the Anio should serve only the neighbours of Rubellius Blandus at Tibur. He ordered the construction of the *Aqua Claudia*, forty-five miles of tunnels and arches from new mountain lakes, changing the river's course, spending huge sums from the treasury, easing economic recession long before the aqueduct itself improved the water supply. The *Aqua Claudia* soared over the lavish tombs of successful tradesmen like Eurysaces the baker.

Tibur was Caligula's birthplace, or rather it was one of the places that claimed the credit. Those who lived near the famous temple of Hercules appreciated the claim that it was the emperor's home. Any connection to Hercules, the most famous half-man-half-god in the pantheon, would appeal to the emperor and might be good for business. Business was important if the flight of cash and credit four years before was not to be repeated. Business throughout the empire improved.

Other changes that Caligula ordered to the natural order were less useful. On Capri he endured the joke from Thrasyllus that he had as much chance of becoming emperor as of riding on water over the Bay of Naples. One of his acts after inheriting the throne and proving the prophecy wrong was to order construction of a three-and-a-half-mile floating bridge over which he rode in the armour of Alexander the Great. His most favoured advisers followed from Baiae to Puteoli in chariots, recalling the processions of eastern kings. Wise courtiers applauded the feat. The watching people, fuelled by feasts from thousands of sacrificial beasts, enthusiastically concurred.

Caligula was a popular replacement at Rome for a recluse who rarely left Capri. His visibility was an advantage. To be tall and pale made a Roman stand out from the crowd. If his hair was thick on his body and thin on his head, if he corrected these defects by threats as well as artifice, this was not a problem for a veteran of Palatine manners. He allowed the exiled actors back to Rome.

Whether the subject was himself or something more challenging, Caligula's mantra was change. For the first six months that change seemed good for the household and beyond. The Palatine had an emperor in residence again, a man whom his courtiers could not only see but sell to the world outside, to ambassadors, to supplicants, to all those seeking an emperor's decision. By explaining

Caligula to those who needed to understand him, they could both earn and exert their own influence.

This optimism at court did not last long. Quite quickly, the now almost traditional role of an interpreter, recognisable even to the few who remembered Augustus, became impossible to play. Some said that Caligula had a sickness of the mind, even that he as well as Gemellus had been poisoned. Whatever was the cause, the subversion of the expected soon became the only result that a courtier could expect. The frail slave from Smyrna, 'Tiberius Julius', already skilled with Caligula's account books, became a master of what was virtually a circus art, the ability to place his head in a lion's mouth and live to tell the tale.

Caligula increasingly needed men to magnify and multiply his pretences. All obstacles became affronts. Like a conjuror gripped by his own magic he began to present himself as one who could challenge any rule of nature. Not only, he said, were his sisters his sexual partners, his sisters had to have sex with his eunuchs. The impossible was possible, the invisible visible. One day came the order for a vast economic construction; on another day for a ruler's artifice, designed to cow and impress, a construction of his own mania for the crowds.

The new normal created new stories. The older men and women of the house remembered having to adapt to Augustus's daughter's and granddaughter's exile for adultery, to Ovid's exile for encouraging it. They now saw an entire section of the Palatine as a brothel for the daughters of the aristocracy, a whim that had of necessity to be wise.

The unfortunate had to join Caligula on a fake invasion of Britain. 'Tiberius Julius' joined a jaunt to a destination as far from Smyrna as any man could imagine. The emperor saw himself in the steps of Julius Caesar, conquering the northern ocean as he had conquered the Bay of Naples. His troops did no more than collect shells on the Channel beaches. The result was proclaimed a triumph.

To survive in Caligula's Rome required a new sense of what was real and what might be made real. Patience was the essential virtue. The careless or backward-looking were quickly caught. Like any returning provincial governor, Lucius Vitellius was regularly under threat, for having been either too successful or not successful enough. He looked after himself. He promoted himself. He flattered himself. He flattered Caligula.

Flattery, like taxation, became ever more necessary for civilised life. It might be deplored, even denounced. There were different kinds of flattery, different levels and purposes, but the exchange of sincerity for advantage spread and flowed from bedrooms to banquet room to business rooms, pervasive like a scent, as natural and necessary as breathing.

25

MAN TALKS TO A MOON

Before the Palatine was a palace it was the home of an old Roman hero, Quintus Lutatius Catulus, a saviour of his city against invading German tribes a century before, one of many models for his fellow citizens to match for vigour and virtue. Catulus was not only a soldier. He was a poet. He read and borrowed from the Greeks before it was fashionable, setting a trail that Horace and Ovid would follow. He was a connoisseur of the theatre, so enamoured of one stage star that he had likened his entrances to the sunrise: 'though he is human, he seems more beautiful than a god'.

In art the human and divine could walk together, heroes with gods, even men and women who were less than heroic. That was what happened in poetry and that was what poets could make happen. Caligula took past precedent – from poets, orators and the merely passionate – and twisted it as no one ever had. He was happy in his own house to be addressed as a god. Sometimes he was insistent. Catulus's sunrise was a metaphor. Caligula presented himself as the Sun itself.

Distinctions blurred. Stories of blurred distinctions blurred into each other. Tiberius had once compared Caligula to the sun as an insult: the young prince was a Phaethon, the Sun god's son, who by reckless chariot-driving came close to setting the mythological world on fire. Caligula, however, spoke of himself as Sun the father, not Phaethon the son, bringing universal light and not destruction. Whether Caligula believed in his own divinity or merely wished to press the limits of flattery was as unimportant as it was unclear.

This presented peculiar problems for those around him. In courtly culture a man who presented himself as the Sun might reasonably imagine himself alongside the Moon. This was a kind of logic. The Sun and Moon were like each other. They were both gods that could be seen, visible by their very nature, not hidden like Hercules or Minerva. Both watched over the seasons for growing food and keeping Rome alive, a constant male and female symbol in the sky.

The Moon was also the goddess of every scheme that came to men at night in their dreams. To Horace, writing as the poet laureate of Augustus's Rome, she was the *siderum regina bicornis*, the twin-horned queen of the stars, a charioteer who drove a two-horse racing chariot, nimbler than the four-horsed kind that had dragged the son of the Sun god too close to the earth. She even had a temple on the Palatine, close to where Caligula spent his nights. In the new realism of the court it might seem natural that the chariot-riding emperor and his neighbour should be friends.

Lucius was quick to absorb these new rules of what was real. He promised prayers and sacrifices, setting a new standard of study for those who thought that humouring alone would be enough to keep them in their jobs. 'I am talking to the Moon,' Caligula told him. 'Can you see her with me too?' Lucius, his head veiled in the eastern style, showed no surprise. He replied that he could not see the emperor with the Moon because 'gods were visible only to other gods'.

This was the wit of an experienced man. It was pitched so as to protect himself, whether Caligula was sane and cleverly testing his courtier or deluded and genuinely believing in his own divinity, or merely experimenting with his own dreams. If he had answered, as the cruder flatterer might have done, that he could clearly see Caligula conversing with the Moon, he risked being drawn deeper into a trap. He might then have been asked what else he could see, which other gods were there, until the laughing emperor could snap out of his pretence and mock him as a charlatan. If he had admitted that he could see nothing, he risked the accusation of doubting the emperor.

Lucius did not know what Caligula genuinely believed about himself. He might have been referring to dining-room furniture, the Moon that was the name for the highest crescent tier of the dining couches. He might have meant almost anything. He might have been simply mad. Men still remembered Tiberius's rival, Agrippa Postumus, fishing and holding the trident of Neptune before he was consigned to his island asylum. In the court of Caligula it was safest to assume that the highest demand for flattery was what the emperor was intending. And, like the crow with the cheese at the top of the tree, he wanted the flattery of those on the ground to be true.

Lucius Vitellius needed to be as insincere as was necessary. Flattering Tiberius had required political calculation, a balancing of factors that the courtier could know. Flattering Caligula required something more. The line that 'gods were visible only to other gods' entered history like one from a famous play. Lucius had to think deeply, drawing from all that he had seen in Rome and in the east, but, most of all, he had to think fast, like an improviser on a stage. When Caligula was the star, everyone had to be in the same play.

As a supporting actor to an autocrat actor-manager, Lucius had an audience of one, the star himself. He had to anticipate, to catch his cues. He had to see the walls and fences within the emperor's mind, between common governance and aggrandisement close to mania, between management of nature and challenge to its laws. Sometimes Caligula saw himself in an oriental paradise of applause; at other times there were the usual garden lines to be drawn, dead flowers to be cleared and damp beds of work to be dug. Lucius learnt fast to serve his master both in his labours as emperor and his delusions about what an emperor was.

A popular professional actor and singer at the court was less nimble than Lucius. Apelles was a confidant of Caligula more in the mould of Aulus Vitellius than Lucius, a companion of play more than administration. When the emperor stood by a statue of Jupiter on the Palatine and asked the unfortunate entertainer which of the two was the greater, Apelles hesitated.

It was not hard for watchers to see why. To say that Caligula was lesser than any god might offend an emperor whose weapons of revenge were closer at hand than any thunderbolt on Mount Olympus. To say that the king of the gods was a lesser god than Caligula might just as surely offend an emperor who affected to be an inti-mate of the Olympian deities.

The greater flattery would have been the lesser risk. Caligula had begun to experiment with putting his own marble head on the heads of statues of Jupiter and Apollo. An extravagant response praising the new presentation of a sculpture might have both pre-served Apelles's self-respect and avoided his punishment. It was the hesitation that brought him down. Caligula had Apelles bound and flogged, his skin falling from his body while his cries and screams brought praise from Caligula for their sweet sound. The singer played his most miserable role – and also survived to tell the tale, to pass on his horror story and to play other roles.

The story spread, just as the quick wit of Lucius had done. Brutal violence was everywhere in Rome. There was nothing unusual in a man with power flogging one who lacked it. But a good story of violence and cruelty was still worth telling.

Caligula was a master of the quick, impromptu reply – in both Greek and Latin. Like Tiberius he enjoyed the company of philos-ophers, although he sometimes tested their metaphysics by execu-tion. Once he had a man killed and for days continued to invite him to dinner. The empty space had its own meaning. The household adapted or died, sometimes both adapting and dying. Lucius was a great adapter, a skill all the more tested when what was real was increasingly only in the emperor's mind.

Phaedrus told a story of a stork who served dinner party food to a fox in a deep, narrow dish where his guest could not reach; when the fox returned the invitation the food appeared on a wide, shal-low plate impossible for the stork. Awkwardness for the guest was comedy for the host. Diners at Caligula's court could see themselves in the fable, as in so many others.

There were traditional dinners for senators, their wives and children where Caligula gave presents, togas for the men, purple scarves for their families. There was the illusion of equality, one of the purposes of men and women taking food together as guests or hosts. There were also novel dinners at which some of the food was made of gold, temptations to one human appetite while destructive of another. His own new clothes included flowing eastern robes and floral tunics. Like Tiberius he gave a huge promotion to a man who had impressed him with greed.

While Caligula played god, Lucius Vitellius became a priest of Rome, a member of the *Fratres Arvales*, the Brothers of the Fields, a body that proudly traced its roots to the prehistory of the city. The Arvals, like the Sun and the Moon, were responsible for the harvest. Few institutions were more determined than the Arvals to boast their importance, producing annual stone lists and minutes of their activities, records of feasts and sacrifices, the rolling of jars down hills and the award of rose petals.

Others seemed not to rate the Arvals as significantly as they rated themselves. At a time when there were many writers of history, handing on their stories to each other, the true and the merely good, the name of the brothers barely appeared in history at all. The Arvals did not matter. Lucius was a pioneer of flattering the man who did matter, and whose place in history was built on some of the strangest stories of flattery ever told.

26

GOOD WATER, GOLDEN MEAT

The Palatine palace was growing fast, piece by piece, house by house. An ancient temple of the Forum became a new entrance. The twin divinities, Castor and Pollux, one with a Greek king for a father, the other sired by Jupiter, were Caligula's doormen. This was a world of blurred lines. A gold statue of Caligula had to be daily dressed in whatever the emperor was wearing, served by priests who were themselves flattered by sacrifices for their table, peacocks, pheasants and black grouse.

Those who had shared the parties of Caligula's youth, like Aulus Vitellius and Eutychus the charioteer, shared the riotous street-rampages permitted by his impunity. Aulus became a charioteer himself, the sport of the Moon and Sun in the heavens, where victory depended on manoeuvring the sharpest turns of the circuit, listening to a man ahead on horseback shouting advice, spinning a pair of wheels made in different sizes to make the turning easier. Aulus's single gashed thigh was a lucky escape.

Caligula also played the benevolent patriarch, restoring elections for minor offices, allowing the candidates to feast and entertain their voters. He held the consulship and allowed Germanicus's brother Claudius to hold it with him in 37 CE. He bought support in cash. Then he squandered what he had paid for. He distributed food. Then he would close the grain stores and condemn the city people to a few days' hunger, just to show that he could.

He had a showman's contempt for the dull. He hoped for a great disaster, like Augustus's *clades Variana* or Tiberius's stadium collapse, anything to mark his reign and ensure it was never forgotten. 'A man ought either to be frugal or a Caesar,' he would say. Guests at his banquets might be hungry if their bread and meat had been made of gold, but they would have something to talk about when they went home.

In the east he appointed Antiochus, Thrasyllus's wife's nephew and another of his party favourites, to be the new king of Commagene, sending him home with the entire revenue exacted during its time as a Roman province. Then he pulled away the throne, hardly before Antiochus had settled on it, as though in a party game. In the west his trophy shells from a beach facing the coast of Britain were just another illusion. He made pearls disappear in glasses of wine, dissolved or cunningly saved for the next show.

He paraded his Julian descent from Augustus's only daughter over the merely Claudian claim of the clearly insane Tiberius. But whatever his family line and whatever the name of the show, the administration of empire had to go on – and the staff of the Palatine had to make it happen. He tried to reduce the power of courtier ex-slaves within the palace. He deemed his own decisions both sanctified and the best. But those decisions could never be enough to achieve results, even the most bizarre ones. Eutychus became suddenly extraordinarily rich – and powerful enough to build a new home for his chariot horses by the labour of Roman legionaries. A Greek freedman, Callistus, corrupt, competent and a close reader of Caligula's mind, became as grand as any courtier of Tiberius.

Long pipes were laid for the *Aqua Claudia*, each section fractionally lower than the last to ensure the smooth passage of water when the testing and then the full flow would begin. Great arches maintained the height of the pipes where the natural terrain would have brought a crashing fall. The treasury paid the slave-masters and the brick-makers, the engineers and their assistants while one of the walks used by Rubellius Blandus on his way from Tibur to Rome became an industrial highway.

'Tiberius Julius' from Smyrna became a quiet accountant of aqueduct projects. Blandus, who had done good service rebuilding parts of Rome destroyed by fire, never saw the result. He had survived the dangers of a marriage above his station. He died before seeing the *Aqua Claudia* deliver any useful water to the hydrants, baths and pleasure domes of Rome.

Caligula approved another imperial marriage. Valerius Messalla Barbatus was a senator, a distinguished grandson of Augustus's sister Octavia, and a loyal servant of Caesar's house. His daughter, Messalina, was allowed to marry the brother of Germanicus and the emperor's uncle, hardly a gracious permission since Claudius was a disabled antiquarian not expected to climb further the career ladder of the Palatine. Caligula, in what may have seemed a disarmingly modest act, married Lollia Paulina, the wife (quickly ex-wife) of a senator from Gaul. Lollia was quickly Caligula's ex-wife too, supplanted by a mother of three daughters, Milonia Caesonia, whom he was said to like parading naked at court. Caesonia won the reputation as her new husband's poisoner – although any dose seemed to make his behaviour even more like a madman's.

The prudent view on the Palatine was that no act of ingratiating flattery could be too much, no applause too loud. A wise man might make a speech in the senate thanking Caligula for an invitation to dinner. Since Gaius could on one occasion spend the annual tribute of three provinces on a single dinner, on gold and liquid pearls to match sums not expendable even on seafood, flamingos and giraffe, this was maybe justified. The practice of senators kissing the emperor's cheek did not return. Caligula preferred to proffer a foot.

A writer of Atellan farces who made a *double entendre* of doubtful taste found himself on a theatrical funeral pyre, deemed to have had the opportunity of flattery and missed his chance. His screams came as interval entertainment. If anyone made a noise during a show by his favourite actor, Mnester, Caligula would have him dragged from his seat and flogged. Sometimes he himself would flog the offender. Antonia, mother to Germanicus, protector of Lucius and Pallas and veteran of the Palatine since its beginnings, committed suicide in a lonely protest. Lucius survived within a shrinking group of those upon whom he could rely.

In the third of his fables of contemporary court life Phaedrus offered a cautionary tale of a man called Princeps, that very useful title invented by Augustus but also the name of a fashionable flute-player. Princeps was a very superior slave who had broken his leg in an accident on stage, an acrobatic soaring that was too high for his own good. After three months in straps he was about to make a comeback, keen to earn a good pay-day, preening himself for the applause he had missed so much in his forced recuperation.

Musicians, unlike actors, did not wear masks. This Princeps was therefore a familiar face. Phaedrus described how a rumour surged around the theatre that the long-absent celebrity was about to appear. Even a rumour brought excited applause. The flautist finally appeared and blew out kisses to his fans.

Unfortunately, at the same time, the real Princeps arrived to take his seat in the stands. The flautist Princeps was unaware. The crowd roared its devotion to their emperor. The flautist thought that the roar was for himself. The crowd delighted in the confusion.

The Princeps in the audience was the master of the *domus divinae*, the holy house. The Princeps on the stage, his leg strapped in snow-white bands, looked more like a server at the Palatine tables. The deluded artist was lucky to escape with nothing worse than a dying on stage, a few catcalls, a kicking back out into the street, a gentler end than Phaedrus himself, so recently so fearful of Sejanus, might have predicted in any other form than a fable.

The new world was a stage. Stealing an emperor's thunder might once have meant winning a military victory that Augustus or Tiberius would have preferred to win themselves – a dangerous enough success. Phaedrus described a different theft of thunder, the mere mistaking of an emperor's applause for one's own. This might be no less dangerous.

The fable was an extended metaphor for a shifting landscape of politics. Just as gluttony had become different from greed, flattery had become different from exaggeration or lying. There was a new pattern which stretched beyond any act or instance. It was a web.

27

TORTURE OF AN ACTRESS

Diplomacy required its own kind of flattery. Flattery was built from lies, and going to lie abroad for one's country was what diplomats did before there was a Roman Empire and for long after it had fallen. Any official from Syria or Egypt might be used to addressing a self-styled king of kings. When representing his country in Rome, the deal was whatever the diplomat had to do.

Caligula's expectation to receive worship as a god was none the less perilous for diplomats at his court. The differences between Jews and Greeks, never-ending squabbles in many tiny pimples of the Mediterranean empire, unusually violent in 38 CE, became much more dangerous when Caligula had to be appeased. An embassy of Alexandrian Jews expressed contempt at any suggestion of a man's divinity. Caligula was even more contemptuous of their disbelief. The rival Greeks responded by giving the emperor even more divine titles.

Caligula asked the Jews why they avoided pork. They replied cautiously that there were also some who avoided lamb. Caligula agreed. He himself, he said, did not like lamb. This small measure of agreement about dinner was as much as the meeting achieved. Caligula showed more interest in the gardens where the talks were taking place, ordering windows and art for his pavilion walls. Adjudication, if it ever came at all, was not immediate. For courtiers there were months of money to be made from taking bribes from both sides.

Caligula saw worship as his right. And, if he were to receive any lesser form of flattery, the decision to do so, he thought, should be his own, not a choice of some barbarian dietary obsessives. When he dictated letters to the new governor of Syria, Publius Petronius, Lucius's successor and one of the Romans who best understood the delicate politics of Judaea, he added threats in his own handwriting. The clash of incompatible beliefs was not long in coming.

Barely eighteen months into his reign the Greek population of Jamnia, the date town of Judaea, erected an altar for the imperial cult. The resident Jews tore it down. Caligula saw a personal insult and ordered Petronius that the great temple at Jerusalem itself should be converted into an imperial shrine. It should house a giant statue of the emperor as Jupiter. The governor was to use two legions to enforce this decree.

Petronius was horrified that what might be harmless, even useful, flattery elsewhere was being imposed where it could cause riot, rebellion and religious war. He used first the bureaucratic tool of delay, easier when in a remote border province than in Rome. He ordered the building of the statue, but told the sculptors not to hurry. When he marched his Syrian legions to the border of Galilee he met a massive demonstration from those who saw the statue as their prime anxiety. The harvest was being neglected. Famine loomed.

Petronius withdrew and wrote to Caligula with a direct appeal to change his mind. This was a dangerous tactic from a distance. Even for Lucius, watching closely at Caligula's shoulder, the emperor's mood was hard to predict. Caligula told Petronius first to obey orders and secondly to commit suicide. But Petronius, in the same way as Pontius Pilate, survived.

Suddenly, courtly expertise had become of no account. Before the suicide instruction to Petronius reached Syria came the reports of Caligula's own death. This was a matter of vital importance on the Palatine, and only a little less in Syria, even if elsewhere the news mattered much less. His fantastical aspirations were a burden to those who had to see and skirt around them, but to most citizens of the empire they meant no more than they did to the Moon. Details of his departure were anyway scarce at first.

Every day, at Caligula's last week of Palatine games, 41 CE, there was some sort of free lunch: apples, pears and pomegranates, dates and figs, beef steaks and chicken wings, live ducks and hens, deep-filled baskets hurled into a tight-packed crowd as bounty from the emperor. It was just like the very best of old times, when men who wanted votes fed those who wanted feasts, or perhaps a parody of those days. On the familiar wooden benches in the courtyard of the marble palace, in the pale January sun, most were not bothered about memory or mockery. Quail and partridge scuttled around their feet to be caught for later.

Before the assassination, anxiety gripped only the very few. Cassius Chaerea was an undistinguished officer of the palace guard, a soldier softened by court life whom Caligula enjoyed mocking as effeminate, giving him erotic daily passwords to hand on to his men, turning his own security into a sexual comedy of cocks and eunuchs. Quintilia was an actress, suspected of knowledge of an assassination plot. Caligula hoped that Chaerea would be so determined to prove his masculinity that he would be her especially brutal torturer.

Chaerea did what he was told to do. Quintilia revealed nothing of whatever she knew about the would-be killers. Maybe she had not known much. Chaerea so wrecked her body and face that even Caligula felt guilty. When the emperor ordered compensation for the no longer beautiful actress, Chaerea was as confused as he was ridden by guilt.

The plotters were disorganised in every way. Each had his own very different reason for thinking that this last day of the games in honour of Augustus, in the place where his body had lain in state, was the day when his great-grandson should die. The chance of success must have seemed low. Among the hopeful who had failed to act before were Cornelius Lentulus Gaetulicus, one of the boosters of Caligula's connection to Tibur, and Valerius Asiaticus, the wealthy Gaul who had endured Caligula's critique of his wife's performance in bed. Many had spoken. Some had spoken to each other. None had acted and time was running out.

Yet when, towards the end of the performance, Caligula left his seat to judge a visiting choir from Greece and take a bath, Chaerea, consumed by his own behaviour as much as by constitutional nicety, followed him into one of the twisting Palatine passages and hacked him with his cavalryman's sword. Others added their blows. Loyal bodyguards briefly fought the assassins, but there could be little loyalty to Caligula once he was dead. Soon there was none.

Chaerea then escaped through the corridors and covered paths to the sometime house of Germanicus. On the side of the Palatine where Caligula's father and mother had once lived there was the usual panic of assassins, echoes of the Ides of March eighty-five years before, the uncertainty whether the killers would be hailed as heroes or killed in turn. At the heart of the court, those who had run the real business of empire under the dead emperor prepared for life under a successor whom they hoped better to control.

Their choice was Germanicus's brother, Antonia's son, Messalina's husband. The new Emperor Claudius was the senior member of the Julio-Claudian house, an unexpected successor except in the sense that the expected successors were becoming rather few, a survivor on account of his all too visible disabilities for office – slurred speech, a limp and a genuine preference for ancient Etruscan texts over the politics of his own time. Palace guardsmen were said to have found him cowering behind a curtain. Maybe he was close enough to one of the plots to have been less than wholly surprised. Certainly he was backed by Callistus, the most powerful freedman of the old court.

Claudius's disabilities and eccentricities would throughout his reign remain a useful cloak, discouraging to those who did not see him operating day by day but of less concern to those who knew him. His ways might not be wholly predictable but, by the standards of the past four years, he was a man who shared some of the reality that others saw. Chaerea was executed on the very normal grounds that any assassin should die to discourage others.

With Caligula's death Aulus Vitellius had lost his friend and fellow charioteer. But Lucius, long-time protégé of Antonia, would work with Claudius and his wife Messalina very well. The status 'friend of Caesar', as the crowd had taunted Pontius Pilate, was the greatest, and most fragile, status of all. The new Caesar found many old friends.

28

GARDEN ORNAMENTS

Lucius did not attract the charges of corruption that clung to many in the court. None of the Vitellii was known for susceptibility to bribes, not even Aulus, whose laxity with money was much more famed than any greed for it. Lucius was wealthy nonetheless. Being a powerful man on the Palatine was still a path to profit. The honest avoiders of risk made money as well as the gamblers. Lucius Vitellius invested in land, as Roman senators always had, and some of it was around his house in Aricia, just a few miles south of Rome on the Appian Way.

Aricia stood for freedom from Rome. '*Egressum!*', 'Phew, I'm out of there!' wrote Horace as he began his part in a diplomatic mission for Augustus during the civil wars. *Egressum magna me accepit Aricia Roma*: Aricia welcomed me when mighty Rome was left behind. But Aricia was also near enough to the capital for messages to flow quickly back and forth and for a cautious courtier to be able to return if the new emperor needed him. The first months of Claudius's reign were calm compared to Caligula's last. It was unwise to be complacent, but the family could still enjoy a few meals under their fig trees.

Lucius in his late forties was still a fit man, known no more for sickness than for greed. He was a more venerable figure in his own garden, less wired within the latest dramas, with his wife Sextilia, veiled and grander in bearing, albeit from a family less close to the *domus Caesaris*, their taller sons, Aulus and Lucius, the first somewhat stouter too, both in their twenties, survivors of Tiberius in Capri and Claudius's Rome. Food was simpler where the country met the city: vegetables in little dishes, salted meat, honey cakes, quince, pistachios, flasks of spring water and spiced wine, and at the table centre statues taller than the flasks, though miniature nonetheless, the household gods of the Vitellii, the wooden Peace and Plenty that his old father, Publius, had worshipped in Nuceria.

Although these guardian witnesses to the family's progress were looked after by more household slaves than Publius would have had, they were still recognisably the same, some painted, some in stone, still garlanded and looking after the food as they did in every family, claiming, like garden birds, the first call on anything that fell from a plate. Old Publius would have been surprised only by a few interlopers among the statuary.

Amid the featureless figures in stone and wood were others in gold, robed in the Greek style and recognisable as individuals: Pallas, *a rationibus*, the accountant, Narcissus, *ab epistulis*, master of the post, and Callistus, *a libellis*, the sifter of petitions. To those familiar with the court there was also Polybius, the speechwriter and secretary, Posides, literary and refined, recognisably the eunuch, all of them former slaves themselves, once victims of vicious assaults, newly loyal outsiders as the Vitellii once had been, the men with the greatest power over every family table. Every public servant had his job. Their statues were a reminder that men could grant favours just as could gods. Rome was not so very far away.

The new emperor was content with the idea of a household being a government. Physical frailty had kept Claudius from following Tiberius into the army or Caligula on to the racetrack. He had few links to the clubs of Roman life. His nervousness in speech separated him from the senate. A crippled survivor of childhood disease and an even more aggressive childhood tutor, at key moments he had been deemed too weak to be even worth killing. The weapons of the weak, insincerity and flattery, were the ones he knew best.

He stared at his courtiers from small, deep-set eyes, short, fleshy and lopsided whether he stood, sat or reclined to eat from a couch. Freed slaves, scribes, cooks and accountants, eunuchs for food-tasting, sex or book-keeping were the people with whom he had passed most of his life. The posts held by the men in Lucius's garden were not new, but it became quickly clear that they were more powerful than before.

Claudius gave out gold rings with his own portrait to designate those who had free access to his presence. As Ovid had pointed out sharply in his exile from Augustus's court, anyone who knew an emperor at all would pretend to be his friend. In a single house, without distinctions of rank or constitutional office, some sort of ordering of intimacy was essential. All were more confident once knowing where they stood, or should be standing.

Gaius Julius Callistus had gained his first two names as a freed slave of Caligula and his third from the Greek for beautiful. He soon became as intimate with the new emperor as he had been with the old. Some said he had himself engineered the change of regime, happy for the doubtful credit of assassination to go elsewhere. Callistus had been as important in Claudius's ascent to power as the guardsmen searching behind the curtain. In an age of only rudimentary maths, he studied risk and accounts and, like Claudius, the art of gambling.

There was the beginning of a career structure for courtiers. 'Tiberius Julius' from Smyrna was freed at this time, promoted, allowed to marry into the aristocracy and prepared for a career as a procurator, the rank of old Publius Vitellius under Augustus. There he showed further the courtier's art of not only serving the emperor but identifying his successors. A machine of new opportunity was being born, as perpetuating of itself as the senate and the army.

In the countryside beyond Aricia, where courtly promotions mattered hardly at all, money moved more quickly from purse to purse, buying support as it was spent and spent again. Claudius held games. He put on shows. He expanded Caligula's projects of public work. He took control of the corn supply from the senate and began a new harbour to protect the transport ships and prevent local floods. East of Rome he ordered the draining of the Fucine Lake through three miles of mountain tunnel, levelling high ground, employing 30,000 men, promising new fields for food.

The *Aqua Claudia* was meanwhile slowly reaching Rome from the nearer hills above Tibur, bending along the contour lines by minutely measured gradients. Rome's imperial *aquarii* worked in a *familia aquarum* of 700 people, both slave and free, funded through

Claudius's own treasury and by water taxes. They were supervised by another Imperial freedman, a *procurator aquarum*, conducting an endless routine of calibrated inspection interrupted by emergency.

Seen from the palace tables, there was a power in applying numbers to politics too. According to the revered Greek thinker Solon, those who had influence with tyrants were like pebbles used in maths, the same stone sometimes representing a very large number and at other times a very small one. So too were the men of a court. To Lucius Vitellius, no great soldier himself and much more comfortable behind a desk, calculators like the men represented in his dining-room shrine were the future.

Lucius flattered Pallas in particular, the chief of the imperial treasury and sometime slave and freedman of Claudius's mother, Antonia. It was Pallas whom she had trusted to deliver her allegations about Sejanus's crimes to Capri. Almost as important was the man who filed most letters as pending, Polybius, the emperor's writer of speeches, a translator of Homer into Latin and Virgil into Greek, or so those claimed who wanted a word said on their behalf. Then, and not least, came Narcissus, who controlled the flow of all letters to and from the Palatine. These men were essential for the working of the empire.

On most days Claudius ate simply with his own children and the children of his friends. The newly prominent freedmen did not need to be invited to the extravagant banquets. Their influence came from more exclusive proximity, becoming notorious for protecting their clients from harm, cancelling any excess generosity by their master, rewarding flattery of the kind that Caligula had demanded, sometimes rejecting it, reversing judgments, altering documents. The year 41 CE was a good year for Antiochus IV of Commagene, reinstated to the throne by order of Caligula, then deprived of it by the same caprice, then restored to his inheritance by the brother of Germanicus.

When Claudius declared war on other people's gluttony, venturing where Tiberius had feared to go, a ban on stuffed dormice was piloted into law, if probably not into common practice. Little more noticed was his ban on stewed meats in the streets. Both were expressions, not exertions, of his power. When Claudius wanted his own seaside dining cave, matching those of Tiberius and the garden-lover, Lucullus, the builders of Baiae received their due instructions.

Emerging bureaucracy brought practical reform. There was a crackdown on theatrical carpenters whose seating failed the spectators, as it did in the catastrophe at Fidenae, or whose stage machinery failed the actors, as in Phaedrus' s fable of Princeps, the flautist with the broken leg. There was more than a moral to be learnt about stealing an emperor's applause. There was a problem and a solution. Sloppy circus builders would be food for the circus lions.

Freedmen and friends took their own homes around the Palatine. The renowned house of the republican orator Lucius Licinius Crassus, with its shady garden of lotus trees, became just another house of a confidant of Claudius. The homes of the freedmen, particularly those of Callistus and Posides, were sites of wonder in themselves. The dining room of Callistus had thirty pillars made from precious onyx and was notoriously barred to the man who had been his master when he had been a slave. Rotundus Drusillianus, from the household of Caligula's sister, Drusilla, was a collector of massive silver plates from Spain.

Posides lived in splendour alongside the eunuch priests of the *Magna Mater*, perhaps gaining his own quiet satisfaction for the crushing of his testicles as a slave child or the cutting of his scrotum as an adolescent, operations that had extended his sexual appeal at the cost of a high-pitched voice, hormonally elongated limbs and a powerful sense of difference. Phaedrus wrote sympathetically of a eunuch's plight in public life, the disgusting jokes and abuse about lost body parts that he had to endure in court, his struggle to argue that he should not be judged for bad treatment inflicted upon him but only for bad things he himself had done.

Phaedrus's fable was formed from a legal quip, the double meaning of a *testis*, the similarity of the words in Latin for witness and testicle. Although eunuch was a Greek word, a keeper of the bed, the fable was not a translation of anything by Aesop. The court setting was Roman, not the only one in the fables, almost as though Phaedrus himself, if he was an ex-slave, was a lawyer too.

Some grandees of Rome found their dependence on former slaves hard to endure; some thought that the damage done to a man by slavery would forever be a bar to virtue; but few thought they could turn back time. Any senators accused of plotting against Claudius found that an obsequious pleasantry to Polybius, Posides or Narcissus, perhaps a payment too, might save their lives.

Within this new system with new rules there was no shame in flattery, and for gluttony no blame. Household management of the Roman world – based on friendship not elections, responsive rather than initiating, more often random than systematic – was set to stay. The machinery of government and its oil were both essential. Both would remain the essence of court life for centuries, the oil lasting longer than almost any act, for good or ill, of the machine itself.

Forged around a court of characters ripe for satire, most of Phaedrus's fables, like Aesop's originals, were not about named human individuals. They were peopled by birds and beasts, safer subjects but sometimes bolder too, subversive, even directly attacking identifiable figures. A powerful animal, a lion or a great ape, would be shown abusing its power over the weak and gullible. When frogs in a pond asked Jupiter for a king and sneered at the god's first offer of a floating log, their next anointed monarch was a frog-eating snake. Men asked who was the old log and who was the new snake.

Canine characters showed the greedy and the flattering in ways that dogs peculiarly can, sniffing each other's arses, chasing their own reflections or being so gluttonous as to give up their own lives and freedom for a snack. A dog swimming with a piece of meat in his mouth would drop his meal to get the meat in the mouth of another dog appearing to swim beside him. A pack of dogs, desperate to lick some meat at the bottom of a river, would nearly drown themselves trying to drink the torrent dry. Dogs accepted the slavery of the collar in order to have fine food from the banqueting tables in their bellies; a wolf, however hungry, would not. Dogs were a means by which Roman readers in the age of Augustus's successors could look obliquely at themselves. Phaedrus was their guide.

Augustus himself had known a very different poet of the kennels, named, though not very certainly named, as Grattius Faliscus. Grattius's work on hunting explained what a Roman master of dogs might more practically expect: not a mirroring of his own morals but help on the hunt. Comparison of the two dog men, Phaedrus and Grattius, however dimly seen through their art, can begin to define what had changed at Rome since the death of Augustus at Nola.

Grattius was more a teacher than an artist. His dogs were only for the chase, not at all for chastising flatterers or gluttons. It was Grattius who set out in huntsman's verse how every country had its own kind of dog and how useful this was for visitors and invaders. Take a Persian dog. It was hard to tame but wild in battle. A Ukrainian dog disliked fighting but had wise instincts. A dog from China was fierce beyond all imagination. Corinthian dogs pursued pigs. Rhine dogs, known to all returning soldiers from the northern frontier, helped men hunt hares.

Dogs could be improved by foreign mates. African dogs had a bestiary of mates. Around the Caspian Sea the bitches bred with tigers, toughening the stock with every generation. Mountain Greek dogs, fit only for barking, would shut up when mated with mastiffs. The British dog, as long as an owner was not too fussy about looks and manners, was usefully careless of its own life in battle, even comparable to a hunting partner of the heroic Greeks.

Grattius was not a court poet like Virgil or Horace. He was not a troublemaker like Ovid. He represented a blunt, expansive, martial Rome. Unlike Phaedrus, Grattius was never a popular poet, his work surviving only in a single long fragment and datable only from a reference in Ovid's failed pleas to be released from exile by the cold Black Sea. In one line among thousands on love and myth, Ovid's essential guide to the Rome of his time, his companions and rivals, stood Grattius the dog-poet, listed in the architecture of place and mind that the universal poet was missing.

Compared to Grattius, Phaedrus's fables were more tricky. Their popularity came, like the Atellan farces which the emperor had banned, from their licensed dissection of old authority. Gluttons and flatterers were both seen as dogs. Phaedrus satirised the strong and also undermined the weak. He was both a flatterer and a critic of flattery, much more than a moral jester, an artist as hard to read with certainty as any of the courtiers among whom he moved.

Grattius had not used dogs to say what a poet might not dare to say about men. His hounds were hunters for food, helpers in war. German dogs were like German people, either to be subdued or to help Romans subdue. All dogs did vital tasks. If they did not, they would not be there. Breeding was a domination of nature. A poisoner could test his arts on the tongue of a dog.

29

LUCIUS RULES THE WORLD

Two years into his reign Claudius divided the senior men of Rome into three groups: those whom he needed for the conquest of Britain, the task in which Julius Caesar had failed and which Caligula had failed to begin; those whom he needed with him to stop them exploiting his absence by a coup; and those whom he trusted to run the city and empire while the emperor was away. The leader of the third group, consul in 43 CE for the second time, was Lucius Vitellius. This was the highest position that the Vitellii had reached so far.

It was almost 100 years since Caesar had twice crossed the Channel, or, as he called it, the Ocean, the name which made his efforts sound fabulously difficult in case he failed, which, unusually for him, he did. Tides had broken his ships. Gauls, not yet knowing the cost in their own deaths, revolted behind his back. Not even Caesar, the great self-praiser and author of his own history, could write that away.

Britain had been a conquest too far. Twice he gave up and went home, satisfied only that the southern British tribes seemed bribed enough to be loyal. What he most immediately wanted was to be richer and more powerful than his son-in-law back home, the irritatingly acclaimed Pompey the Great. Britain had not helped. Caesar's carefully edited version put his failure in the best possible light.

Augustus later considered another try. His flatterers even promised for a while that he would finish his father's task. But he had always bigger problems than a mere tempting irritant. Conquest had to justify its cost and the conquest of Britain, he thought, would not. Tiberius continued this policy of long oblivion and as his favourite island preferred Capri. Caligula thought about Britain briefly before finding easier fantasy schemes.

For Claudius in 43 CE this unfinished business was a chance to fashion himself in the best tradition of a Caesar, a great-great-grandnephew of Julius Caesar, as long as Rome could be kept secure while he was away. Neither Tiberius nor Caligula had dared to leave Italy as emperor. Claudius was the proudest writer, observer and thinker to rule Rome since Caesar. He knew how he might flatter himself – and be flattered – when he came back in triumph.

Claudius chose as the leader of the invasion force his commander in distant Pannonia, Aulus Plautius, one of his key supporters after Caligula's death, a man of no great family himself but a former consul, allegedly trusted by Tiberius, and related to the Vitellii. Plautius seemed a sound choice and proved to be so, neither too close to the grandees of Rome nor too far away.

Narcissus had to leave the comfortable Palatine tables where he sifted the empire's letters to its emperor. He too took the road to the mysterious island where the priests were Druids and people were their sacrifices. Plautius brought his nervous army to the pebbled beach of northernmost Gaul, showed them the shifting sea, and they refused to cross. Britain was more unknown than any place they had ever been, more bizarre than anywhere of which they knew. They needed reassurance.

Plautius stood on a podium, not a famous face except to the men who had followed him from the Danube, and visible only to a few. His speech failed to change their minds. Impatiently, and it did not at first seem wisely, Narcissus tried his own plea on behalf of the emperor. Nothing changed until the horror of taking orders from such a man became clear to the troops. An ex-slave affecting to lead an army was a crossing too far from Palatine to camp. Such reversal of roles had once been kept to the one day in the year when the low lorded it over the high, the festival of Saturn. '*Io Saturnalia*', they shouted, 'Happy holidays', mocking both one of the most powerful figures in the empire and themselves. The ships sailed for Britain.

Posides the eunuch sailed too, further outraging traditionalists in the army when he was given one of their highest bravery awards, the *hasta pura*, an ornamental spear, probably not, it was thought, for bravery: there were to be no last-ditch struggles on this British campaign, nothing to require a writer to become a fighter. Also on the trip was one of the many Palatine doctors, Scribonius Largus, famed for whitening Messalina's teeth and easing Antonia's tonsillitis. Claudius's personal doctor, Stertinius Xenophon, was one of the highest-paid members of staff. Even greater than his loyalty to the emperor was his devotion to his home island of Cos in the southern Aegean. The mud of Kent and Essex must have been an even greater ordeal for him than for the rest of the travelling court.

Claudius in Britain was an emperor in a hurry, not in the way that Julius Caesar was always in a hurry, circling and extending the edges of the Roman world, but in a hurry to get home. All his problems were at home, apart from those he had brought with him and would have to stay with him, the rivals whom he needed closely to watch. Those who reluctantly made the trip included Valerius Asiaticus, the rich Gaul who had tentatively plotted the killing of Caligula, Lucius Livius Galba, the heavy-faced favourite of Livia whom Tiberius had deprived of her legacy, and Titus Flavius Vespasianus, both protégé and protector of Narcissus. Vespasian was a politician and general whose mistress was Antonia's secretary, Caenis. Behind his military demeanour he was a fierce flatterer. With or without Caenis's advice, he had once made a senate speech thanking Caligula for a dinner invitation.

Lucius Vitellius was left in the *domus Caesaris* to run the normal business of government as best he could. His son, Aulus, had learnt early about power, swimming with Tiberius in Capri as a child, gambling and racing with Caligula. But his first close sight of administration came while Claudius was away invading the island that every predecessor had failed to win. Aulus, from his great height, was free to watch.

For all those left at Rome there were the permanent problems of corn supply, the new harbour at Ostia, the slow, snaking progress of the *Aqua Claudia* from Tibur, the drain for the Fucine Lake which for 1,900 years would be the longest tunnel in the world. Abroad there was the plan to end discontent in Judaea, the funding of a small war in Mauretania to the south of the straits of Hercules, and some consolidation of the tax base in Gaul. Senators had to be flattered that they had at least some of the power of their ancestors. The people always needed to be fed – and a new system of dated tickets for collecting the free corn was designed to prevent the queues at the end of each month.

In Britain itself there was little to interest the Vitellii except the glory that Claudius might find there and, if he didn't find, Lucius would have to promote and invent. Druids, their secret language and human sacrifices, were of much more interest to Claudius than they were to his hard-working man in Rome. Flattering the old antiquarian that he was also a great general was the central aim of the project. How much Claudius, an emperor with new military clothes, believed the flattery or merely pretended to believe it, was never clear.

Britain had oysters, mysterious creatures which grew fatter and thinner with the phases of the moon. That was indeed clear. There was tin in the western British mines, gold allegedly in the hills, several friendly native kings and even those that were unfriendly had sons who might betray them. There were traders who knew Rome well and were well known at Rome. There were slaves every-where. According to Caesar the British population was immense. So too was the number of its animals for human consumption, a class that did not include chickens, geese or hares, which the people kept as pets.

The less civilised Britons lived inland and clothed themselves in skins. Even Rome's friends on the coast wore blue tattoos. The hair on their heads and upper lips was long. Otherwise they were close-shaved. Groups of up to a dozen men, including fathers and sons, took to bed the same women, the children deemed always to belong to whichever man had done so first.

The British dogs, according to Grattius, Augustus's poet of the kennels, were usefully courageous, although they had well-known limitations: ugliness, ill-discipline, just like most of the people. It was necessary to penetrate the Britons to bring home their dogs, as he had ambiguously put it. Rape and enslavement were what Romans abroad did so routinely as to be rarely worth mentioning.

Claudius, whose own favourite was a small white dog, would have read his Grattius, omnivorous student that he was. Aulus Plautius might have pretended to know this author's list of national dogs which, behind its canine growls, was a window into how its writer and his readers saw their expanding world. The doctor, Scribonius Largus, made a speciality of treating dog bites. But otherwise the expectation of the courtiers was of nothing much bar mistletoe and superstition, surrounded by the same vicious waves, clinging mud and cloud that Publius Vitellius and his men had found on the German shore.

Good things, especially good food, came from the east. Those campaigning in Britain never felt further from Rome than when they ate. But, through good planning, Claudius and his travelling court had to eat in Kent and Essex for only sixteen days of a six-month absence from Rome. They landed on what was still then the island of Thanet, crossed the oyster-filled channel to the mainland, marched with elephants to what was not yet London and on to Colchester, where the local tribes, knowledgeable about Rome and well understanding Claudius's temporary need to be flattered, made a tactical surrender.

It had been a gamble, the kind of calculated risk that Claudius and Callistus understood well. Their men knew about gambling too. In the ground behind the invasion beach they left behind squares made from Italian marble, a rarity for Kent, their surface scratched with crosses within smaller squares. There were also pieces of a box made of bone, a simpler game, holes at top and bottom and slats inside to ensure the random falling of dice. For the many soldiers who preferred a still greater simplicity of decision there were wave-worn pebbles for the palm of a hand: make a fist, take a guess, two stones or one, one or none, in or out, easy money.

As soon as the Danube legions had subdued Britain's flat lands, with a respectable count of bodies on what could be deemed battlefields, Claudius could leave with a victory and forget the rest. The lands that were newly Roman were the only parts of Britain that anyone would know or care about. His elephants had shown the showman's touch that few would forget.

On his return, via the dedication of a fountain for himself at Lugdunum, the Gallic town of his birth, Claudius awarded himself what his courtiers agreed was a well-deserved triumph. This was his chance to be driven in a chariot through the streets of Rome, accepting applause like the heroes of old for an achievement which, while not wholly real, had more substance than the imagination of Caligula. He issued commemorative coins to praise himself for conquering the Ocean. He did not give himself the name Britannicus, bestowing it instead on the young son whom Messalina was obsessively protecting from rivals.

Claudius was grateful to his commander. Aulus Plautius would nonetheless have to live off the damp northern fields for a little longer, the diets of himself and his men supplemented from the holds of a chain of transport ships, a virtual wooden bridge across the Channel. He would be allowed an appropriate lesser honour at a later stage.

All Claudius's companions, the eager and the pressed, won honours in Britain to secure their loyalty. These honours were of far greater importance on the Palatine than anything happening in Colchester. After Julius Caesar's failures in Britain, Augustus's caution and Caligula's fantasies, success was a fact. An emperor had made a difference in the empire that everyone had to recognise.

30

ASHES OF A SWALLOW

When Claudius was back in Rome, Lucius again had to balance the roles of the flatterer and administrator, the dark arts of the courtier's day squeezing practical governance into whenever it could be done. Flattery is always an inefficient use of time, requiring watchfulness and patience amid bouts of high activity. Gluttony is for some an easy accompaniment, a way of spending wasted time and obliterating the sense of its consequences.

This was, however, the way that Lucius's world was run. His sons were still in good positions to learn for themselves. The wife of Lucius, his younger son, was the ambitious Junia Calvina, a great-great-granddaughter of Augustus whose family saw itself as no less entitled to rule than the throne's recent occupants. Alongside the court of freedmen were also the rival grandees. Again there arose the older jealousies within the *domus Caesaris*.

Claudius's wife, Messalina, was the figure whom Lucius watched most closely. While somewhat easier to understand and predict than Caligula had been, she was behind much of the palace turbulence and accused of being behind it all. Lucius made her his special object of flattery, different in form from humouring Caligula about his place in the heavens but in outcome, he hoped, the same.

Messalina had turned Claudius against Julia Livilla, one of Caligula's notoriously beloved sisters, who was briefly recalled from exile after her brother's assassination. Livilla was executed while her alleged lover, the Spanish orator at court, Lucius Annaeus Seneca, was exiled to Corsica. This was a generous fate, though rapidly unappreciated by Seneca himself, whose flamboyant letters from exile, widely read later but not at the time, were a masterclass in flattery. Their recipient was the freedman Polybius, a man of literary taste who may have appreciated their style but did nothing to ease their writer's return home.

The new empress also moved early against Tiberius's grand-daughter, Julia, whose husband, Rubellius Blandus of Tibur, had died before enjoying his imperial status for very long. Julia had a son, Rubellius Plautus, who was about ten years old. Tiberius had ordered Julia's marriage to Blandus to keep her heirs out of the succession race. But a provincial background was an insufficient guarantee to the anxious empress, who had hopes for a two-year-old son of her own.

Julia was charged with incest, immorality and use of poisons, persuasively enough for the newly triumphant Claudius to order her execution. The woman who for thirty years since Augustus's death at Nola had been married to a regal son of Germanicus and a respectable man from Tibur faced an executioner's sword. The object of Augustus's last anxiety made no defence. Her friend and relative, Pomponia Graecina, wife of Aulus Plautius, never forgave Claudius.

Pomponia might have herself suffered for that but instead sur-vived for a further four decades. Her path of survival was twisted and dark. She may even have worshipped the man whose cruci-fixion Pontius Pilate had been incompetent to prevent. Christians were becoming a small problem. Jews and Greeks were still a much larger one. Quickly there would be the not-very-conquered Britons too.

Much banqueting marked Claudius's return from his conquest. Scribonius Largus had new experiences from his trip to Britain to improve his textbook, soon to be dedicated with due flattery to Callistus, some useful thoughts on damp and cold, snake bites and yew tree juice. Back home his more valuable expertise was once again in cosmetic toothpaste, breath fresheners, earache, vomiting and the cure of those whose excrement signalled their excess.

Like Apicius and the Palatine cooks, Largus used dozens of rare ingredients because his patients could afford them – and maybe because his rivals could not. His recipe book of drugs showed a man keen to assault the reputations of others while promoting his own.

'*Bone deus!*', 'Good god!', he interjected at the failings of those he deemed to fall outside the profession. Like Phaedrus, but with sage and saffron rather than satire, he gave his readers an insight into the daily jealousies of the court.

Time with the emperor brought a doctor profit just as it did for a diplomat. If a drug was popular with the imperial family, it was saleable beyond the Palatine. Largus mixed celery seeds, cinnamon, myrrh and the ashes of an overcooked swallow to calm the throat of the emperor's mother Antonia. The protector of Lucius Vitellius, Pallas and Caenis, destroyer of Sejanus, had a throat much used in the interests of the *domus Caesaris*. Her satisfaction was a profitable sign for others.

In remote Britain there arose a temple to the Divine Claudius. Colchester was distant enough from Rome to fit the convention that emperor worship be permitted to those far away. Augustus had set that rule, not explicitly but clearly enough. Britain was in the west, not the east, but there could hardly be any place where the natives were stranger. Even Tiberius, who did not become a god after his death, had permitted some of the wilder northern Gauls to flatter him with worship. The Britons would have the same privilege to prove themselves loyal.

There may have been also a tactical purpose – as in Alexandria, where an altar to a Roman gave Greeks a weapon with which to irritate the Jews and balance local power. Perhaps it was hoped that the new temple would replace the Druidism that Aulus Plautius and his legions saw as their enemy in the mist. Before he took the throne the emperor would have had a greater interest in studying Druids than in substituting himself for them. But his brief trip to the mud of eastern Britain, and the grovelling welcome from its chieftains after their defeat, may have encouraged him to advance the process of civilisation.

There were benefits from dividing the loyalties of foreign worshippers. At Rome those who benefited most from a changing face of flattery were the flatterers themselves, protected by their arcane knowledge of what was right or wrong and prepared to sell that knowledge to outsiders. Scribonius Largus, who used Augustus's name to promote an ointment that the first emperor had used on his weak left eye, called Claudius *deus noster Caesar*, Caesar our god, a phrase that Augustus would not have allowed in Nola except from an Alexandrian sailor.

31

FLATTERY'S TEXTBOOK

Just as flattery was a means for survival at court, so was anonymity. When Phaedrus published his fables he dedicated them to a man called Eutychus, a figure hardly less mysterious than himself. Maybe this Eutychus existed or maybe he did not. Quite likely he was a type of man, not an individual. Many of the missing occupants of the halls where Aulus was to hide in the December of 69 CE were types of men, book-keepers, bakers of white bread, breeders of dogs; or types of women, wet-nurses, voluptuaries or magicians. Their names were their work; their work was their identification and all the mark on memory they would make.

Eutychus was a common name for a slave. It meant good luck, appropriately for the Eutychus who had been one of Caligula's charioteers, even more so for the Eutychus who betrayed Sejanus. It was possible, though never likely and maybe never known, if Phaedrus's Eutychus was one of these lucky men or just a type. When Phaedrus dedicated his book of fables, with a sideswipe at the monstrosity of the safely dead captain of the imperial guard, some readers would have seen a connection between two real men. More readers, perhaps those enjoying from further away Phaedrus's flattering foxes and arse-licking dogs, would have just seen Eutychus as any slave on the make, anyone that they might know.

A lucky slave was a particularly popular type for Roman readers. It was natural for a master to think that a man was lucky to be his slave or, at least, lucky not to be someone else's. Sometimes that thought was justified. A loyal slave might be truly lucky, well paid, promised freedom and then officially freed, slapped around the face in a ritual act of sending him or her on his way. Freed slaves would often then stay on in the master's house, still telling the master what he liked to hear about himself, maybe more likely to be believed, fortunate in a different way, particularly so if the household was the sprawling Palatine and they could profit from knowing its rules. An unlucky slave could be kept enslaved or cast out into an unwelcoming world, not just profitless but starving.

Phaedrus might have been a slave or former slave himself, or a witty Roman citizen pretending to be an ex-slave, a lawyer perhaps of some kind (there is a lawyerliness about some of his jokes) with an interest in Aesop and a desire to entertain. Whatever the truth, Phaedrus was sufficiently cautious about his own anonymity that the learned Seneca could claim never to have heard of him. Writing one of his pleas to the powerful freedman Polybius from his exile in Corsica, he could claim that the task of translating Aesop into Latin had still to be undertaken. Polybius, despite all his burdensome duties, was, Seneca argued, the perfect writer to make the attempt.

This letter later became much more important for students of flattery than any fable by a man known as Phaedrus about an animal or even an emperor. Seneca was a courtier of rare breadth of intellect, an orator, teacher, pioneer playwright, hypocrite courtier and elegant justifier of hypocrisy, a revolutionary guide to the interior of characters' minds, soon to be perhaps the most powerful and richest great writer of all time. Seneca's letters taught philosophy and politics and the etiquette of how to survive. But, at the time when Claudius was newly back from Britain, the author was still in Corsica and as low as a hungry fox at the bottom of a tree.

Messalina was implacable against Seneca. Courtiers might rule upon most of what mattered at court, the tax queries, the building contracts, the diplomatic give and take, but on personal matters they were wise to stand a little further back. Managing the personal (much of it with origins that were obscure) was as important as managing the political. The two might sometimes be the same. Lucius knew the arts of anonymity. Seneca was not in the least anonymous. He was a courtier in very public disgrace.

Corsica was a larger place of imprisonment than the Mediterranean islands on which so many junior members of the *domus Caesaris* had starved. It was a trading post between Italy and Gaul. It had fertile fields as well as malarial swamp. There was familiar food for a man who had been a vegetarian until, in the reign of Tiberius, vegetarianism, like so much else, became a potential sign of dissent. Messalina may have thought she was being generous. She might have incited Claudius to be much harsher. He would probably have done what she said.

Seneca's nights were much warmer than Ovid's on the Black Sea had been. Ovid had died in exile. Seneca feared the same fate. He was not a fit man. His chest heaved every day of his life. His throat was a cave of coughs. Much worse, he claimed (almost certainly falsely) that there was no audience on Corsica for his words and no readership for his work. Any passing ship might bring an executioner as well as letters from friends. He was hardly less determined to be back in Rome than if he had been on Pandateria or Ponza, the harsher prisons used by Augustus, and he thought he knew the levers of release. Even in his faraway place he heard that Polybius, Claudius's secretary, speechwriter and minister of many portfolios, had lost his brother. In around 44 CE he sent back a letter of extraordinary flattery, a *consolatio*, a knowing manipulation of the only world that he thought worth knowing.

To anyone ever studying the flattery required for court life this letter would be an essential document. Lucius Vitellius might easily have left such an embarrassment behind, but he was lucky; he was never in exile and he left the arts of writing to others.

Seneca's opening thoughts were about the need for humility. After some conventional words about the nature of life and the inescapable reality of death, he moved swiftly on to his gratitude that Polybius might be reading his letter from distant Corsica at all. There were so many in the empire who needed the genius of so great a man as he, the power he had earned both by his love of his master and his translations of the poetry of Homer into Latin prose and of Virgil into prose in Greek. Literature, he wrote, elevated Polybius even higher than did the letters of business and politics, from all over the world, that he sifted each day for the emperor's eyes.

Seneca knew, as only politicians who are writers knew, that a speechwriter prefers to be praised for his art than his power. The pressures of the Palatine, he went on, were preventing Polybius from using his more important literary talent. Like Claudius, who had lost his freedom for the sake of the world, so too was Polybius kept from his books. Both men were like planets, pursuing their course without rest.

Seneca advised that Polybius be wary of letting his grief for his family loss keep him from the *domus Caesaris*. Only outside the Palatine did he risk despondency. A dead brother did not much need to be mourned. In Seneca's kind of *consolatio* the dead man was irrelevant and did not need even to be named. The mention of him was merely to provide the appearance of honest criticism that gives flattery its greatest power.

Since Polybius always said that Claudius was dearer to him than even his own life, still more his brother's, it was wrong, wrote Seneca, for the courtier to complain about the triviality of death while the emperor's divinity was by his side. Polybius should instead, with dry and happy eyes, continue to write his works that equalled the greatest poets, even exceeding their stature by bringing them readers in the Roman world. And then, with his best powers and with his emperor as model and guide, Polybius should compile an account of the deeds of Claudius himself, so that, being herald-ed by one of his own household, they will be repeated throughout all ages.

But, he added, Polybius also needed a rest, or at least a change of pace. After such weighty matters as Homer, Virgil and Claudius, Seneca had what might seem some lesser suggestions, the highest of these in Seneca's mind being his own liberation, but that ought not to be raised too early. He had a little idea. He hardly dared venture to suggest (but he did anyway) that Polybius might agree to turn into Latin, with his characteristic elegance, the Greek tales of Aesop, a task that 'Roman intellect has not yet tried'.

That was not quite true, but in a piece so full of falsity it was hardly the worst offence. Perhaps Seneca didn't see Phaedrus as Roman intellect. Perhaps Phaedrus was still writing in the shadows, not a member of the Roman writers' club. Perhaps Seneca hoped that thinking about Aesop would be good for Polybius, bringing him down to earth from his pretence to be a planet. That would have been a subtle point, certainly by contrast with what was to come next once Polybius was caught by his own vanity.

Lift yourself up, Seneca continued with his *consolatio*, 'and every time that tears for your brother well in your eyes, fix these upon the emperor. At the sight of the splendour of his divinity they will be dried. His brilliance will dazzle them so that they will see nothing else.' This was a grotesque advance on Lucius's advice to Caligula that he could not see him talking to the Moon because gods were only visible to each other.

Seneca went beyond Thrasyllus's reassurance of Tiberius's longevity on the throne. He predicted Claudius the lengthiest imaginable reign. 'May gods and goddesses lend Claudius long to earth. May he rival the success, may he surpass the years, of the god Augustus. So long as he remains among mortals, may he not learn that any one of his family is mortal. May he offer his son as ruler to the Roman Empire and see him ruling by his side before he is his successor. Known only to our grandchildren may rise the day on which he rises to the skies.'

He went on in words taken from the same books used by those following the crucified 'King of the Jews'. 'Suffer him to heal the human race, that has long been sick and evil, suffer him to restore and return all things to their place from the madness of the reign now past. May this sun, which has shed its light upon a world that had plunged into the abyss and was sunk in darkness, ever shine.'

Only at this point did Seneca slide his praise towards less weighty matters, though not less weighty to him, his own predicament as an exile in Corsica. He did not, he said, wish such messianic events to occur in his absence. He too wanted to be a witness to the emperor's glory. That was his reason for adding to the millions of words on Polybius's many desks.

He was confident. 'The Emperor's mercy raises the hope that I will not fail to see his glories. For he has not thrown me out with no thought of ever lifting me back. Even when I was first hit by Fortune and was falling, he checked my fall, and with his divine hand let me down gently.' That was why he was alive in Corsica rather than the decaying corpse that Messalina, with Lucius Vitellius at her side, would have preferred.

'Meanwhile,' he moans, 'my great consolation in wretchedness is to see his compassion spreading across the world. Since his mercy has unearthed many who were buried long years ago, I do not fear that I shall be the only one it will pass by. He himself knows best the time for each man's rescue. I shall strive that he should not feel ashamed to rescue me.'

Seneca did not show any sign of shame himself. He was not too proud to beg attention from the emperor who was 'the consolation of all mankind'. He was anxious only that the form be right. He appealed to Polybius writer to writer. He had composed his letter 'as best I could, with a mind now dulled by long rusting. If it shall seem to be ill suited to your intelligence, or to fail to heal your sorrow, think how he who is gripped by his own misfortunes is not at peace to comfort others, and how Latin words do not suggest themselves easily to one in whose ears there is nothing but the noise of barbarians.' The language of Corsica, he complained, was distressing even to the more civilised barbarians, still more so to himself.

And there he stopped, with himself, where he had hoped to direct attention from the start. Much of Seneca's language about 'the universal consolation of all mankind' would soon become more familiar. Some Christians became sufficiently impressed with it to pretend that Seneca was somehow a Christian himself, an exchanger of letters with Saint Paul, struggling nobly to escape the shackles of his place and time.

For Seneca, however, in the pressing present of Corsica in 44 CE, even this rhetorical command of flattery was not enough to free him. Perhaps he had misread Claudius's appetite for praise. Being a courtier at a distance was always hard. Lucius Vitellius preferred to stay close. Being close was all. Perhaps Polybius, piled around with papyri for his attention, never even read the *consolatio*.

32

A BEDROOM SLIPPER

Gaius Julius Polybius controlled the letters, but Antonius Pallas controlled the money. Both men were former slaves, both bearing proudly the Roman names of the families who had freed them. Pallas was the most powerful freedman at Claudius's court, the prime minister of the empty rooms, known to the emperor since he was a child in his mother's house, vastly wealthy, proud of his reputation for virtue, prickly about any contradiction suggested between these two.

Pallas was increasingly a person of suspicion to Messalina, too close, she thought, to Agrippina, the granddaughter of Augustus's only child, the most direct descendant of Augustus still alive. Agrippina and the former slave were lovers, it was also said, a smear against each of them, the same smear by which the empress had put Seneca on a beach in Corsica.

Lucius took the contrary side, the side of the established power. That was his way and his skill. He was the most powerful man at Claudius's court who was not a freed slave. Like Polybius, his sympathies were with Messalina, who was also in the imperial bloodline as a direct descendant of Augustus's sister. More importantly for the present, she was Claudius's wife and the mother of his son.

Polybius and Messalina, the secretary and the empress, were also allegedly lovers, an allegation about freedmen and their mistresses so common as to be worth repeating only as gossip. As gossip, of course, it was very frequently repeated. There was never a suggestion that Messalina and Lucius were lovers, although her slipper was often in his hand, on occasions ostentatiously kissed, to show whose side he was on.

Lucius preferred to be a fixer than a player. Court life was more complex under Claudius than in the reign of Caligula. There was not just one man with the Moon who had to be humoured, there were two women, Messalina and Agrippina, and their open champions. There was less space for the role of diplomat in the shadows.

The senate too tried to adjust itself to the changing times. It was not helpful to grandees for them to look down upon Pallas, the freed slave who was establishing his own household of freed slaves, the Pallantiani. Anxious senators passed a decree welcoming him to the status almost of a former consul. Lucius seemed to his colleagues to be a man moving in the opposite social direction, a senator who behaved like a flunky at a court of Commagene or Persia, simpering over the toe of an imperial shoe. Old social distinctions were blurring, a marker of bureaucracy's birth and the new courtly life.

Neither Lucius nor Aulus Vitellius ever had a reputation for sexual excess. Both were known as uxorious in a place and time when fidelity was more a political aspiration than an individual one. But at this perilous part of his life at court Lucius could not avoid being drawn into the charge and counter-charges of who was sleeping with whom. He did have one passion, it was said, for the saliva of one of his own ex-slaves which he mixed with honey for his throat after a hard day at work. This was at a time when his champion, Messalina, was accused of competing with prostitutes for the prize of greatest sexual staying power. Lucius's sin seemed more like a medicine by Scribonius Largus, honey, herbs and bodily fluids – without the ashes of a swallow.

Sexual charges, like charges of gluttony, were verbal weapons whose relationship to reality was often the least important fact about them. Any kind of oral sex – with man, woman or footwear – was especially good to use against a man whose words needed to be brought into disrepute. In the rhetoric of the street a befouled tongue could not be trusted as a conveyor of truth. Medicinal saliva was, however, hardly much of an entry in the annals of food and flattery. Lucius was still a problem-solver more than a problem in himself.

Messalina herself was the rising problem. She was fast succumbing to imperial fantasies of her own, flattery from a younger husband (there were various candidates), a firmer position at the head of the

Palatine tables, and maybe a more official form of power behind the same throne. It was never fully clear whether the empress or Claudius himself was the prime executioner when prominent senators began to disappear. But the death of one distinguished senator who had rejected her initiated a terror in which she denounced other senators too. It became a lasting mark of courtly law that an accused might never know who was whispering to the judge. Julia, object of Augustus's dying concern and widow of Rubellius Blandus, was just a preliminary victim.

Lucius found a new role when Messalina wanted ownership of what were seen as Rome's finest gardens. In the eyes of her enemies, using the same hostile language once used against Germanicus's widow, Agrippina, she was gasping for them, gagging for a possession that she desired as though it were the latest delicacy or a new lover. Getting the gardens of Lucullus, the site of cherry trees and other pioneering luxuries a century before, required a man who could work both the law courts and the imperial courts, comfortable when both were sometimes the same. Lucius was a friend of the gardens' owner, an unwilling seller, as well as of the woman who coveted them. He could no more avoid Messalina's commission than could his brother, Publius, have avoided the prosecution of Piso for the murder of Germanicus three decades before. He had to betray his friend to stay alive.

The name of the latest owner of Lucullus's pleasure park was Valerius Asiaticus, the senator from Gaul whose wife had once been insufficiently imaginative in bed to please Caligula between courses at a banquet. Caligula had then expressed his dissatisfaction to the rest of the guests. Asiaticus, a calm and popular man, became subsequently sympathetic to the conspiracy to murder Caligula but had held back from acting himself. Like Lucius he preferred realism to revenge.

Claudius was neither hostile to Asiaticus nor keen to extend his wife's collection of vines and shady trees. He was also strongly in favour of more senators from Gaul as a dilution of the power of old Roman families. None of that, nor his record of generous hospitality, was any help to Asiaticus. The charge chosen by Messalina was that of attempting to supplant the House of Caesar. Lucius's task was to portray the owner of the gardens not as a sympathetic observer of Caligula's death but its prime instigator.

Lucius's co-prosecutor was a professional lawyer, Publius Suillius Rufus, despised by traditionalists in the senate for earning high fees but supported by Claudius on the grounds that legal practice should not be preserved for the already rich. Suillius, like so many in the empty rooms of this story, was either a sleazy man-on-the-make or a breaker of tired moulds, depending on who was writing the history. For most writers he was a man of sleaze.

The trial took place in late 47 CE, not in the senate house where Publius Vitellius had once done his duty in denouncing Piso, but in Claudius's private rooms in the *domus Caesaris*. Messalina was one of the few spectators. Lucius led the main charge. Suillius tried to humiliate Asiaticus by accusing him of passive homosexuality (the only kind that was deemed humiliating). Asiaticus was as calm as when Caligula had humiliated his wife. He said that Suillius's sons had their own direct knowledge of his active sexual performance. Before slitting his wrists, he added that he would rather have died under Caligula or Tiberius than by words from the mouth of a Vitellius who had licked and sucked between so many women's thighs.

In treason trials the language of sexual abuse came in from the street. It became a legal commonplace to compare the foul mouths of informers to those who fouled their mouths in sex. Phaedrus had a fable about it which the censors of his only surviving manuscript found too strong for survival. Asiaticus's last act was as cold and calm as his last words, ordering a new site for his funeral pyre so that the flames did not damage the trees for which he had died.

For Lucius the price of survival was higher than it had ever been before. He was angry at what Messalina had made him do and the abuse he had received in return. He was no longer above the fray. He was a highly visible actor on a stage in which food, flattery and sex were combined within the vocabulary of farce.

Meanwhile, away from the emperor's chambers, the court had more matters to consider than merely itself. There were food riots in Rome, a political threat at all times. The first water flowed into

Rome from the *Aqua Claudia* and, although the work was not completed, it was continuing well. The gardens and bath houses of Rome gained water at a minimal expense to Tibur but, in a court increasingly divided at the very top, good administration did not win much advantage. The man who made an art of walking the tightropes was risking everything on one side. Pallas and Agrippina saw clearly how close Claudius was to rejecting his wife. Lucius stayed almost too long with Messalina's slipper.

The empress's hopes for continued power lay, securely it once had seemed, with her and Claudius's son, the newly named Britannicus, the boy whose succession Seneca had insincerely urged should be smooth, unopposed and far into the future. Agrippina's ambitions lay in her son, Lucius Domitius Ahenobarbus, known as Nero, her supporter, Pallas, and her own growing popularity with her uncle Claudius.

Messalina had her personal hopes too, and not only in her desire for finer vines and shadier trees. She was said, sometimes with sympathy, to prefer the beds of actors and aristocrats to that of her older and disabled husband. She was not very discreet. She pursued the same stage star, Mnester, who had captivated Caligula, arranging his obedience to her by means of an imperial decree and a statue of him cast in bronze.

In 47 CE, Lucius was consul for the third time, a rare distinction, but the focus of political attention was not on Syria and Judaea, where the Christians had a new promoter in Paul of Tarsus, nor even much on Britain, where Aulus Plautius was finally allowed to leave his post, but on the bedrooms of the Palatine. Messalina's reach was beginning to exceed her grasp. Mnester was an unwilling seducer. He had to be ordered into her bed. After his much-rumoured role in the end of Caligula he maybe thought that another political performance would be one too many.

When the empress's attention turned instead to the consul designated for the following year, Gaius Silius, Mnester's name, usually familiar only from programmes for the stage, appeared on the lists of those charged with conspiracy. The famous actor, beloved by palace and public alike, was condemned to death in

Claudius's private Palatine rooms, his silent plea for mercy a final success in dramatic effect but a failure in saving his life. Life was exceeding art. Phaedrus's fabled stage star had merely stolen an emperor's applause: Mnester had stolen rather more and met his end like the tragic heroes he liked to play.

Pallas, Narcissus, Callistus and Polybius, still the senior four among the Palatine freedmen, were in growing disagreement about the damage that Messalina was bringing to the *domus Caesaris*. The containment of dissent within his household court was, for Claudius, one of the system's chief advantages. But when Messalina secured the execution of Polybius too, the courtiers closed ranks. Lucius, staging a diplomatic retreat, discarded the slipper and moved against his patron.

Narcissus seized the opportunity to move decisively further, convincing Claudius that Messalina and Silius had held a public wedding ceremony and were plotting to seize the throne. On his own authority, ensuring that neither Pallas nor Callistus knew what was about to happen, he had Messalina murdered by a freedman called Evodus, a victim in her own new gardens, dying in such a way that Claudius, calming himself at a drunken dinner, did not have to be implicated himself.

Lucius too was kept away from the final act. He did not see Messalina being wheeled around in a cart like so much garden rubbish. Narcissus suspected that long service as the empress's slipper-holder might bring him to her aid at the critical time. Claudius called for more wine. Public response was quiet. Messalina had not been an empress with popular appeal. The work of building alliances and aqueducts continued. As well as developments in Syria and Britain there were revolts along the Rhine and struggles within the courts of Commagene and Parthia, all of which, like the water supply of Rome, needed attention from behind a Palatine door.

33

OF UNSHAKABLE LOYALTY TO HIS EMPEROR

Rivalry between the freedmen did not cease. They each had their prime responsibility but, like senior officials in future courts, they did not fear to stray beyond their allotted roles. Some were famous, others virtually unknown beyond the Palatine, others still anxious to climb the greasy poles of early bureaucratic power. Some stayed in the background: Dionysius, a rich Greek eunuch, was so anxious for a role that he abandoned his free status in order to insinuate himself into the court. Others were flagrant: a freedman called Arpocras was proud to gain permission for a luxurious private carriage, for slaves to carry him through the streets and for personal sponsorship of games and feasts.

There was broad agreement that Claudius would at some point need a new wife. The issue was who it should be, the kind of question where senior freed slaves, intimates of the family, had a stronger responsibility than those, like Lucius, who had their own families and stood at a greater distance. The whole *domus* needed clarity on who would succeed to the throne. The prospects of Britannicus were dimming with the demise of his mother. Three men, Narcissus, Callistus and Pallas, played the main parts in a marital selection story that became both theatrical and mythical in its retellings.

The power of Narcissus, the writer and reader of Claudius's letters at home and abroad, had also dimmed from its peak after Messalina's murder. The role of assassin was insufficient to counter his previous loyalty to the empress he had killed. His benign suggestion to Claudius was that he remarry a woman to whom he had been married before, Aelia Paetina, a sister of Sejanus and already the mother of Claudius's daughter, Claudia Antonia.

Callistus, the chief official in charge of the law courts, had been both close to Caligula and part of the plot to assassinate him. But after a successful career on the line between the two kinds of courts he was increasingly an invalid. The dedicatee of Largus's book of cures was in constant pain with kidney stones. Showing a conservatism hardly less than that of Narcissus, he proposed a previous wife of Caligula, the usefully wealthy Lollia Paulina.

Pallas, the financial secretary and at most times the senior of the three, proposed Agrippina, whose big advantage was her son Nero, grandson of Germanicus, at the centre of the line of the Caesars, and, unlike Britannicus, almost ready to succeed. She was, however, arguably too close to the family. A special law would be required to make a legal marriage between the emperor and his niece.

Thus, as it seemed, there were three plausible candidates: Paetina, maybe too familiar, Paulina, surely very tolerant if somewhat scarred by her six months as Caligula's empress, and the third certainly the most trouble. Paetina had the weakest backer and was still maybe tarnished by her connection to Sejanus. Paulina's disadvantages included her not unreasonable suspicions of life at court and her fondness for astrology. Agrippina would need a change in the law on incest for her to have the right to Claudius's bed. This was where Pallas needed Lucius Vitellius.

Lucius sensed that Agrippina was the one most likely to succeed. There was no greater courtly art than seeing the immediate future. But the mere kissing of a slipper was not the kind of loyalty Agrippina required. She needed a false prosecution and a change in ancient law. Thus, late in his career, Lucius Vitellius had to risk himself out in the open in the courts where household and senatorial politics met, where his brother had first fought the family cause in the trial of Piso almost thirty years before.

The first task was to make possible a teenage marriage between Nero, whom he knew as a friend of Aulus, and Octavia, the daughter of Claudius and Messalina. This would strengthen Agrippina's cause. The only obstacle was that Claudius had already promised Octavia to someone else, Junius Silanus, another descendant of Augustus, popular, respected and not readily shifted from his place.

Lucius had no subtle way forward. Silanus suddenly found himself accused of incest with his sister, Junia Calvina. Incest was about to become Lucius's speciality. He had some credibility in proposing this slur since Junia had only just been divorced from his own younger son, Lucius. On this occasion neither the legal niceties nor the bedroom evidence needed to be tested. Before the case was heard, Silanus chose to resign his public offices rather than face public humiliation.

Lucius and Pallas were now firmly in league to promote the interests of Agrippina and Nero. This was good for the Vitellii and conveniently, Lucius could argue, in the best interests of the *domus Caesaris* and the empire that it controlled. Claudius remained indecisive. It became necessary for Narcissus, Callistus and Pallas to make their cases directly before an emperor whose role was both presiding judge and subject of the case. The process must have looked like a fraud, though, by the standards of the recent past, not perhaps an egregious one.

Some real testing of arguments certainly took place. Paetina was maybe too arrogant: she had earned a fearsome dowager reputation since Claudius had divorced her two decades before. Paulina's experiences with Caligula had left her too crazy. Agrippina would be hardest to control even if the legal obstacles could be removed. The rhetoric moved back and forth. How much the outcome was genuinely in doubt was hard to say.

The choice seemed more like a work of art than a personal or dynastic plan. The judgment of Pallas was a parody of the Judgement of Paris, the mythical beauty competition between three goddesses for the Golden Apple, the argument which began the Trojan War. The mythical question was would the winner of the apple be Juno, the queen of the gods, offering Paris the bribe of power, or Minerva, the goddess of fine design, offering the gift of victory in exquisite armour, or Venus pimping out Helen, the peerless beauty married to a Greek king and causing the maximum chaos. There was only one answer, but the plot required at least the possibility of others. This was one of the founding stories of Rome. Without Paris taking Helen as his prize to Troy, there would have been no war, no

Trojan defeat, no Trojan Aeneas to flee to Italy as the hero of Virgil's epic poem.

Claudius deliberated and followed Pallas. His empress would be Agrippina, the Venus of the debate. One popular version of the Judgement of Paris, written early in the reign of Augustus, was by Ovid before he became himself a victim in the sexual politics of the Caesars. His poem showed Helen happily taking part in the pimping process, though with proper reluctance at first. Agrippina was not reported as having the slightest doubts.

This was a major household victory for Pallas, the former slave who had so faithfully served the emperor's mother. While the theatrical show was going on perhaps he already knew best what Claudius's real wishes were. Agrippina was an acknowledged beauty, favourite of the court sculptors and possibly already sharing the bed of her uncle. Lucius had the final job of making the planned incest fit with the law – and quickly, before the question could loom too large.

Inside the senate Lucius had certain formal privileges as censor, an antique office which Claudius the antiquarian had revived and given to his trusted counsellor. In addition to vague responsibilities for public morality, he could initiate and control business. He again exercised this power, which he had already used to drive Silanus from office, requesting that he be allowed to speak first on a matter of highest importance to the state. While Claudius waited at the palace, Lucius made his argument for the new marriage, beginning with how much a hard-working emperor deserved a wife, gaining easy agreement for this uncontroversial proposition, then moving on to how only a woman of the noblest birth, the most proven fertility and the best of character would suffice.

Agrippina's right by birth was as high as it could be in the imperial family. The name of her father Germanicus was the most popular in memory bar that of Augustus himself. She already had a son and might have more. Her good character might readily be debated but was superior, everyone would now agree, to the promiscuous dead traitor she was attempting to replace.

Lucius's switch from Messalina's slipper-bearer to Agrippina's advocate was smooth. He argued that marriages within families were a protection against emperors becoming sexual predators on outsiders. The senate, he said, should always be consulted on such vital decisions. Marriages with the daughters of brothers might be unfamiliar in Rome, but in the great imperial families of the east such unions were common. Why should the *princeps* of Rome have any less freedom than the princes of Commagene?

The speech was a triumph. The senate voted its agreement. Individual senators rushed out towards the Palatine gates to demonstrate. Enough people joined to allow the claim that the full SPQR was behind the marriage. Lucius won his case – and with it a new lease on power under the new regime.

Aulus Vitellius became consul in succession to his father, whose final term in office was his third. The family was entering the aristocracy, new men no more. The father helped the son, as the son in Capri had once helped the father. As censor, Lucius could keep a close watch over his consular son. There was need for some delicate argument over whether Claudius's personal representative in Syria or the Jewish authorities owned the robes of their high priests that Lucius had returned to them while he was governor. Aulus never became known for tact, but he survived without dishonour.

On the first day of 49 CE, Agrippina and Claudius were married. Junius Silanus, who had unwittingly stood in the way of Nero's marriage to Claudius's daughter, killed himself in protest on the same day. His sister, Junia Calvina, was exiled. No longer the wife of the young Lucius Vitellius, she was barred from Rome by the determination of her ex-husband's father. She would not see either Lucius of the Vitellii family again.

Agrippina, aged thirty-three, was empress. She was already a veteran of imperial high society. Her mother had been a formidable, if finally failing, fighter. Her previous husband, the father of Nero, dead for eight years, was the son of Lucius Domitius Ahenobarbus, the wealthy promoter of married women on stage whose extravagant shows had so alarmed Augustus. The Ahenobarbi were prominent, sometimes controversial, but she had surpassed them all. Her new husband was ruler of the *domus Caesaris* and of the Roman world. Her son was married to her new stepdaughter. Together Nero and Octavia were well poised for the future. Admirers noted Agrippina's double canine teeth, a further sign of her sudden great good fortune.

The face of the new empress became famous. She was portrayed in pale-green translucent stone, her tiny nose and mouth suggesting modesty and a high moral tone. She spread her good fortune to her supporters and even to the small town in Germany where she was born. It became Colonia Claudia Ara Agrippinensis – Cologne as it later came to be known, with the letters 'g' and 'n' in her honour. Those who had feared Messalina's anger could sleep more easily. More than thirty senators had been executed or murdered since the death of the more famously murderous Caligula but, with Messalina dead too, the killings almost ceased.

There was particular good fortune for Seneca. The self-interested comforter of a freedman's grief was brought back from Corsica to give political tutorials to Nero. The need for an educator in rhetoric produced success where Seneca's rhetoric itself had miserably failed. A year later Nero was adopted as Claudius's son as well as his son-in-law. Messalina's son, Britannicus, whose easy glide to the throne Seneca had called for in his *consolatio* to Polybius, was now yesterday's prince.

Lucius joined Claudius in a census of office-holders and citizens. They barred a distinguished Greek judge because he knew no Latin. They purged the senate of some of its more dubious members by an unprecedented 'volunteer' programme of retirement. As a flatterer Lucius had lost none of the agility that had kept him alive under Caligula. 'May you often do it,' he said when Claudius opened Secular Games that would not be expected again for around 100 years.

Phoenix birds were supposed to appear even more rarely than Secular Games. A new sighting like the one a mere fifteen years before in its flaming nest of cinnamon was best ignored in order to maintain due order. The people were given other entertainments.

Nero's coming of age was celebrated by stage performances. In the spirit of Agrippina's impresario father-in-law there were strict decrees against barracking young aristocrats who appeared as actors. One of these was a rising star, more ambitious in the military and sexual arenas than on stage. His name, not yet famous, was Fabius Valens. The *Aqua Claudia* had its formal opening. Claudius could take the credit for the permanent supply of more clean water past Tibur into Rome.

Pallas's brother, Marcus Antonius Felix, became the latest governor for the Syrians and another sign of outsiders taking over the traditional centres of power beyond the *domus Caesaris*. Those in the senate who would have liked – and profited from – the job themselves accused him of unreasonable corruption, a charge that would be amplified in Judaea. Lucius remained close to Pallas, continuing to buy information for their shared ends and ensure that the sellers were paid.

A successful prosecutor from a undistinguished family, Eprius Marcellus, dedicatee of Columella's wine guide, was promoted to the rank just below the consulship to replace the unfortunate Junius Silanus. He served only for a single day in an office normally held for a year. Even those who despised his origins and his work had to agree that he could not do much harm. But his appointment, to critics of the household in the senate, was just one more case of changing times and people of whom they disapproved.

Callistus gave up his struggle for life as well as power. He had backed the wrong contestant in Claudius's Judgement of Paris. The long-time stone in his bladder was a condition only curable by the knife, a process as dangerous as that which had once taken the testicles of his Palatine rival, Posides. Scribonius Largus advised a diet of insects from stone quarries for bladder stones, a sympathetic cure by the rules of Roman medicine, maybe especially sympathetic for a man notorious for his taste in rare marble, but in Callistus's case not an effective one.

No mere doctor could stop the statuette of Callistus being the first of the Palatine courtiers to leave the dining-room shrine of Lucius Vitellius. There was no point in having an image of a dead freedman among his household gods. Callistus's head, if it were deemed too recognisable, could be lightly recast for a successor. The master of the courts had been a huge cog in a government machine; he had a daughter and a grandson ready for imperial service in the court he had helped to create; his name was on lead pipes bringing water to Rome. But Callistus, the bureaucrat behind the scenes, was not going to last in flattering memories, nothing like a god of Peace or Plenty, one of the statues of plaster, wood and pastels that would be passed down as an heirloom for the Vitellian dining rooms of the future.

Lucius himself had not long to live. Still influential, he was also approaching his sixtieth year and vulnerable to new versions of himself. Accused of treason and designs upon throne, he could not avoid the day in court he had so often watched destroy others. Agrippina protected him from execution and outlawed his unfortunate accuser, but two days after his arrest he died, peacefully of a paralytic stroke. A credit to his trade, he was awarded a marble memorial statue by Claudius inscribed 'of unshakable loyalty to his emperor'.

34

GOD-GIVEN MUSHROOMS

When Lucius Vitellius died in 51 CE, his elder son had already achieved as much as his family had expected of him and more. Aulus was thirty-nine, a courtier of the *domus Caesaris* who was also a former consul and senator. Being a former consul was not what it had been when his grandfather first came to Rome, but it did not mean nothing. His father had been three times consul. This was a record which Aulus showed no wish to match. He did not live in the past, even the very recent past. He did not ape his older senate colleagues in distant nostalgia. He cared nothing for ancient times when there were no Vitellii except those imagined by the gullible. Aulus lived in the present, with a survivor's half-closed eye on the near future. He was a large and genial man with a limp, a low-slung belly and long experience of watching his superiors. He understood power. He knew what the powerful wanted. In that respect, if not in intellectual range and subtlety, he was his father's son.

In his single consulship, three years before, he had successfully promoted Claudius's plan to appoint 'long-haired Gauls' to the senate. Opponents then argued that, because Gauls had sacked Rome almost five centuries before and then resisted the divine Julius Caesar, their experience, power and, most of all, their money should be denied to the highest offices in Rome. Aulus spoke for the emperor. He introduced to the senate the very proposal that so many of its members, in fear and in their own interests, opposed. His was not the speech that counted. Only Claudius's words told their hearers how they ought to vote. But when Claudius lacked support – in the senate and even among his own freedmen – a Vitellius had been with him.

Aulus took over his father's place in the social and religious clubs of Rome. A Vitellius would still be one of the twelve *Fratres Arvales*, the Brothers of the Fields, who had their ancient duty, traced to earlier than Rome itself, for making sure that the gods smiled on Italy's food. Their own feasts, celebrated in the country four miles west of Rome, were notorious for ensuring their own food supply: each brother dined wearing an ear of corn on his head secured by a white band.

The revival of the club had been part of Augustus's reinvention of Roman history, the connection of his own favoured institutions with ones which may or may not have existed in the past. Claudius was a Brother of the Field, as, soon, was the teenage Nero. Aulus also joined the Club of Fifteen, the *Quindecimviri Sacris Faciundis*, another priestly college famed for its banquets as much as for its responsibility to read secret books of prophecy in the present interest.

At around the same time as his father died Aulus remarried. These two events were probably connected. His relations with his first wife, approved by Lucius in the Roman way, had been fractious, not only financially. His second wife, Galeria Fundana, was more tolerant.

His brother, the younger Lucius, was also divorced – from Junia Calvina, the imperial wife whose faked incest had helped their father destroy Messalina. He was soon to be married to a second wife, Triaria, whose vision was also more forward than back – sometimes, it seemed, the most militant Vitellian of them all.

With their father safe among the respected dead, the two brothers were more free to enjoy the dining rooms of the Palatine and the surrounding streets of bars which Aulus in particular preferred. This was a time of imperial peace, except in Britain and Parthia, which were far enough away not to worry much the people of Rome. Shortages of food, not always prevented by the fine-dining Brothers of the Fields, were of greater concern than conquest.

Aulus made it his business to know Nero well. He did not share the new heir's passions for poetry and theatre, but for more than two decades Aulus had watched and learnt how to live among the powerful. Gluttony was a family trait for which he was already known, but flattery helped him to the positions from which he was worth knowing at all.

*

The Vitellii had survived the deaths of Augustus at Nola, Tiberius at Misenum and Caligula in the palace corridors. Aulus and Lucius, the new leaders of the family, had next to survive the aftermath of Claudius's death, hastened, it was said, by poison. The administer was possibly Xenophon, his ungrateful household doctor, or Locusta from Gaul, on whom many poisonings were blamed, or Halotus the eunuch food-tester, maybe bribed by Claudius's wife who was, now more importantly, Nero's mother. The poison was probably atropine, the cosmetic of Cleopatra and the spice allegedly sprinkled by Livia on Augustus's figs. The deadly food for Claudius was a mushroom.

Halotus was one of the most successful survivors behind the office doors of the Palatine. Food-tasting, like many specialised responsibilities at court, was conducted by a hierarchy of slaves and former slaves. Just as there were different bakers of bread and cakes, headed by the most high-skilled baker of white bread with expensively refined flour, so too there were junior and senior food-tasters. Together they operated a reverse version of the normal pecking order at table, the grander being last to taste and the lesser first. Halotus was the senior taster, just as Locusta, surviving in and out of prison according to her rates of success, was the highest-regarded of the poisoners. Neither's task was as simple as it was sometimes made to seem.

Claudius died while being less well than usually watched. Narcissus, his most loyal courtier and constant enemy of Agrippina, was conveniently convalescing away from Rome. He was taking the warm volcanic waters around Vesuvius for relief of his gout, the glutton's disease, as his many enemies might have been tempted to say. The emperor himself was watching the performance of a farce at the time he took his mushrooms, not going as far as Augustus in making an actor's last request for applause, but continuing the theatrical theme of the Caesars. His last reported words were a joke that he had 'shat himself', a standard from the comic play-book of the street.

Claudius was deified in death. Nero, aged sixteen and still out to impress his mother with his wit, joked that mushrooms must be the food of the gods because Claudius had become a god by eating one. Most mushrooms were simple food, not much favoured in the recipes of Apicius. Some were greater delicacies. Green-capped, white-gilled *Amanita phalloides* were the most useful for promoting an elevation to Mount Olympus, their venom impervious to the heat of cooking.

35

AULUS THE EDUCATOR

In October, 54 CE, the *domus Caesaris* was not united in its acceptance of Nero as the fifth emperor of Rome. Although Pallas remained strongly in support of Agrippina and her sixteen-year-old son, Narcissus led a faction which preferred Britannicus, aged only thirteen but with the potent claim that he was the grandson of Germanicus. Narcissus's influence was not what it once had been, but gout and ill temper had not completely cut the web that he had spun around the Palatine in so long a term of service.

Either boy, the senior courtiers agreed, would need experienced guidance. Nero had his mother while Britannicus did not. Agrippina, even to her greatest critics, was a woman determined to educate her son and there was hope – as there was always hope at a transfer of power – that youth would be an opportunity for improvement. Aulus was characteristically in the party of hope and established power, a rejecter of nostalgia, fear and subversion. In that he was truly his father's son.

Aulus was an educator in princely play. Nero needed his mother's praise, his tutors' praise and his playmates' praise; if he could not have all three, the third came to be the praise that mattered most. He was not drawn to gladiatorial shows: this form of Roman theatre provided no opportunities for himself. He wanted stages on which to tread, not an imperial box to sit in. He wanted flatterers to clap him, not just friends who would join him in applause.

Nero's studies were directed first by two freedmen from the pool of court teachers. Seriousness quickly became the responsibility of Seneca, who repaid for his rescue from Corsica with both lessons in the rhetoric of politics and speeches which made it appear that his efforts had already borne fruit. Seneca gave his pupil lessons on clemency and constitutionalism that aimed to revive the best memories of Julius Caesar and Augustus.

Their shared effort was at first much admired. Nero enjoyed the flattery he received as a generous constitutionalist and Seneca played on that need for applause. As long as the flattery that Nero received was for doing good, Seneca saw himself as a success. But in order to stay successful a tutor had to be more than a virtuous bore. That was the more difficult task.

Seneca made little use of direct flattery of Nero, preferring instead to contrast him with his predecessor. He composed a vicious assault on the dead Claudius, a contemptuous reversal of the flattery he had sent to the Palatine from exile. The tutor who soon became Nero's closest adviser mocked the 'pumpkinification' among the gods of Olympus of the man who had condemned him to Corsica. In a short satirical essay, the *Apocolocyntosis*, Claudius was depicted in a heavenly court where no one took any notice of what he said: 'You would think they were his freedmen, so little attention did they pay him.' The man accused of killing 'as easily as a dog shits' became deified as a vegetable, not one of Tiberius's little cucumbers but a pumpkin, a desiccated gourd never seen on a decent table, a hollow joke whom the gods of Olympus were horrified to receive.

In life Claudius never believed in the ultimate flattery that he was divine. Unlike Caligula, he discouraged convoluted deceits and allowed temples to himself only in places, like Britain, where the natives themselves might be flattered by a Roman deity in their midst. Only in death, in Seneca's theatrical imagination, did he become a god, a slobbering, slurring, incomprehensible monster, greeted by Hercules as a hairy sea-beast, convicted of mass murder and condemned by his new colleagues to their worst imaginable fate, living in the Hades household where Caligula was rightly eking out his own afterlife. Claudius's new servants were the same as the old, the freedmen whom he had 'sent ahead' to look after his needs, individually named and known to Seneca's audience. Polybius stood ready to the fore, but there was also Myron, Amphaeus, Pheronactus and Arpocras, the former slave who had been allowed his own carriage through the streets and to put on entertainments like an ambitious vote-seeker of a century before.

The occasion for the 'pumpkinification' was Nero's first Saturnalia on the throne, the traditional time in the centuries before the *domus Caesaris* for household roles to be reversed, for masters to serve their slaves, for abuse and flattery to flow against the normal tide. Claudius's reversal was exceptional even for a Saturnalia.

At the same festival Britannicus sang what he hoped was a witty song about his failure to succeed his father. Maybe Agrippina encouraged him, fearing that she had served her purpose in the life of her ungrateful son and making Saturnalian threats that Rome had the wrong young emperor, that the grandson of Germanicus was the better man. These were mistakes in a court where to use traditional subversion was a naivety. Ovid was not the last to learn the courtier's truth that what was funny one day might be fatal the next.

By the evening of his fourteenth birthday, Britannicus had already survived attempts on his life in the new era. He was cautious. He had watched the ways of the table as carefully as had Aulus Vitellius. Finally, a way was found, but Locusta the poisoner failed to provide a strong enough dose. For that failing she was racked and whipped by Nero himself. Shortly afterwards, four months after Nero's joke about the god-given mushrooms, Britannicus was in the part of the imperial dining rooms reserved for children and succumbed to sudden sickness. The son of Messalina and Claudius, both his parents vilified and dead, asked for a hot drink tested by his food taster. He found it too hot and asked for it to be cooled. The poison, a higher dose this time, came with the cold water.

Nero said that Britannicus was suffering from an epileptic fit. The dead boy was not only an emperor's natural son, as his song had made clear, but he had also sung his offence in a fine singing voice. This was a double affront to Nero, the second a deeper cut than the first. The death was in full view. The pyre was already built. The funeral was held quietly on a rainy night.

*

The methods of the Vitellii were changing with the times. Aulus's father flattered Caligula like a doctor humouring a patient. When Claudius came to power, Lucius sat alongside the secretaries for correspondence and finance. He helped the emperor to be a statesman and to feel like one when he was not. Aulus's method was more to be a companion in eating, drinking and incognito wanderings around town. He saw what made Nero feel good about himself and ensured that he had it. Nero wanted praise for his poetry, inspired by and maybe borrowed from the best in the empire. Most of all, what Nero wanted was applause for his frail and husky singing, practised with great determination, with diets of leeks in oil, laxatives and lead weights on his chest.

On certain days each month Nero ate nothing but leeks. Chopped with their vegetable cousin, chives, they were for Nero what figs were for the first Roman emperor and cucumbers for the second. In Greek Nero was the *porrophagus*, the leek-eater. Apicius recommended leek with laurel berries wrapped in cabbage leaves, a vegetarian voice-tutor's version of the ducks stuffed with dormice enjoyed at more traditional banquets at court. Augustus and Tiberius were trying to signal their simple Roman virtues. Nero was trying to be a Greek singing star.

The successful at court were, as ever, those who sensed the latest truth. When others cavilled to pretend that they were in the presence of a musical genius, Aulus flattered Nero's voice and lyric skill. He joined Nero's teenage parties, in and out of the Palatine, helping the new head of the *domus Caesaris* to find an audience that his predecessors had never sought.

Aulus was a tall, strong, heavy man. Nero was slight and frail, with distinctive deep-set eyes. Even as a thirteen-year-old he had been a subject for sculptors, dressed in the toga of a man beyond his years, stretching his hand downwards in acceptance of respect. His young face was easily recognised on the coins that Aulus exchanged for food and drink. Out in the streets Nero would sometimes protect himself by dressing as a slave. This was not necessarily so demeaning a role to play. In the court where he had spent his childhood some of the most powerful men and women were slaves or former slaves. If a Caesar so required it, everyone might be a slave.

When greater security for the emperor seemed necessary, their revelling band was backed by guardsmen and gladiators disguised in the everyday dress of Rome. With them too were the sons of senatorial families, ideally the poet sons or those prepared to pretend themselves poets or, if without even the slightest literary aspiration, to applaud Nero's lines.

Prominent among these was Marcus Salvius Otho, the defence advocate who had failed to save Publius's wife, Acutia, after the fall of Sejanus. Otho was from an ancient Etruscan family and had a wife, Poppaea, whom Nero came to covet as a mistress. The period of coveting did not last long. Otho retreated into a distant but respectable banishment as a twenty-six-year-old governor of Lusitania. Without his wife he survived and waited for applause of his own.

Being applauded was becoming almost synonymous with being an emperor. Nero jealously guarded his flattery. He did not only want it, he wanted it for himself alone, just as emperors had long demanded every bit of military glory. Nobody but an emperor could celebrate a triumph; nobody but Nero could please an audience.

What made actors dangerous was not so much what they said and did, the satirical crimes of the Atellane farce men, but the sound of their being clapped. Their masks, as Phaedrus had pointed out, might have no brains behind them but their celebrity was a threat in itself. The dying Augustus had used actors' language to ask for the traditional reward from an audience to a stage. The last in his line preferred not to have to ask.

Seneca tried hard to keep both control and good relations with his pupil. The theorist of flattery was no purist. He urged what he saw as philosophical restraint. Preserving the body, like preserving Rome itself, was a matter of balance, with pleasure to be had in the low parts of the city and virtue to be won on the high ground. The whorehouses and the cookhouses, the temples and the Forum were all part of the body politic as long as proportion was maintained. Nero's way of life was a useful education in the lives lived around him.

A good emperor, Seneca said, should show restraint in accepting cheap praise from the senate. Nero did not need the title *Pater patriae*, father of his country, that Augustus had held. Nor did he need the calendar to be restarted in December to mark his birthday. What he needed was a reputation as a reasonable man. Some small degree of unpredictability was acceptable in a ruler. When Nero held his morning salutations, he might dress down while others dressed up, dress Greek when he was expected to dress Roman. That kept his people alert. But excess was the enemy, excess in gluttony and vanity the worst.

Hypocrisy was essential to politics. Strictly speaking (that was whenever Seneca was writing essays of general instruction), a proper Roman man was supposed to be devoted to the gods, his family, and to the state – not to his lust or belly. From his Corsican exile he had directed some of his harshest critical theory at those who spent their fortunes on exotic dishes: 'They vomit so that they can eat, and they eat so that they can vomit. They don't even consider the dishes which they have assembled from across the earth worthy of digestion.' Excess in food or sex was a sign of inner moral laxity. If Romans desired anything more than basic food and drink for sustenance, they were fulfilling not their needs but their vices.

In less strict practice (when Seneca was giving personal advice), the lessons were more forgiving. A useful philosophy also included elegant arguments about why beliefs need not be put into practice in every case at every time. That was the means by which Seneca hoped both to survive and be useful. His influence, both in theory and practice, grew and then gradually faded. The likes of Aulus Vitellius were more amenable counsellors.

36

OEDIPUS AND ACTORS

As a former consul, Aulus remained a senator. That rule had not changed while so much else was being transformed. Early in Nero's reign it became even easier to combine the roles of senator and courtier. A senate meeting was held at the palace so that Agrippina could listen from behind a curtain. When the senators used coins to borrow, lend and gamble, they might see Agrippina as the obverse figure and Nero relegated to the back, or sometimes the two heirs of Augustus together like a kissing couple.

But Agrippina, like Seneca, began running out of ways to control what she had created. After losing Britannicus as a lever against her ungrateful son, she looked for others who might keep him in line, perhaps Aulus Plautius, the real hero of making Britain Roman, or, more threatening, Rubellius Plautus, son of Blandus of Tibur and Julia, memorably one of the last names on the lips of Augustus.

As her influence further waned, the mother was reduced to seeking any affection from her son that she could. She played the seductress – whether by sex or heavy flirtation, few could certainly say. At least one writer at court, Cluvius Rufus, whose books included a history of acting, was a close observer of Agrippina's roles as an incestuous mother, her boasting about her success after a heavy lunch, and the confusion that this caused.

Even in the Palatine court incest was something of an affront, a practice that, though fine in Commagene and further east, was alien to Rome. Sex between mother and son was a plot line of myth and tragedy, safest kept to the stage, ideally to the very private stages where Seneca's own plays, including his *Oedipus*, were performed. Seneca had to send a warning to Agrippina that an Oedipal *princeps* of Rome, paraded in lurid accounts to all, would be intolerable to the distant legionaries whether or not they were true.

Seneca waxed and waned as master of both flattery and its opposite. His intellect gave him power. He wrote much of what Nero said,
criticising Claudius not just in pumpkinifying farce but in early para-
graphs pronouncing on good government. He understood money.
He was a rare force within the *domus Caesaris* at this and any time
– with his own personal staff, his Spanish background, respectable
but not part of the Roman aristocracy, and his memories of exile.
He also had two useful brothers: an elder, Gallio, who would claim
a place in later histories by rejecting a lawsuit in Greece brought
by the Jews against the Christian leader, Paul of Tarsus ('but Gallio
cared for none of these things') and a younger, Mela, who acted as
one of the emperor's personal representatives, a procurator as old
Publius Vitellius had been.

Aulus, with his own brother actively alongside him, watched and
weighed the family loyalties. Their father had been too loyal to Messalina for almost too long. Their uncle, Publius Vitellius, had stayed
too long in the shadow of Agrippina's mother. The next generation
needed to avoid the same fate with Agrippina, the formidable but
weakening daughter.

Less than a year after Nero's succession, Pallas left the Palatine,
a further sign that Agrippina's power was falling. Pallas had been
her man as much as Claudius's. Marcus Antonius Pallas departed
with his head held high, with the name of a Roman of the imperial
house, the status of a Roman praetor, almost that of a consul, and
a deal that no questions be asked about the sources of his wealth.
He would owe the state nothing and nothing would be owed by the
state to him.

This was a relief for Nero. Power for freedmen was part of the
legacy from Claudius that he wanted to reduce and, rhetorically at
least, to end. Pallas had been envied, even hated, by senators who
resented the influence of a former slave and hoped that their own
influence might rise to fill the gap. Some of those hopes were met,
since Nero preferred to keep business out of his bedrooms. He had
little interest in bringing policy battles into his palace. Opportunities for bribery fell.

Seneca supported Pallas's departure. It was increasingly his sole task to manage both the machinery of the Palatine rooms and a maddened mother of the emperor. He had to warn Agrippina against her too-public affections, a dangerous task for Seneca in itself. Agrippina claimed to be protecting Nero's wife, Octavia, from threats to her position from outside the imperial family, an argument which must have tested the most flexible master of philosophical argument.

Agrippina's chief target was Claudia Acte, a former Greek slave with whom Nero liked most to share his nights. The daughter of Germanicus railed against even the slightest chance of a servant in the *domus Caesaris* joining the masters. Seneca agreed, but thought that Acte would be less trouble than many alternatives. He fabricated a story to protect her claiming that she was instead the lover of his relative, Annaeus Serenus, the chief of Rome's fire brigade. Nero supported the deceit by wooing his mother with even more expensive gifts than those for his mistress. Agrippina had the same appetite for gardens that had signalled the end of Messalina, a bad omen it seemed to some. Serenus, an emotional man whose moods belied his name, was rewarded by Seneca with the dedication of a treatise on how to acquire a quiet mind.

The humiliation of Octavia, Nero's wife and Claudius's daughter, sent danger signals to the court. Aulus Vitellius, educated in Capri, had learnt to watch the doors to the bedroom as well as the banqueting hall. A female former slave might be less threatening than a male, but the emperor's mother was not alone in seeing the risk to Nero's legitimacy from abandoning Octavia. Without her he would have no children in the direct line of succession from Augustus. Agrippina, appeased by grand fabrics from the emperor's wardrobe, returned to uneasy favour, but not for long. Her open-mouthed ambition, as her critics complained, began to recall that of her mother as well as her predecessor.

Two years after coming to power, Nero ordered the exile of all actors. Maybe he felt that he was being mocked on stage. Maybe he saw unwelcome competition or sensed, farcically even in the realm of farces, that the actors saw competition from him. Popular actors, like popular fables, were inevitably subversive and an easy affront to those who affected the higher arts. Those who won applause in the streets risked the double wrath of a jealous politician and an even more jealous artist.

Nero's grandfather, Lucius Ahenobarbus, had famously produced farces. Nero wanted to go well beyond that, to take the stage himself, not at first in Rome under the eyes of his hostile mother and a suspicious senate but in one of the theatres around Nola or in Greece. This would be a parody of the Roman virtue of living up to one's ancestors, certain to meet censure from Agrippina wherever his show took place, but an ambition even early in his reign.

Aulus was an encourager of that ambition. His great-uncle, Quintus, had lost social standing by his performances in public. Fashions had moved both back and on since then. A courtier had better to be nimble than frank. Survival required seeing how Nero saw himself. The most necessary skill was not only flattery itself but a careful observation of the flattery of others.

With his hopes of acting operatic parts held back by his mother, Nero settled first on literature to show himself in what he considered his true light. When the poet Calpurnius Siculus praised both Nero's literary skill and his commitment to lower taxes, his likeness to Apollo and his love of world peace, that was – and still is – a fair indication of how his subject wanted to be seen.

Siculus was a bucolic poet whose other subjects were safely in the realm of nymphs and shepherds. His predecessor, Virgil, in the time of Augustus had succeeded in introducing subversive commentary among the shady trees and flocks, but under Nero the bucolic was back where it began. Siculus's most striking innovation was replacing the standard peasant farmer with a more metropolitan gardener.

Nero planned to match Virgil's greater work, his twelve books of the *Aeneid*, the authorised foundation myth of Rome, honoured by readings aloud as work in progress at Augustus's court. Flatterers of this new project to write an epic on the deeds of the Romans urged that it should comprise at least 400 books. Another relative of Seneca, Annaeus Cornutus, prolific in Latin and Greek poetry himself, retorted that no one would read so many. This rare impatience in the imperial presence became merely an opportunity for further flattery. Did Cornutus not know that Chrysippus, one of the most distinguished of all Greek philosophers, had written on a Neronian scale? Why should the emperor do less?

Many at court knew the work of Chrysippus. He was a writer highly regarded in Rome. He wrote on the philosophy of almost everything and was also famous for drunkenness at banquets and dying of laughter at his own joke about feeding figs to a donkey. Cornutus snapped back that Chrysippus's 700 books on morality and logic were at least useful to people's lives, an act of candour about the contrasting likely usefulness of Nero's epic which won him both further fame and exile.

Nero liked to share his dining rooms with poets. He encouraged spontaneous composition and appropriated others' best lines. He was keen on poets who satirised other people, the fat, the thin, the incompetent, particularly the medically incompetent. He financed a Greek epigrammatist who dedicated to Nero his second book, telling the gods that he would have been nothing if the emperor had not been his paymaster. Nero himself wrote a poem attacking a young courtier as 'a one-eyed man', a penis, a prick, a Cyclops blinded by Odysseus in his cave. To weep with one eye was to ejaculate. There were many allusive possibilities for students of Greek to pass carefully around a table.

Aulus Vitellius was at the centre of this literary salon. He promoted a book of Nero's poems, the *Liber Dominicus*, the Master's Book. Gallio, the eldest Seneca brother, introduced Nero's public readings. Mela, the youngest, more than made up for his aversion to public life through his son Lucan, Marcus Annaeus Lucanus, a highly political poet who hailed Nero as divine, though not, of course, the son of the newly reviled 'pumpkin god', Claudius – without whose adoption of him Nero would not have been emperor at all.

Lucan declared that every horror of civil war had been worthwhile because it led to the new reign. At the first literary festival in Nero's honour Lucan won a crown for verse flattery. Nero's own themes included a mistress's fair hair and a rewriting of the Trojan

War with a new hero, Paris, the judge who gave Venus her apple for beauty. He took the Latin poetry prize himself.

Some of the tactics of these poet flatterers were not as new or necessarily shocking as their critics claimed. Poetry and praise had for centuries been the same. If a politician could find no one to be his flatterer, it was not unknown for him to write the poem of eulogy himself. Some of the best-loved Greek poets were professional flatterers, praising for pay, sometimes asking for money in the poems themselves.

A mercenary approach did not make a poet bad, either in the judgement of his peers or of later critics. Pindar, who 500 years before had profited from praising princes and charioteers in central Greece, was still much admired despite the difficulty and density of his language, sometimes because that difficulty restricted its appeal to the few. Poetry was perfect for both the flatterer and the flattered. It was ritual even before the addition of rituals from the court. It was reciprocal. At Nero's table a poet gave praise and accepted praise. He flattered and hoped to be flattered in return.

The dinner table itself encouraged a sense of idealistic Greek equality, though it was a brave man who used it. Flattery was like a deterrent weapon. No one could opt out since, if they did, their rivals might not. It seemed safer to increase the power of praise rather than reduce it. This was the new Roman way. Phaedrus's hungry fox was more pleading in Latin verse than Aesop's had been in Greek prose. Cornutus used Latin for his day-to-day works while reserving Greek for anything subtle or important. Greek eulogy had its ancient rules which great Roman poets could adapt into high art and which the mere hungry versifier could copy for a living, for a free meal and to stay alive.

World peace was, meanwhile, an ambition not merely boasted by Calpurnius Siculus and his fellow artists but almost achieved. This was a result of reduced Roman ambition on the advice of Augustus, a secure succession by the skill of Agrippina, the lack of need for Nero to show military prowess and his personal preference for other skills. Seneca's Gallic ally, Sextus Afranius Burrus, commanded the palace guard. There seemed no risk of a return to the age of Sejanus.

Around the Mediterranean there were still a few skirmishes between Jews and Greeks, the former rejecting any kind of worship of the emperor, the latter flattering Nero all the more in order to do their rivals down. This brought not public expense but profit to certain parts of the court even when opportunities for lesser corruption were lower. Beryllus, one of Nero's freedman and, like Seneca, a former Palatine tutor, took massive bribes from the Greek side for an imperial judgment denying Jewish rights in Caesarea.

Between Roman Syria and Parthia lay the disputed state of Armenia, whose king had to be kept independent. But the Parthian king, whenever there was potential disturbance, preferred diplomacy to battle. Nero's court offered numerous diplomatic avenues. Commagene, restored to independence by Claudius after its troubles under Tiberius and Caligula, remained quietly loyal to its liberator, its dissidents driven out and stateless further east.

In Britain there was desultory progress in creating a firm border, a merely rhetorical ambition to conquer Wales and some minor trouble among the then little-known Iceni tribe on the eastern side of the country. Claudius had gained all the easy kudos likely from penetrating the land of dogs and oysters. The best hopes of expansion were financial, the building of towns in the civilised south of the country, a concern for Seneca more in his personal role as banker than as senior adviser to Nero.

As long as the *domus Caesaris* was providing a source of unambiguous authority, it was serving its function. In Syria and Britain, even in Tibur and Nola, it mattered much less who was Caesar, less still whether they ate peacocks or had sex with their mothers, than that there was an emperor whose decisions could (or just as frequently could not) be received.

37

DISH OF MINERVA

The Great Food Market on the Caelian Hill south-east of the Forum, the *Macellum Magnum*, was one of Nero's prized projects, a square of shops arranged two storeys high around a courtyard, with a ring of domed columns, a marble-countered area for butchers with drains to sluice away blood, a separate place for selling fish, and fountains for discarding small change to the gods.

Nero was a great banqueter but not a notorious glutton. He had other vices by which he would be defined. He did care about feeding the people. He promoted himself on his coins alongside Ceres, the goddess of corn, and Annona, the spirit of the free food by which the emperor kept the poorer citizens from starvation. Closer to the mood of the streets than any of the Caesars since Julius, he knew what would keep him popular and what would not.

He knew too that the court and its Palatine guard was even more important than public opinion. The new *Macellum* was more for the delicacies of the rich than the needs of the poor. Like the riverside market of Tibur, it was a temple to fine food. Families who wished to boast of their best businessmen built shrines to them among the shops. Lucius Calpurnius Daphnus would have been as unknown as so many thousands in the Palatine rooms had not his heirs portrayed him in stone, prosperous and chubby, with a fish in one hand and a banker's book in the other.

A fresh mullet was a major asset, but a fading one. A live fish, transported in water barrels from the coast, might rate the same price as gold, weight for weight, *uncia* for *uncia*, pound for pound. A dead fish was worth less every hour. Salted fish, the kind sold by Horace's canny father as he began to make his fortune, had a much lower price but held it over time. The *Macellum Magnum* was for lenders and speculators. From the marble slabs anyone might become an Apicius for a night, buying spiny lobster with lovage and pepper, diced crab, pumpkin in the style of Alexandria, melon in raisin wine. Aulus Vitellius became a notorious abuser of credit.

Nero needed his new buildings to be big successes. In March 59 CE he had made the biggest mistake of his reign. His courtiers knew nothing in advance of the plan to murder his mother. They needed every possible means to distract attention from what they had not stopped. Nero was harder than usual to distract. Applause did not work when night after night there was dinner at which the shade of Agrippina, dead for days, weeks and even after months, still loomed in her long-allotted place.

The scenes were all familiar, Halotus the food-taster, still hovering, two of Nero's childhood tutors present, Anicetus and Seneca, Nero's mistress, Poppaea, on the couch where Agrippina would have been if Anicetus had not run his sword through her womb and Seneca were not left with the task of explaining the murder to the senate and the people of Rome. Nero, more panicked than liberated, was still seeing his mother as a very angry ghost.

Not even the dining room's keenest flatterers could persuade Nero that his plan to rid himself of Agrippina after a party on the Bay of Naples had gone well. The emperor had been too nervous to ask for help. He considered various ways of removing the main obstacle to his singing stardom and a new marriage, not to Acte but to Poppaea, the ex-wife of the comfortably exiled Otho. He ended with absolutely the worst way.

A poisoning in public seemed impossible. Agrippina had too many clients who owed her loyalty. She had seen too many deaths by deadly nightshade to fall for an atropine cocktail. Seneca was still a determined protector of the empress who had rescued him from Corsica when his flattery of Polybius failed. Burrus backed Seneca. They saw Agrippina as the only brake on Nero's worst ambitions.

The *Quinquatria* banquet for Minerva, Italy's goddess of wisdom and memory, was held at Baiae, the notorious resort where Caligula had once begun his equally notorious water walk. It was part of a women's festival for the goddess, a chance to highlight feminine values, to praise Minerva's protective shield over Rome, to eclipse for a night the rival swords of Mars, the war god. It was a party for enjoying the fruits of the sea, for silver shields to be used as dishes for lobster, crayfish and sturgeon – and for prophets to tell the peace-loving guests their most intimate futures.

To Seneca, who for once knew nothing, Baiae was where girls went to play at being girls and where men and old women played as girls too, an unpredictable and almost public place, unpropitious for a killing even if the killing were a good idea. The plan of the more biddable Anicetus, Seneca's predecessor in Agrippina's school for her son, recently promoted to command the imperial fleet, was to murder Nero's mother on her quiet sea journey home.

Anicetus took the job. His method was more ingenious than practical, more like a rhetorical exercise than the plan of a ruthless killer. He used his position as admiral to build a sinking ship. On board was a lead-weighted, collapsing bed in which Agrippina would sleep off the fine wines of the *Quinquatria* before quietly drowning in the wreck of a broken cabin.

For all its ingenuity on a classroom blackboard, the accident failed to happen, the bed merely tipping its occupant overboard for a short and easy swim to the shore. Anicetus had to stab Agrippina himself as she stumbled to what she thought was safety. Seeing death instead, she opened her legs to his sword. She screamed about the ingratitude of a son to the mother who had given him birth. There were many witnesses to the murder.

Even within a few days a mass of myths and stories had attached to the daughter of Germanicus and mistress of the *domus Caesaris* whose lucky double dog teeth had let her down after a night under Minerva's tragically inadequate shield. Not even Seneca, drafted from Rome to write an explanation for the senate, could claim an accidental death. Not even Nero, a man trained at blurring art and life, could deny to himself what he had done.

Seneca did his best. The killing, he said, prevented Agrippina's own plans to kill Nero. The messenger she had sent with the news of her lucky survival at sea was carrying his own assassin's sword. In and out of the Palatine, most saw no choice but to accept the story and move on. Only the emperor himself was struggling. Star of the stage in his own mind, free without his mother's disapproval to become a bigger star, he was in that same mind a mother-killer, a matricide, an unforgivable criminal who in the great Greek plays was forever pursued by avenging spirits.

Seneca's own plays, composed in some of the quieter times throughout his life, were masterpieces of deep emersion in minds distorted by excess and guilt. He wrote Greek tragedies in his own dense Latin, an *Oedipus*, a horror story of sex between mother and son, a *Medea* about a child-killing mother and a *Thyestes* in which a king banqueted on his own children. But neither his literary genius nor his political skill could help Nero once Agrippina was dead. No new marketplace for food, no banking or business, could drive a mother's murder from the minds of the men and women of Rome. Art and flattery were not enough to undo what the desire for art and flattery had done.

Nero ordered a new villa at Sublaqueum in the hills where the *Aqua Claudia* began its route to Rome. This was deeper in the countryside than Tibur, too far to be reached from the Palatine in a single day. When the court moved it had to stop for the night. The farmhouse that had once belonged to Horace, his symbol of the simple life, was newly aggrandised, with more bedrooms and a bathhouse fit for a small town. In front of the court's latest country home a vast artificial lake improved the emperor's view without improving the supply of water to the city.

At Sublaqueum Nero gathered his courtiers to dining tables where his mother had never reigned. There was still Halotus, the food-taster, Poppaea and Aulus Vitellius but also poets, singers and masters of oratory. Orators were increasingly popular for prosecuting Agrippina's alleged accomplices, particularly those who were rich and whose wealth was deemed due for redistribution. Food was an accompaniment to singing and dancing, an obliterator of unpleasant necessities, blasting away the news of the latest trials for fabricated treason.

Chicken breasts were softened with oil and shaped into cakes, lampreys stewed with coriander. Others might praise the choice of beans from Baiae, a paste of peas with ginger, hard-boiled eggs and honey, duck scalded in its feathers with turnip. For readers of Greek comic melodramas (and Nero was an avid reader), eating a favourite eel or fowl was as close as anything could come to making a man feel like a god. Food could bring back the dead to life. In Nero's mind his murdered mother was always on the brink of new life.

Sublaqueum was a hotel hard to leave. Seneca wanted to spend more time at his own country houses. He blamed the constant banqueting for damage to his health. Nero wanted his former tutor at his side, citing the long loyalty of Lucius Vitellius to the Divine Claudius. Praise of Lucius was a commendation of Aulus too. Any mention of Claudius was worth a smirk at Sublaqueum. His daughter Octavia, still Nero's wife, was rarely at the house where recipes were a rejection of reality, a reinforcement of status, a reminder of what it meant to be on the inside rather than the outside.

This was the world which Seneca had helped to create and never wanted to see again. He had had enough. He had done enough. The offices of the Palatine still worked well. Burrus was keeping the guard under control. But Nero's closest companions had become a bodyguard of mirrors, men and women who reflected both his view of himself, his hopes of a yet more celebrated future and the threats that they saw all around.

There was no longer a chance of the clear succession that the court needed above all else. With the death of Nero's mother, and the consequent collapse of his marriage to Octavia, the *domus Caesaris* lost its hope of a new Caesar. Some new family had to be standing ready, just as Augustus had considered at Nola. Seneca wanted no part of that future.

When the companions came together in the hills above Tibur, the ghost of Agrippina was best not mentioned. The spirit of the local landowner of Tibur, young Rubellius Plautus, was all too present too. When Nero looked for threats to himself Plautus was arguably, and ever more visibly, the greatest threat.

38

BLACKENED TABLES

It was almost thirty years since Tiberius had scandalised the grandees of Rome by marrying his disgraced granddaughter, Julia, to the respectable, but hardly grand or ambitious, Rubellius Blandus from Tibur. Even in a time of food and water failures, sudden debt and economic collapse, the wedding had been a social offence. And if the aim had been to weaken Augustus's most direct descendants, to dilute the line with an outsider merely of good repute, it had been an even bigger failure.

The son of Julia and Blandus, Rubellius Plautus, was still seen – fearfully in Sublaqueum and hopefully elsewhere – as a man who might rule Rome as it had not been ruled since the death at Nola. For four months a comet fell across the sky, the sign that Augustus had used to show his own right to take the place on earth of Julius Caesar. Gossips had time to speculate who Nero's heir might be. It was a dangerous time for a contender, however retiring Plautus might be, however content to continue the local antiquarianism of his father.

Nero was well aware of Plautus's potential to rule. Agrippina had taunted her son with his name. Plautus himself may have played no part, but Nero's flatterers fanned his insecurity. Seneca advised caution in dealing with Plautus but Seneca, increasingly, was in retirement. Nero was becoming happier to accept his excuses.

Nero's rights to rule included his being both the adopted son of Claudius and the husband of Claudius's daughter. This had once looked incestuous, but was now accepted. Had he and Octavia had a son together, there would be no need to gossip about Plautus. But there had been no child at all, and no sign of one. If Nero were to divorce Octavia, who was popular at Rome, he would lose part of his legitimacy; if he were to stay married, he was risking his chance of a legitimate heir by a new wife.

Maybe marriage to one's sister had been wrong all along, acceptable only as long as it was useful. It was the sort of practice that Romans still associated with the eastern kingdoms of Commagene and beyond. The legal arguments of Lucius Vitellius had been more expedients than precedents. Poppaea, who had proved her ability to give birth with a previous husband, had her own supporters at the dining tables, demanding divorce and remarriage for herself.

Seneca wanted to protect Octavia and saw his advice as far superior to anything in the past from Lucius Vitellius. The man celebrated in the Forum for loyalty to Claudius had indulged his patrons too much. He had encouraged Caligula to see himself talking to the Moon. A desperate exile might be excused for placing his patrons among the planets but Lucius, unlike Seneca, had never been an exile.

Even more importantly, Lucius was dead. His son might as well have been dead too for all the good he did. Seneca's advice was subtle and fragile, vulnerable to being overturned in his own ever-longer absences. He stood for maintaining the awkwardness of the match between sister and brother. It was hard to be heard.

While the comet was still low overhead, a new contribution to the argument came from the sky. A night of autumn lightning lit the road from Sublaqueum to Rome, illuminating the temples of Tibur, the new lakes behind new dams and the new course of the *Aqua Claudia*. The waters were in black shadows split with jagged flashes. In the morning the tables by the lake where Nero and Poppaea had entertained themselves and their friends were black-scarred and smouldering.

Professional prophets for an emperor, like Thrasyllus for Tiberius, were skilled at improving the most unpropitious signs. But no one at Sublaqueum could see the shattered wood above Tibur as anything but doom for the emperor and a mark of heavenly approval for Rubellius Plautus. Nero ordered a letter sent to Rome advising that his reluctant rival would be safer in the fields of Asia that he had inherited through his imperial wife.

Plautus might have expected worse. He swiftly followed the travel advice that might easily have been for suicide instead. He would never see Tibur again. For two more years Nero refused to decide between his younger and older courtiers, the crudest flattery and the subtler kind he had been educated to expect, between divorce and staying married, eliminating Plautus and letting him live.

Shortly after the lightning storm, the emperor fell ill at Sublaqueum after bathing in the upper pools of the River Anio. His coterie expressed the classic fears of the flatterer's repertoire, asking how will the empire survive if its great leader is gone? Nero rebuffed rather than rewarded the idea of such dependence. The system would cope, he told those anxiously observing his sweats, before naming as his heir a man called Memmius Regulus, Rome's oldest ex-consul, a man of otherwise no great distinction whose closest link to the *domus Caesaris* was a brief and unprotesting loan of his wife to Caligula.

Like Rubellius Blandus, Memmius was known as modest in wealth and talent. He had not even married into the edges of the imperial family. His naming must have aroused comment about others similarly lightly connected, men such as Aulus Plautius, commander of Claudius's British campaign, cousin of Claudius's first wife, a war hero linked closely to the Vitellii. There was also Galba, almost a son to Augustus's wife, Livia, and Otho too, if his ex-wife Poppaea were to become Nero's empress as she intended.

There was a Cassius, descended from Julius Caesar's leading assassin but married to a granddaughter of Augustus. With the options spread so wide, anyone might dream at Sublaqueum of someday taking the head of the table. Success would produce any number of flattering genealogists and prophets to improve their claims.

Aulus Vitellius was part of no one's calculations. He had no tested talents. There was rumbling local warfare around Nuceria, his family's home town, but Nero did not choose him to bring peace when attempts by the senate failed. Instead, the son of Lucius Vitellius was about to take a gentle job abroad, one requiring little but loyalty, his first job of any kind since serving as consul under the watchful eye of his father twelve years before.

In 60 CE Aulus became Nero's governor of Africa, the quiet province based on the lands of Rome's greatest old enemy, Carthage. The fields of Africa were important. They provided most of the corn that Nero needed to give away in Rome. But the province was not usually challenging to administer; Blandus and Julia seemed to have had no trouble there. When Augustus had allowed it to be rebuilt after the defeat of Hannibal 200 years before it was as a grandiose version of what he hoped Rome might become, filled with marble and men loyal to himself.

Carthage was still a place of dreams, the mythical home of Dido, the queen whose passion for Aeneas had failed to prevent the founding of Rome. There was always the hope that Dido's magnificent mythical treasure, rescued from the murderer of her husband in the exotic east, made famous in Virgil's *Aeneid*, might be found and be more than a myth. Aulus took his brother, Lucius, to Carthage too. Together they managed their domain of bread-flour, pomegranates and hopes of ancient treasure. Aulus's wife gave birth to their first son.

In Sublaqueum and Rome succession anxiety eased. Nero recovered from his cold. He ordered the death of Pallas who, in prosperous retirement, with a grand tomb prepared on the road to Tibur, was still too much a reminder of Agrippina's grip on his life. When Pallas left the Palatine it was a major political event; when he left his life it was not. That was one of the differences between those who inherited power and those selected to serve it.

Nero had already tested the appetite of himself and the people for a modest Neronia festival of sport and poetry, hosted by the consuls of the year and attended, with their due blessing, by the Vestal Virgins. Both the popular appetite and his own were high, although the crowd would have preferred more Atellane farce and less poetry in Greek. Nero was next planning grander stages, celebratory banquets, charioteering around the *Circus Maximus* and mass spectacles starring, if he dared, himself. There were great Greek parts for matricides like Orestes, murderer of his mother Clytemnestra after the Trojan War. Nero was going to play them.

Seneca was still available when needed, taking care of his own great fortune and the fortunes of the state, balancing them and sometimes allowing one to influence the other. Britain was the biggest test in his preparations to retire. In 61 CE, in distant Colchester the temple of the Divine Claudius was suddenly as blackened a ruin as Nero's picnic tables at Sublaqueum.

As many had predicted when Aulus Plautius led Claudius's invasion, Britain had proved as dangerous and useless as Africa was profitable and peaceful. Nero gave the job of subduing Wales to one of Claudius's favourites, who died after only a year, leaving a long and flattering will in favour of the imperial treasury but little else of strategic use.

The most threatening rebellion against Rome, by Queen Boudica and her Iceni tribe, began in the east of the country, reduced London as well as Colchester to damp embers, and spread terror everywhere before finally failing in the west. Boudica killed herself. The legions restored order but there needed to be new determination, and new military leadership, to finish the job that Julius Caesar had so long ago begun – or, at least, to decide what finishing the job might mean.

One reason for the revolt was the sudden withdrawal of credit from Rome, sharply rising rates of interest and brutal retribution upon those who could not pay. Seneca, in the midst of reorganising his affairs, was prominent among those demanding rapid repayment, a leader of financial opinion not just because of his wealth but because he was held to know whether Nero might be considering a withdrawal from Britain altogether. Even Nero's dispatch of a personal ambassador to Britain, his freedman, Polyclitus, with a massive retinue of lesser courtiers, succeeded chiefly in showing how much bureaucracy had been born, how little progress made in emptying the Palatine rooms. The Romans stayed. So too did the trade in slaves and dogs.

Dog-racing came to Rome – or at least the threat of it during a dispute between chariot-owners and the emperor about prize money. Grattius had set out the ways in which dogs and foxes of different national characters might be bred to produce a greyhound. A British and an African might be a winner. On this occasion the row ended in negotiated compromise with the owners of the horse-drawn chariots before any new sport could come to the stadia.

The Palatine had new connecting tunnels between bedrooms and banqueting halls and a new and influential *arbiter elegantiae*, a style counsellor, Petronius Arbiter, who made decisions about what was appropriate for the emperor's table and what was not. Petronius also wrote a secret satire on his own role, the *Satyricon*, a surviving story of food raised to art and of slave boys' hair used for washing after defecation. He did not live long but left a lasting fantasy. The court remained enough of an attraction for Nero to impose financial penalties on those who pretended to be imperial freedmen when they were not. This was a new and unusual problem.

Two years of light duties later, Seneca asked Nero if he could move in the opposite direction and withdraw from court altogether. He wanted to write more about the theory of flattery than to exercise his old-fashioned flatterer's skills, to portray guilt-haunted characters in tragedy rather than live a life with the ghost of Agrippina. He wanted to live more like his nephew, his brother Mela's son, who was rising in reputation as a poet. He cited the example of how Augustus had let go his own long-serving counsellors. Nero responded with a detailed rebuttal, referring again to the example of Aulus's father, Lucius Vitellius, who had stood by Claudius till he died.

Seneca remained at court, a further diminished force. There was a successful response to the mass sinking of corn ships in the Tiber, subsidies and other moves to stop panic. Images of the *Macellum Magnum* food market began to appear on coins. But Seneca could not stop the murder of Rubellius Plautus in Asia in 62 CE after he was rumoured to be plotting a bid for the throne. Nero sent his eunuch freedman, Pelago, to ensure that the suicide happened as required. When Nero held Plautus's head in his hand he mocked how frightening its long nose was. This was not the *clementia* he had once claimed to prize.

Nor could Seneca stop the divorce of Octavia, her execution on the grounds of an alleged relationship with Agrippina's killer, Anicetus, and the extravagant marriage of Nero and Poppaea. His relative, Annaeus Serenus, who had pretended an affair with Acte so that Nero could progress his own, died after eating mushrooms at a palace banquet. Nero's freedman, Doryphorus, successor to Callistus as *a libellis*, sifter of requests for imperial help, was poisoned on suspicion of organising public opposition to the marriage.

The Brothers of the Fields sacrificed a cow with gilded horns to Minerva, adding the offspring of Nero and Poppaea to their list of those who would ensure health and happiness for all. 'Their end is destruction, their god is their belly,' Paul of Tarsus, promulgator and propagandist for the new Christianity, wrote to his followers from Rome, warning of gluttons, evil-doers and dogs.

39

FOOD AND FIRE

When fire raged through Rome in the summer of 64 CE, it was not an unusual disaster for a city built of more wood than stone. It lasted ten days, but the firefighters had better access to water than those who had done the same job in the past. Nero's managers of the corn supply organised food to be brought in from the fields at public expense. Subsidies were paid and prices controlled. The emperor's lasting failure was what he himself saw as his instant success, his personal performance of *The Capture of Ilium*, the song of the fire at Troy from which Rome had arisen through the heroic virtue of Aeneas, the theme of Virgil's *Aeneid*, the poem which had brought lasting glory to his ancestor, Augustus.

Nero expanded his repertoire of epic heroes from Troy, strengthening his lungs with bricks piled on his chest and calming his throat with honey and spiced wine as well as leeks. He played Nauplius, the mythical Greek who avenged his dead son by luring sailors on to rocks with false fires and slaughtering any who swam to the shore. Niobe was one of his female roles, a mother whose pride brought divine destruction on her children and whose husband was the son of Zeus and played a golden lyre.

After the fire an audience was invited to watch Nero play the part of Hercules, not as a protector of Italy in the temple of Rubellius Plautus's family but as a madman in chains who had murdered his wife and children. A vast palace of theatres and banqueting halls, revolving ceilings and stages was added to the imperial domains in Rome in place of what the fire had destroyed. Nero's builders ordered coloured marbles from across the empire. Glass sparkled in the mosaic ceiling like night sky. Frescoes and floors filled with sea monsters. More houses of the old senatorial elite disappeared.

The *Domus Aurea*, the Golden House, was a wonder of the age. It was not a disaster until Nero's other failures made it so. It provided employment before it attracted opprobrium. Its workers were proud of their roles. Some of its increasingly specialist staff, Eumolpus and his daughter, Claudia Pallas, planned memorials to boast their responsibilities for its furniture. Others tended the rare fluorspar glasses that reputedly improved the taste of wine. There were new jobs for *triclinarii* around the dining-room couches, *fornacarii* to stoke the furnaces, *ministratores* for the many demands of administration. The successors to the slave who combed the hair of the dying Augustus were *tonsores* and *ornatores* or holders of other grander titles.

When critical citizens began to suspect that Nero himself had deliberately set Rome ablaze so as to rebuild it in grander style, there were feasts to placate them. Imperial expansion brought more public benefits than did the houses of the senatorial elite. There were garden parties like stadium games. Walkways were lit with Christians clothed in burning pitch. Two decades after the disgrace of Pontius Pilate, Rome finally had a hideous use for those who worshipped the 'King of the Jews'.

The fire caused more damage than at first sight to the *Aqua Claudia*. Nero ordered repairs and then diverted its water to make a great lake. He wanted power for a revolving domed banquet chamber to represent the earth and the sky, the paths of the Moon and Sun gods, new water to spray scented fountains and to sluice a block of forty lavatories, more than in most large towns. The stories of the *Domus Aurea*, good and bad, spread wider and faster from Rome than did the imperial edicts and replies to tax questions which occupied most of the men of the Palatine.

The impact on normal administrative life, even on the management of disaster, was small. The cogs in the Palatine machine continued to turn; most of the empire did not need the Palatine machine or rarely asked for its verdicts. The *Aqua Claudia* still brought the fresh springs of the Anio into Rome. A new extension of the underground pipes ran west into the Palatine and beyond.

*

If Nero had to be an entertainer, Seneca would have preferred him to be a charioteer, the sport of the Moon in which Aulus Vitellius had both proven skill and a thigh wound to prove it, than a singer following Apollo, the Sun. Racing, like singing, required its own unusual diet. Draughts of dried pig shit, mixed with water to strengthen muscles, were just part of the regime. The track was a much lesser disgrace than the stage. The *Circus Maximus* was central to old Rome, the view of every emperor from the windows of the Palatine.

The chariot was a sport of ancient kings and epic heroes. The poet Pindar produced some of his most florid praise for charioteers. Seneca loathed everything that happened in a stadium, but he still saw the wearing of a high Homeric helmet to drive horses as less offensive than wearing olive leaves to recite poetry and play the lyre. Nero did not agree. In his final years at Nero's side, Seneca had no choice but to praise his former pupil's skill as a musician, comparing his voice to that of Apollo, watching while his initial high hopes fell further.

Nero wanted to compete on merit and was confident that he could. In quinquennial games in 65 CE he played the harp, obeying every rule followed by other competitors, using only his cloak to mop his brow, and waiting with a persuasive display of nerves for the inevitable announcement of his victory. In suburban streets supporters founded clubs called the Neropoppaenses to show their approval of the emperor and his new wife.

Although Nero lapped up these layers upon layers of flattery, as for any addict it was not enough. He began to resent Seneca's own literary skill and that of his nephew Lucan even more. The object of flattery envied the very skills used to flatter him. Petronius Arbiter was forced to suicide. The emperor wanted the applause of both the court and the public too, a lust for artistic celebrity which drew him gradually further away from the *domus Caesaris* at home and to entertainment abroad.

Aulus Vitellius was a loyal booster of Nero's showmanship. The first of the emperor's personal performances on stage were in a regional experiment around Naples, close to his family home, and to where Augustus had died among the adulatory Alexandrian sailors. Popular demand soon brought a transfer to Rome. Aulus's own personal service was to rouse the crowd to demand what the emperor affected shyness to supply. When Nero left a theatre without performing, he could rely on Aulus to ensure that the retreat was merely a tactic. Aulus was never a competitor. He played no instrument except, like his father, the emperor himself, whom he wanted to sound good, look good and be good too – as long as the third was consistent with the first and second.

The audiences of Rome were flattered by Nero's attention and happy to reciprocate. Whether or not Nero was a good tragic heroine (opinions varied even at the time), he must have made an extraordinary spectacle, well worthy of Phaedrus's pen. This *princeps* was not being merely confused with a preening musician of the same name, winning the applause that a comeback flautist thought was his own due: this *princeps* was himself the musician. The son of a great courtier, Aulus son of Lucius Vitellius, was the master of the ceremonies. No one needed Augustus's fat men of Atellane farce – or cared whether Mr Glutton and his friends were exiled or not – when there was entertainment like that.

Aulus stayed away from even the best-supported opposition to Nero in the senate. There was a plot to replace the emperor with a member of the same Piso family that had been disgraced and driven to death by the efforts of his uncle, Publius. Piso was himself a noted singer but avoided the charge that singing was his only love. One of Nero's Greek secretaries for replying to citizens' petitions, Epaphroditus, was the first to see the danger. Seneca was accused of involvement, probably unjustly, and had to take his own life. His subversive nephew, Lucan, a flatterer whose poetry protested too much, was more likely to have been a plotter and died in the same way.

Out in the provinces and in the army, attitudes began to be harsher and louder. A centurion on the Rhine did not need to believe every bizarre story from the Palatine, but there was no doubting that the emperor was a singer and lyre-player who had murdered his imperial mother and humiliated his imperial wife.

Piso's conspiracy caught the innocent as well as the guilty in Nero's revenge.

Epaphroditus bought grand gardens by the Golden House with the financial reward for his detective work. One of his personal court of philosophers, Musonius Rufus, a friend of Rubellius Plautus and a critic of gluttony, took the punishment of exile. A promoter of a simple diet, Rufus suffered from association with Seneca and, like Seneca under Claudius, had to do his thinking on a distant island. His gains, he said, were to his Stoic understanding of deprivation.

More distant observers included the elderly Galba in Spain, supported by a flamboyant and much younger financial secretary, Caecina Alienus. Further west in Lusitania was Poppaea's banished husband Otho, more famed as an effeminate fop than a warlord, a gourmet whose use for common bread was as a paste to keep his body free from hair. Neither was a feared man of resistance and Otho, like Aulus Vitellius, had been one of Nero's intimates on their nightly riots through the Roman streets. Aulus Plautius, the hero of Britain, was a candidate for some. No one would have thought of Vitellius himself, especially not his closest family and friends.

Nero took hope from the arrival of a conman from Carthage who claimed to have seen the location of Dido's treasure in a dream. Like the emperor with no clothes, Nero was easy prey. His courtiers shared the enthusiasm and the hope. When Nero believed, his flatterers pretended to believe. Aulus, the courtier most recently in Africa, must have had his doubts – but also the best command of the story. Quite quickly the fact was exposed as fantasy, but not before Nero had spent the new money anyway on new stages on which to perform and receive applause.

40

TUTOR IN VICE

The last time that an emperor had left Italy was when Claudius went to Britain in 43 CE, leaving Lucius Vitellius to manage business in his absence. Almost a quarter of a century later, when Nero left for a singing tour of Greece, Aulus did not get the chance to match his father. Left behind in Rome was Helius, one of his freedmen, a less successful pair of eyes and ears. Every member of Nero's entourage was in the wrong place to sense the events on the Palatine and in the empire that would bring the year when four men were emperors, none of them an heir of Julius Caesar.

The focus for the planners of the trip was that all the main Greek festivals should be rearranged into a single season. Nero had to be able to win every possible prize in the shortest time that it was safe for him to be away. The stages had to be perfect, the audiences appreciative but not too obsequious. The competition had to seem to be real.

Nero's sexual and emotional needs also needed court attention. Poppaea had survived only three years as empress, leaving a daughter and dying, it was said, during a violent row about the time Nero was spending at the races. He was taking to Greece his less controversial third wife, Statilia Messalina, also Sporus, a boy castrato who had to be dressed like Poppaea. Among his closest courtiers on the journey was his African 'mistress of the Imperial wardrobe', Calvia Crispinilla, known to her enemies as Nero's 'tutor in vice'.

By the final years of his reign Nero's bodyguard of mirrors was a musical troupe the size of a legion, a parody, to his critics, of Augustus's young soldier bands, but to Nero a sign of progress and civilisation. Its purpose was art, not war. Its numbers rose quickly to some 5,000, rehearsed to provide synchronised applause of the kind that Augustus had once heard from Alexandrian visitors to his beloved Naples. Those with memories as long as the Vitellii's could recall those last days of Augustus, the clapping of the sailors and their reward in new clothes from their emperor. Nero enjoyed a triumphant tour. His hosts were expert at creating the greatest dramatic tension before hailing Nero Victor. Crispinilla organised his marriage to Sporus.

Back in Rome, there was a rather different reality. Helius had to deal with a more than usually serious revolt in Judaea and the defeat of four legions. There was a massive earthquake. A tidal wave destroyed corn ships and warehouses and damaged the *Aqua Claudia*. New gold coins displayed Nero's elegant new marketplace. In gold the emperor's face was just as symbolic and imperious as in his youth, if somewhat fatter around the neck. His eyes were deeper in his head, with just a slight tilt upwards to the sky as though the master were solving every problem.

Aulus Vitellius began another of his rare public roles, the supervision of contracts in Rome for the repair and rebuilding of temples. There were complaints that gold and silver ornaments, candle-holders, lamps and plates were being mysteriously swapped for tin and brass copies. Whether this was the result of incompetence or corruption was never clear. Throughout his life Aulus was never accused of greed for money. In Africa he was deemed unusual in his probity, even if frequently short of cash. Unlike his father and uncle, he was no orator and could not earn legal fees.

The treason courts were still profitable places to work. Vibius Crispus, a dangerous wit, and Eprius Marcellus, the gourmet friend of Columella the wine writer, were newly rich men in Rome. Aulus's friend, Silius Italicus, designated to be consul in 68 CE, prosecuted many men whose private wealth the emperor thought would be better public. Nero personally took over 'half of Africa'. The estates that had made Rubellius Blandus rich and paid for the ornamentation of Tibur gained a different function for Rome. Italicus was also planning their appearance in his inspirational epic of the war against Carthage.

These trials were not for the incompetent. The arguments had to be persuasive, some of the substance real. Italicus was an artist.

Marcus Aquilius Regulus, an orator whose art was comparable to the best of the old Republic, won a death sentence for three members of the senate and massive transfers of wealth out of the old order. But, without Seneca, Nero had no one in the cowed ranks of the senate who could do what Lucius Vitellius had done for Claudius, getting his master's bidding done while making the senators feel that they still mattered.

Aulus was certainly not that man. Mildly mired in scandal, he retired as best he could with his wife and brother. His son was five years old, tall and gangling and had a nervous stammer, probably not the only member of the court so afflicted.

Revolts within the Gallic legions – the kind of protest beyond the palace walls that Tiberius and Claudius had crushed without too much trouble – led more quickly than anyone expected to a collapse in Nero's support and the end of the dynasty. Some in the court began to sense the winds from the world outside. Others looked only inwards. Calvia Crispinilla, a true mistress of costume changes, helped to turn a legion against him in her native Africa. Rome again faced famine from the blocking of African corn.

Nero heard the news of the revolts at a dinner in Naples on the ninth anniversary of his mother's murder. He overturned the table, smashed two crystal cups engraved with scenes from Homer and for a week abandoned the normal business of replying to letters. He ordered corn ships to carry stage sand needed by his court wrestlers.

On his return to Rome he sent a letter to Spain ordering the death of Galba. He spent the rest of the day discussing how organ pipes could be powered by aqueducts. His inner court was quickly reduced to four former slaves, Epaphroditus, the loyalist who had saved him from danger before, Sporus, the castrato who looked like his second wife, Neophytus, hardly known outside the Palatine, and Phaon, his financial controller and the last of Pallas's successors. Phaon owned a villa outside Rome where they thought they might hide if the news from the armies required retreat.

It took three weeks for Nero to learn that Galba had somehow intercepted his death sentence and was still alive. The movement of other commanders was unclear, but their lack of loyalty to himself was not. The last band from the Palatine court set off for Phaon's villa and waited. It did not take long for Galba's soldiers to reach Rome, for the senate to recognise the right of might, and for Nero's whereabouts to be known. On 9 June 68 CE, Nero heard the horses approach. His box of poison was missing: one of his household had taken a final payment before fleeing into the future. He attempted to stab himself in a more suitably theatrical suicide. His last recorded words were *Qualis artifex pereo*, 'When I die, what an artist dies.' Epaphroditus assisted him to ensure success.

PART THREE

Take a cooked sow's belly, with the teats still on it, fish, chicken, breasts of thrushes, strictly fresh eggs and raisins. Boil and spread on pancakes. An expensive silver platter would materially enhance the appearance of this dish.

Apicius (attr.) (first century CE)

41

MR STINGY

The news of Nero's death was at first uncertain. It blew from room to room through the Palatine, from house to house and town to town less like the 'smoke for sale' at the death of Augustus than the smoke that had seeped through the roof tiles in the great city fire, twisting, turning, changing colour and substance. The first reports were sharp, those following ever more blurred, more bloody and also more bloodless. Not everyone believed that Nero was gone.

Household members, few of whom were ever popular, took much of the blame for the perilous uncertainty. The dead emperor still retained respect on the streets he knew so well. There was hunger for food but not necessarily for a new Caesar, even if one could be found. The fear of the unknown was still strong. His nurse, Claudia Ecloge, and his long-time lover, Claudia Acte, arranged a suitable funeral pyre, dressing him in white robes embroidered with gold, laying him in a white crystal coffin in the family tomb of his fathers.

If Galba were to succeed, he seemed certain to repudiate Nero, his friends and his works. Aulus Vitellius slipped into obscurity as best he could. He had lost his last sponsor among the heirs of Augustus.

Aulus's wife, Galeria, was possibly of some assistance. She was no Neronian. She was famed for virtue just as his father, according to the inscription in the Forum, had been. She had her own connections to Silius Italicus, the would-be new Virgil of whatever era came next. But she was linked to the age of Nero, if a successor chose to purge the court too far. Men would later accuse Aulus Vitellius of many crimes against convention and good taste, but neglect of his second wife was never one of them. His first had paid money to keep him from their children. He was determined to care for his second.

In the early days of enforced retirement Aulus could also assess how the last successor to Augustus had ended the family line. Nero and his court had been looking out for the wrong kind of opponents in the wrong direction. On his triumphant tour of Greece the emperor had won hundreds of competitions in poetry and singing, scattering the competition from coast to coast. Meanwhile, an unknown Roman Gaul called Julius Vindex was leading a revolt.

Vindex himself had not defeated Nero, but he had encouraged Roman generals to think that they might do better, or to fear that someone else might do better if they did not. Servius Sulpicius Galba, with a nearby army in Spain and already one of the consuls designated for the following year, had been just one of these. Another was Marcus Salvius Otho, former husband of Nero's murdered wife, Poppaea, who was still in comfortable exile in the furthest part of Spain as governor of Lusitania.

Aulus was twenty years younger than Galba and did not know him well. Otho had been his companion at Nero's court, sharer of banquets, concerts and flattery of their master's voice. Those who sought certainty of succession wondered if Galba, who was abstemious, strict, vain and, most importantly without living children, might adopt Otho. Aulus might hope for future advancement if such certainty could be achieved. So might his stammering son, the highest of Aulus's concerns.

But this was primarily a time for survival, seclusion and forgetfulness in the hope that others would forget. It was a time for family matters. A stammer had to be cured. The boy needed calm. Romans distrusted those with impediments to speech. In whatever way a man spoke – as a public orator or as a court flatterer – a stammer was a handicap. Aesop's stutter had not contributed to his reputation for wisdom, only for being a clown. Claudius had not made disability fashionable and even Claudius, along with Lucius Vitellius, his faithful minister, was slipping into the distrusted past. Ahead was the new and unknown.

What was already certain was a fact more significant than the choice of any particular emperor. The new truth was that the choice for the first time since the death of Augustus need not, and would not, be made at court. The *domus Caesaris* no longer had a Caesar in Julius Caesar's line and would have to wait for whichever successor might choose the name (or another name) as his title.

The future was clouded by distance and ignorance. Soldiers in different places, from west to east, stood ready to take the decisions that for more than fifty years had been made within the palace. Senior officers whom he knew, such as Fabius Valens and Caecina Alienus, previously judged on the Palatine by what they might do for Nero, became suspected of conspiring in their own interests and against one another.

Aulus did not have many friends in the army. In his time in Africa he had no direct responsibility for the legion in the province. Valens had made his first public appearance at Rome as a volunteer performer at the Neronia festival. His home was a holiday resort in the hills south-east of Rome and his reputation was as a libertine, as notorious for taking the sexual opportunities of power as was Aulus for exploiting the kitchens. He had thrown his weight into turning troops from Nero to Galba and was expecting a rapid reward. He was one of many.

Caecina was also prominent in Galba's service, a younger war hero, tall and eccentrically dressed in multicoloured coat and Gallic trousers, fast-talking in the officers' mess, conspicuous on the battlefield, dangerously so if his superiors were looking too long in his direction. He was the kind of adventurer who, in earlier days, would have appealed to Julius Caesar. A mutual loathing made Valens and Caecina very useful allies to anyone else. But this was of no immediate concern to Aulus.

Galba, the new man of the moment, had the advantage of looking as an emperor ought to look, even if few ever did. He was tall and blue-eyed, with a downward-curving nose. He was bald and sensitive about it, and as soon as he had the chance he added hair to the image on his coins. Even before he was emperor, he had a family tree claiming descent from Jupiter and the Sun, a distinction which others had to wait for until they reached the throne.

Galba had prospered in his youth as a protégé of Livia, Augustus's wife. He was sufficiently dangerous to Claudius – or possibly valuable too – for the invasion of Britain to be postponed until he was fit enough to travel. (Aulus could remember that well, the high point of his father's career in service.) He survived the enmity of Agrippina, who allegedly wanted to marry him. Many absences abroad came to his aid. He was rich, not least from Livia's legacies, but notorious for frugality, an antique virtue all the more appreciated in the senate, which gratefully acclaimed him as Nero's successor. His army then waited for the money that a new emperor traditionally paid his troops. This menacing military presence close to Rome made the senate's gratitude useful, but not absolutely necessary.

Galba had used secret informants at the court of Nero. Prime among them was Calvia Crispinilla, the woman from exotic Africa seen as Nero's 'mistress of vice' but with influence well beyond the bedrooms and banqueting halls. It had always been the most important courtly skill to sense the direction of the political wind. Crispinilla was the mistress of that art, as well as those for which she was better known – and had no need to worry if grander people thought her merely a pimp.

The new emperor was neither a courtier nor the master of an influential court. He was a man who presented himself as the past. In an antique custom, he made all his slaves and freedmen parade before him twice a day. He had an inner circle of only three, an undistinguished soldier, his lawyer and his male lover. Supporters could only hope that this group might be widened by the pressures of power.

Otho, hoping to exploit his knowledge of how a court ought to work, offered the newly acclaimed Emperor Galba an early gift of some of his own most cultured slaves. He met with a sharp rebuff. Vitellius kept himself out of the way with his wife and children.

News at Rome was scarce. In Galba's army it seemed that Caecina had suffered a setback, an investigation on suspicions of theft and fraud. Otho and Valens were more visible on the march south from the Alps, joining in the massacre of a force hastily produced by Nero on the last bridge into the city; the emperor's mind had still been on the stages of Greece. His battalions of ballerinas dressed as Amazons put up appropriate resistance. A key last concern for Nero had been the escape of himself and his Greek theatrical equipment. That was what Aulus and his friends knew. That was what Galba soon learnt, and some of it was true.

Galba did not care for the machinery of the stage. In as much as he had a taste for theatre it was closer to that of the dying Augustus at Nola. At his first celebratory games, designed to show himself to the people, a team of Atellane satirists played the stock roles of Mr Glutton, Mr Fool, Mr Toad and Mr Chew. These were characters who had entertained in Italy before the arrival of competitors from the highbrow east. There was an especially enthusiastic response for a figure called Onesimus, Mr Stingy, the parent who is mean to his children. The audience joined in and the line was sung that *Venit Onesimus a villa*, 'Onesimus is back from his farm', a sign that might have sounded good to the new emperor but quite quickly was not. His soldiers wanted their money.

42

A GOOD JOB FOR A GLUTTON

Galba's only autumn in power was mild before what would be an unusually warm winter. The mosquitoes of Rome rolled in clouds around the damp alleys. The house of the Vitellii was poor by the standards of Aulus's childhood. He was no longer part of the *domus Caesaris* which Nero had so confidently expanded beyond the Palatine. He had lost his creditworthiness at the fall of his guarantor and his creditors were pressing him hard. It was a good time to be leaving and Galba, solely for his own interests, gave him his chance.

One of Aulus's distant and wealthier relatives, notorious for little more than his indecisiveness, had already received the governorship of Pannonia and its possibilities for plunder along the banks of the Danube. Tiberius in his youth had made his military reputation beside the border river which ran west to east across Europe as the Rhine ran south to north. That was no part of Galba's plan. A general who had just led an army to Rome did not want other generals with the initiative to do the same.

Lower Germany was an even more strategic province than Pannonia. It stretched down the Rhine from the North Sea to its capital at Colonia Agrippinensis, a camp that had won its walls and towers from being Agrippina's place of birth during Germanicus's campaigns. To general surprise, even of Romans for whom the new world was nothing but surprise, Galba gave Lower Germany to Aulus Vitellius – with a brief to do as little as possible.

It was hard to see what advantage Galba thought he might gain from this. Perhaps the most immediate was that Aulus did not belong to that large class of the imperial household whose ill-gotten gains Galba was hoping to recoup for the treasury. If, as was occasionally alleged, he had swapped gold ornaments for bronze during a minor administrative role, there were no gains remaining. Or, as

his wittier critics remarked, he had eaten them all. Galba was appar-
ently content that his governor should gorge himself on the food of
the northern seas as long as that was the extent of his ambition.

Aulus's departure was less than elegant. He had to move Galeria and their children, Aulus and Vitellia, into a small apartment,
borrow a pearl from his mother and dodge those who thought he
was merely fleeing his debts. He was lucky that the moneylenders in
Rome, like the food traders and the builders, faced a range of much
bigger problems than himself in the new age without the Caesars.

There was no longer even the very limited certainty for the
future that was necessary for banking and building. There was
again no clear succession. A necessary decision, pressing before
Galba had found the slightest comfort on the throne, was whom he
might identify as his son and heir. Otho looked the man most likely.
Almost as impoverished as Aulus, he was highly enthusiastic for the
role, borrowing money and distributing it at a banquet to the palace
guard, hastily organising a marriage for his daughter with a senior
adviser to Galba.

But there were other hopefuls too to test the moneylenders'
confidence. In the last weeks of November the issue was still unre-
solved. Aulus left Rome, feasting, glad-handing, showing an early
common touch and leaving his debts behind. When locals along the
route north asked if he had enjoyed his breakfast, he belched loudly
to prove it.

Aulus was a man for all men. He saw nothing wrong with a belch
or a fart. These bodily functions were forces of nature, and many of
the grandest philosophers he had heard at the tables of emperors
had argued for following nature's calls. A dish of beans in sweet
and sour sauce, attributed to Apicius himself, became known as
the Vitellian. Stoicism was about more than a stiff upper lip; it was
about the undigested decay of food.

Within a month he was at the birthplace of Agrippina, Colonia
Agrippinensis. The welcome for Aulus was at first no warmer than
the weather. About half his troops claimed loyalty to Galba, but the
other half, much noisier, felt that there was more plunder to be had
from the tribes whose opposition to Nero had brought Galba to

power. They wanted to fight Germans, not call a halt on the orders of someone whose authority was hardly that of a Caesar.

The legionaries did not trust the locals, whose married women wore their hair in turbans and worshipped goddesses that did the same. Their most profitable German partners were the local traders in slaves, the *mangones*, who bought captured prisoners and dressed them up to get a higher price in Rome. This was a business that a man could proudly boast on his tombstone.

Few wanted the inactivity which Galba's representative was demanding. To a visitor from Rome – and Aulus's military inexperience made him little more than a visitor – the Roman soldiers in Germany looked disconcertingly like Gauls and Germans themselves. The legions seemed like just another tribe wanting war. The flamboyant Caecina, resentful at his accusation for fraud further south, was not alone in wearing multicoloured patched Gallic trousers any more than he was alone in disaffection with Galba.

Aulus set about making himself popular as best he could. He had always liked to be liked; it was the skill that had kept him alive. The officers of Aulus's new legions ate from field tables without the couches and entertainments of Capri and the Palatine. Dogs chased hares across the white clay mugs from which they drank the local beer. He ensured that they ate well. Their best wine glasses may have been stamped with the head of Augustus, in glowing bottle-green, but their devotion to the line of the Caesars did not extend as strongly to anyone who merely lived in Caesar's house, particularly if his policies did not seem profitable to themselves.

It was not yet clear how much loyalty and discipline was at risk with the loss of the last man to boast the imperial bloodline. Julius Caesar himself had cleared the land of Cologne in retaliation for a native uprising and massacre of his soldiers. One of his many daggers was a talisman in the temple of Mars. This temple itself was a gift to Cologne because of the birth there of Agrippina. Cologne was a town of the Caesars from its creation.

No living soldier had served anyone but a descendant of the victim of the Ides of March, 44 BCE. The grid of streets was built around the east–west line of the sunrise on the birthday of Augustus.

Capricorn, Augustus's constellation among the gods, adorned the temple to the dead. It was more than 100 years since a teenage heir had discovered the power of his father's name and defeated larger armies that lacked that unifying force. Caligula and Nero had many failings as commanders, but the Caesar in their name was not one of them.

After the suicide of the last of Caesar's line, a laudatory red-lettered inscription to Nero was used as a sewer cover. There was panic and uncertainty. But all loyalty in Lower Germany was still fluid. Galba was little more than an ungenerous disciplinarian to those who had served him. He looked like an emperor, but he lacked the capricious generosity which troops had come to expect. He was grim and antiquarian in his brutality. He was not a Caesar, and he was a long way away in Rome. From the capital came rumours of demotions, decimations and a dogged refusal to pay bounties and bonuses which the legionaries believed they were owed.

Aulus looked as much like an emperor as Galba did. He was just as tall. His nose bent towards his chin. He was inexperienced in warfare but highly experienced in survival. He had never been a flatterer with words as his father had been. But he was a master of making himself popular by deeds, by cavorting with Tiberius, riding chariots with Caligula, applauding Nero's poetry and organising others to applaud. He had known hard times. He understood people whose times were much harder. If one set of soldiers could make Galba emperor, another might do the same for someone else.

43

FILL ME UP!

Rumours of how Galba was consolidating his power reached as far as Cologne. It seemed that in the *domus Caesaris*, which no longer had a Caesar, the new emperor was keen to clean house. Locusta the poisoner, mistress of the atropine, was condemned to a more public death than she had dispensed to others. Galba ordered her to be led in chains through the city before her execution. Along the same route clanked a long line of courtiers whom he deemed 'the scum that had come to the surface in Nero's day'.

Acte survived, escaping to Sardinia where she freed her own slaves as Actiani. Crispinilla too survived; she had helped to give Galba the confidence to challenge Nero. The people knew her name from stories of the Neronian court but she was close to Otho too, both of them sharing information that those seeking success under Galba would prefer to stay hidden. She knew what was in the food, and who was flattering whom in the bedrooms. She was as quick-witted as the consummate courtier needed to be, a quality no less valuable because Romans attributed it to the blood drawn to her brain by the African sun.

Once his purges were over, Galba began the task of staying in power, but little of his thinking leaked out into the army, not even to the part of it that had raised him to the throne. He still had no court himself, only three advisers of whom one, his former slave Icelus, was also his lover. No one in either of the German provinces knew anything of his plans. It was known that Galba would at some point name a successor, but not when or whom. Only one fact seemed to be agreed. Six months into his time in office, Galba was ever more certain that his task was a break with the recent past, not a continuation of it.

The armies of Germany were anxious most of all for the tradition of buying their loyalty. If there was not to be expansion of the empire, with the opportunities for plunder they had tasted against Vindex's rebels, there had to be gifts in cash paid from some part of the world that was already under Roman rule. Nero had heavily depleted the treasury and Galba had what looked like a principled objection to new public expenditure.

Otho had been popular with his legionaries in Lusitania. He was said to see himself as the man next in line. Many doubted this. Galba, it was feared, had not brought discipline back to Rome, financial and otherwise, in order for the throne to pass after his death to a playboy friend of Nero whose only military experience stemmed from Nero's desire to get him away from a woman married at different times to them both.

The result was a vacuum of the kind that the soldiers of the age without a Caesar, like the courtiers of the *domus Caesaris* before them, most abhorred. The idea that Galba might consider Aulus Vitellius, another playmate of the Caesars, seemed even less likely to the men of the German camps, even to those of them who had considered that option at all. When a wholly new name appeared in the rumours it was an equal shock.

Unknown to the legions of Germany, like almost every other fact in Rome, Galba was beginning to turn against Otho. He was settling instead on Lucius Calpurnius Piso, from one of those many old families who, from the beginning of Tiberius's rule, had considered themselves just as worthy of the throne as any adopted son of Augustus. Several members of the Piso family, for half a century from the death of Germanicus, had paid the price of their presumption.

Piso's family stretched back to Julius Caesar's colleagues and rivals, to Pompey the Great, to Crassus, crucifier of Spartacus's army, and to far beyond. In Galba's mind a young Piso would add lustre to his own line just as the youth's grim seriousness, hardened by the execution of his brothers and his own exile, would continue the style of rule that Rome would continue to need.

The watchwords of his new heir, Galba hoped, would be 'honour, liberty and friendship, the chief blessings of the human mind', and not what he had found on the Palatine, 'flattery, adulation and that worst poison of an honest heart, self-interest'. Otho in Rome, borrowing more and more money on the basis of his imminent adoption, had no more knowledge of the coming rebuff than did the armies far away.

Aulus commanded his own soldiers from his base in Cologne, but most of them lived in scattered camps throughout Lower Germany with little action required and little entertainment beyond grumbling about their prospects. This was a frontier army whose closest contact with the local peoples was with those trading them as slaves. Its great wall, three miles long and six feet thick, with nine gates and nineteen towers protected hardly more than the staff of the governor himself. Triple arches separated military traffic from pedestrians. There was little variety in the local stone – sandstone studded with quartz, dark varieties and pale – and less variety still in the amenities added in the twenty years of Agrippina's colony.

And whatever bars or bath houses there were in Cologne, most of the men were not even near them. They spent the days patrolling the mud of a river bank. They had no Caesar, no action and no certainty of new money. Easily disgruntled with Galba, they also lacked an obviously willing replacement. Aulus Vitellius was accused by his critics of many crimes, but arrogant ambition was never one of them. His men waited for a lead from somewhere else.

In Upper Germany, the part closer to Rome, there was the same disgruntlement but also an ambitious, charismatic commanding officer, Caecina Alienus, who needed a survival strategy of his own. Caecina was only in his mid-twenties. He had neither the name, age nor position to seek the throne for himself. He faced a death penalty from Galba for corruption and little opportunity to defend himself in the purge of those deemed corrupt at Nero's court. He began agitating on Vitellius's behalf. So too did Fabius Valens, once an enthusiastic participant in Nero's military parades for youth, now free for new enthusiasms.

Results came fast. At the new year of 69 CE Aulus learnt that two of the Upper German legions, standing between himself and Rome, had refused the traditional annual oath of allegiance to their emperor. He treated this news with care. Although his formal duty was to enforce that allegiance, that was not necessarily the best way to survive. He had no control over Caecina or Valens. He was not agitating for himself, but excessive modesty might be as dangerous for him as excess ambition.

Anyone who knew of the auguries at his birth could, by the rules of the age, have been reasonably cautious. Anyone who knew the balance of power after the death of Nero had to recognise that an army might want to be the power, not merely follow a leader. Aulus at first showed some of the caution he had learnt on the Palatine and in Capri. From Cologne he sent a message that legions of Rome should either prepare to enforce allegiance to Galba on dissenting colleagues or prepare to support a new emperor.

Aulus maybe hoped for a lengthy period before a reply. If so, he was disappointed. On the second day of January, barely twenty-four hours after the first refusal of the oath, Fabius Valens brought back an answer, not one Aulus had been actively seeking but one he could not for long ignore.

The troops in Upper Germany would not coerce their colleagues who had rejected Galba. Instead, encouraged by Caecina, they had broken such few statues of Galba that they had and declared themselves loyal only to the letters SPQR on their standards, to the Senate and People of Rome. This was a meaningless cover for rebellion. There had to be an emperor for them to accept or deny. The Augustan state could not keep the peace merely by existing, by pretending that the SPQR was still in place. That kind of peace was gone.

In Rome many members of the senatorial aristocracy, former governors and generals or their descendants, would have seen chances for themselves in these events. But none had soldiers at the time when soldiers were needed. On Aulus Vitellius's behalf, the troops in Germany became their own leaders. Valens's route to the centre of Cologne was up the vertical axis of a cross, directly through the south gate of the massive walls, along the muddy north–south road towards the east–west road lit perfectly by the sun on Augustus's birthday. Escorting him was a band of Roman and local cavalry, a ragged retinue of tiny horses and sword-swinging riders. Almost as though Galba were no more alive than was Augustus, they hailed Aulus as emperor.

Valens entered the governor's mansion in search of the beneficiary of his efforts. It was hardly an imperial palace. It was closer in appearance to the cold stone of Julius Caesar's Rome than the marbled splendour that five subsequent Caesars had bequeathed to the Capitol, Forum and the Palatine. Its bricks were stamped with *Ex Germ Inf*, the sign of the brickworks where too many of his soldiers had to labour. The view east to the Rhine reminded no one of that to the Tiber.

The dining room was heated by a wood-burning stove, the bedroom damp and cold. The new Emperor Vitellius had only the authority that he was about to be given. He was following orders, not giving them. He had to emerge from his quarters in trousers and tunic, without time to change into a general's uniform, still less a toga. An enthusiastic soldier handed him the dagger of Julius Caesar that he had taken from the shrine to Mars, the war god.

On his first morning of elevation Aulus was carried high by his troops on a tour of the sodden town, the grim, grey towers, the temple to I.O.M. that was neither Optimus or Maximus to anyone used to the Capitol of Rome. He waved Caesar's dagger as the only visible sign of the difference between that day and the day before until he returned to his headquarters to find it in flames.

It seemed as though Galba or the gods had taken instant revenge. The dining-room stove was quickly decreed the culprit, not the last time that Aulus Vitellius would be pursued by legends of the table. The superstitious troops still saw the blaze as an ill omen until Aulus found sufficient wit for a tricky moment, hardly the sophistication for which his father had been famed but good enough. 'Do not lose heart,' he declared. 'To us a light is given.' He then led his followers to a dining room that had been spared the flames and to a large lunch, with wines from the south, reported and recorded for posterity.

Aulus did not send any announcement to Rome. He neither claimed the throne for himself from the senate and people, nor claimed that he was taking over to end the tyranny of his predecessor. He acted as though wholly satisfied to be emperor of Cologne, enjoying food and drink fit for his new status and delaying the date when he might be required to do anything else.

He saw no need for haste. There was wine from the south as well as local freshwater. There were forests of game, fish delivered from the north, a military harbour, quartz quarries for glass, long pipes from the hills and vast sewers into the Rhine. There were kitchens and echoing halls. The money that Agrippina had released for her birthplace colony had been spent in more useful ways than if she had been born in Tibur. Cologne was ready for a man ready to use what others had built. Drinking cups carried the mottoes *VIVAS*, 'To Life and Health', and *REPLE*, 'Fill Me Up'.

44

A HARD MAN TO FLATTER

Even if Aulus was not communicating with Rome, it was clear to Valens and Caecina that Galba would soon learn of events in Germany, the refusal of the new year oath and the elevation of Vitellius, the first an unwelcome but manageable surprise, the second doubtless a cause for incredulity. It would not have been hard to imagine the mockery at the news that the master of the fowl and seafood courses was claiming the mastery of all lands and seas ruled by Rome.

The legions of the Rhine needed fast to live up to their fearsome reputation in order that Galba's tiny court of advisers, his fellow soldier, his lawyer and his lover, should fall as fast as it had risen. Fortunately the winter stayed warm, the conditions for marching south much easier than in a normal season. Caecina and Valens, sticking to their preference for keeping as far away from each other as possible, divided between them what could now be described as the Vitellian forces.

Caecina was the keenest to leave, Valens as determined that his rival should not race ahead. Caecina took the shorter, more arduous route through the Alps. Valens, with a convenient eagle flying for his soothsayers, took his soldiers, with his personal train of camp-followers, on the longer march through Gaul to the Mediterranean coast.

Aulus needed little persuasion to stay in Cologne with a largely fictional main force ready to follow when required. At his personal communications centre, rebuilt and restored from the fire that was his own 'light' from the gods, he would receive bulletins both on the progress of his army and how Galba was planning to respond.

Soon enough there was news. Soon it was a time of bloodshed like no one had known since Caesar's conquests. Valens, he learnt, had been unable to stop his men from slaughtering thousands of German tribesmen. For most years during the empire, the madness – or even the sanity – of succession politics at Rome made little difference to life in the provinces. But in January 69 CE the men of what would later become Metz succumbed to mass murder driven not by greed for plunder but by a political transformation. The horror was hardly a credit to Valens's authority. Aulus might hope, and see it as a warning against future resistance. Hoping was all that he could do. From Caecina there were few reports of any kind.

Then, after only a few weeks as emperor of the sodden Rhinelands, there was news for Aulus from Rome that was more dramatic than anything from his armies. His enemy on the Palatine, he learnt, was no longer Galba but his old friend from the days of Nero, the newly proclaimed Emperor Otho. Galba had made a massive mistake in preferring the aristocrat over the playboy as his successor. In announcing his choice of Piso, he had not even flattered the palace guard for their exemplary loyalty while the Rhine army was in revolt. Nor did he promise the cash that they still believed was theirs.

Otho had not accepted the demotion of his hopes. He was deep in debt, his creditors were everywhere, even his house was collapsing, and he had secured just enough of a final loan to pay for a team of assassins. He appointed one of his freedmen to organise the murder. He appointed another to be his head of the navy and chief agent for ensuring the loyalty of any unreliable senators.

He and his agents bribed a group of guards to proclaim a new regime and agree to accept their due financial reward as soon as the stingy Galba was dead. Their code word, which would have aroused no suspicion, was that it was 'time to meet with the master builder'. Otho needed many meetings with his master builders for his notoriously crumbling house. He had no money to pay them, but intended that he would soon be housed at the public expense.

By the time that Aulus was reading his dispatches in Cologne, Otho was already master of the halls where both of them had served in the very recent past. Even in faraway Carthage, a freed slave called Crescens was holding a huge feast in support of Otho's claims, a new reminder of how politics and banqueting had been linked in the previous century.

The first plan had been to kill Galba while he was at dinner, not usually a long opportunity. Galba got away and had been confident enough to climb to the temple of I.O.M to give thanks for his preservation. This preservation was not long. An emperor without a court, he had been dragged from his litter while passing through the Forum, finally and desperately telling his attackers that, if they spared his life, they would be paid.

The urban civil war had been short. If Vitellius had any doubts about the launch of a longer war on his own account, it was already too late. Otho, it seemed, had handled the heads of both Galba and Piso and was particularly delighted with that of his aristocratic rival for the succession. Galba's head had reached the palace with a soldier's thumb in its mouth for easier portability.

Aulus knew his new enemy. He knew the courtly facts about him, that he was a small man, with spreading toes, thinning hair and face whitened by make-up. Aulus had been with Nero when the emperor wanted Otho's wife Poppaea as his empress. Otho was not unlike Nero; he was not ashamed of that and at first used the name Nero Otho in his letters.

Otho would not risk being the enemy to the palace guard that Galba had become; the early news was clear about that. At an extravagant banquet, designed to win senatorial support, the eating was interrupted by a revolt of Praetorian soldiers who feared that Otho was planning a surrender. He had to climb on to a couch to calm a revolt that had been launched on his own behalf.

The senate was successfully flattered. Otho was happy to appear as an old servant when he was the new master. That was an easy deception for a veteran of the Palatine. Early news suggested that there would be no purge of Galba's supporters, more a realistic acceptance that men and women had to make their peace with power.

Crispinilla was still surviving the calls from the mob that she be executed for her stewardship of Nero's orgies. Galba's lover, Icelus, had ensured Nero's last wish not to be decapitated before burial.

This had not helped him. He had been crucified as a slave even though he was a freedman. There was no great concern at Rome for a freed slave, however rich he had become by Galba's side – richer, it was said, and certainly more rapidly richer, than any freedman of Claudius or Nero.

Letters directly from Otho began to arrive at Cologne. Aulus's brother, Lucius, was now a hostage. Otho offered safety for Lucius and a luxury retirement for Aulus if the march on Rome by Caecina and Valens were to cease. Assassins began to arrive too, easily identifiable among the tiny population of the army town but a clear statement of intent.

Aulus sent back letters and assassins of his own, threatening dire consequences to Otho's family if any harm befell his mother. The safety of his wife, Galeria, was assured, he believed, because a senior member of Otho's court was a member of her family. His letters offered Otho the same retirement terms that he had been offered himself. His assassins were slightly more likely to survive in crowded Rome than Otho's in Cologne, but there was little expectation that the outcome would be decided by a single dagger.

Otho would not be an easy rival to dislodge. The new emperor, hailed like Galba by a senate without soldiers, was knowing and cunning. When it seemed that Nero's name was not as popular as he had supposed, he stopped using it. Otho knew much more than had Galba about the mechanisms of making a house a place from which to rule. He was hard to deceive by flattery. He knew its rules too well.

Aulus had no option but to stay behind his generals and, since he could not retreat, aim to defeat him by older ways. Little happened in Lower Germany. His few imperial duties were to try prisoners sent back by Caecina. In preparation for what he hoped would be a respected reign ahead, he acquitted several troublemakers who made good speeches before the soldiers' juries.

45

BROTHER BEHIND THE LINES

Lucius Vitellius was the younger brother of Rome's new emperor in Cologne, but that did not necessarily make him an enemy to Otho in Rome. The two brothers had worked together in Africa, Lucius following Aulus as governor in what to the Africans must have been one unbroken regime. But, when the stakes were the rule of the whole empire, it cannot have been obvious to Lucius that his brother was the right man to back, that Aulus would win if he fought Otho or even that he would fight at all.

Lucius knew enough about Aulus to think that he might prefer doing nothing to doing anything. To have two emperors, neither of whom had known about the other's ascent, was clearly ludicrous. It was disorienting for the palace guard, who depended on a single emperor and did not have one. It was a misunderstanding that caused chaos whenever a suspicious guardsman saw something untoward. But it need not lead to civil war.

No one should want civil war, certainly not anyone trained in the *domus Caesaris* that had emerged from so many civil war years. Otho was no Julius Caesar. Aulus was most certainly no Augustus. One of the two might back down and Aulus, feeding his face far from Rome, was perhaps the man more likely to choose luxury retirement.

Aulus's soldiers might want to fight. But civil war was both harder and less profitable than terrorising northern tribesmen. Civil war brought with it not just the prospect of killing former friends but the convention which prevented the defeated being ransomed or enslaved. Neither Otho nor Aulus were from a world where Romans fighting Romans made sense. Otho held the throne in Rome. It made no sense for Lucius to assume that he would lose it. Accepting flattery for himself as a Vitellian, a man of new and greater interest might, temporarily at least, be enough.

Throughout the warm January there was ample time to consider these assumptions and enough ignorance of the facts for encouragement of theory. There were more immediate distractions too. The Tiber was in constant flood, a city bridge collapsed to become a dam and river waters destroyed gardens and shops. The possibility, or not, of hostile armies emerging from the north was a problem for Lucius much further away.

Food may have been plentiful in Cologne, but in Rome prices were soaring, apartments were tumbling into flooded basements and the people were nostalgic for Nero who, while debasing the currency, at least gave them Caesar's bread. Otho, like Nero, ordered the minting of silver coins linking himself to Ceres, the goddess of the corn. It was soon requiring silver even to buy a loaf. Otho's own silver was reserved for paying his troops and avoiding the fate of stingy Galba.

Lucius was probably free to leave Rome for the north and join his brother's forces, but it was a probability that he did not test. There were rumours, no more yet than that, of legions of the Rhine, loyal to Aulus, popping from the Alpine passes like stoppers from a jar. It was all almost fantastical. In Cologne, even if he reached that far, he, Lucius Vitellius, would be merely the younger Vitellius yet again. By staying in Rome he could best be useful to Otho, if required, useful to Aulus, if that seemed appropriate, useful to their mother, which Aulus would surely approve, and useful to himself whoever was the winner.

Otho, however, had no need of Lucius except as a hostage. He already had the service of many Romans who considered themselves useful, even invaluable, and were not the brother of the friend who had become his enemy. The servility of senators and junior officials to a new emperor was astonishing even to those who had attended the court of Nero. Statues of Poppaea, who had been wife to them both, sprung up again as though at a party she had never left. Aulus was no longer part of the party.

In the middle of February the first reliable news came to Rome of the twin attack by Valens and Caecina. Rome itself had no military defence apart from palace guardsmen more effective at court politics than against defenders of the Rhine frontier. Otho summoned the best imperial legions from the Danube, assembled his best generals and prepared for what seemed, unless a deal could be done, to be the most likely battlefield – on the long, broad plain north of the River Po.

For the legionaries from the Rhine Rome would be their destination, not the source of their power. Otho knew enough not to rely on the young men of the Palatine who dressed themselves as Greek heroes and packed their travelling kits for feasting and fornicating along the way. One of his courtly soldiers was Gaius Julius Antiochus Epiphanes, prince of Commagene, nephew of Aka, the wife of Tiberius's Thrasyllus. Antiochus was just one of the many fish struggling without the political water that was all they knew and needed.

Otho needed brute force to meet the brute forces against him. He prepared his own uniform as a regular foot-soldier. He had learnt more in Lusitania than those who remembered his Palatine days expected or would know themselves. He hoped to join his Danube legions and deal separately with Caecina and Valens, either by diplomacy or by battle, before they could unite. Their mutual enmity was his own best friend, he hoped.

His last speech in Rome was a triumph, possibly too good to have been written by its speaker. The likely writer was the orator Publius Galerius Trachalus, whom Aulus was relying upon to protect Galeria, his wife, who was still in Rome with their children. Otho did not even name Aulus and accused the Rhine legions merely of restless credulity. It was met with lengthy applause of the kind given to Nero's singing and Caligula's virtuosity on the chariot. Lucius Vitellius prepared to join Otho on the journey north.

By the middle of March, Lucius was one of some 5,000 men who had marched out with Otho, stopping fifteen miles behind the main forces ahead. His final destination, not of his own choice but very satisfactory for him, was Brixellum, a small town in the fertile flat fields south of the Po, home to farmers of pigs, vines and wool. The land was slowly drying in the spring winds, every day becoming easier terrain for fighting.

A war was beginning but neither Aulus, still in Cologne, nor Otho, nearer but no better an example to his men, would witness the first battle for their futures. Lucius and Otho had to wait in Brixellum for news brought back by messenger to the drainage ditches and grape trellises. Aulus would learn nothing till all was over.

In the first week of April Otho made one brief visit to what had become the front line outside the small town of Bedriacum on the north side of the Po. He did not stay long. Only when he returned to Brixellum with a large escorting force were Lucius and Otho's other camp-followers able to know what had happened since the Vitellians arrived in Italy.

It was a picture without clear prediction for the future. Caecina had been active for almost two weeks. It was no longer a magical success to bring an army through the Alps (Hannibal's pioneering journey was almost 300 years before), but it was still a surprise to the detachments of Otho's force whom he had quickly overwhelmed. Just as reportable, and maybe more disturbing to Lucius, was the arrival of Caecina's wife, with a full cavalry escort, on a horse decorated in purple as though she, not Aulus's wife Galeria, were the next empress.

Caecina had then, it seemed, been beaten badly in a rushed assault on the town of Placentia. He had been keener to defeat Otho's armies before Valens arrived than on any victory itself. Otho's men, by contrast, felt that their own generals were too patient and had not pressed their advantage. Caecina had won a cavalry battle. His men had wounded the prince of Commagene, the kind of detail that looks good in dispatches while making no difference to any outcome. Otho's men were close to revolt again over the caution of their commanders, whom they accused of being at heart on the side of the Rhine army, if not of Aulus Vitellius himself.

Little was clear. The arrival of Valens had not immediately helped the Vitellians' cause. His troops, like those of Otho, accused their commander of insufficient loyalty to their emperor and, even worse, of hiding plunder beneath his tent that should have been shared with his men. They forced him to escape dressed as slave and dug up his quarters, from bed-tents to banqueting tents, before allowing him back. Caecina referred to Valens as 'a disgusting old git' and Valens called Caecina 'a pompous prat'. This was not an alliance that, to Lucius, seemed a secure investment for himself. Until the facts were less like smoke, the peace of Brixellum suited him well.

Otho's own response was to stay in Brixellum too. His brief council of war had decided on a rapid attack while the Vitellians were in disarray, and a role for himself that was wholly behind the scenes. He feared that if Aulus were to be following Caecina through the melted Alpine ice, the soldiers of the Vitellii would be yet further emboldened. Aulus was still in Cologne and in no hurry to leave, but neither Otho nor Lucius could be sure of that.

Bravery would have been foolhardy for Otho's cause. He had announced no heir and thus a victory for his forces in which their commander died would be a total defeat. Lucius too saw no advantage in declaring his loyalty. Brixellum, its vineyards, pig fields and wool-carders, was to remain Otho's base – and Lucius's too until such time as he saw both an opportunity to leave, and a benefit in leaving.

The next news to reach Brixellum, only a few days later in the middle of April, was of the total defeat of the forces fighting for Otho. When Otho's supporters at his base camp showed themselves ready to fight on, Lucius quickly saw the dangers of the rear becoming the front line. He and other senators retreated, bickering and backing further down the road to Rome. Fortunately for everyone, Otho killed himself at dawn after the news came. His last words for Vitellius were that he should enjoy his family. His last part in the drama of court politics was soon deemed his finest.

In their early days on the Palatine and at Capri, both Otho and Aulus had learnt to present themselves for theatrical effect. Otho's death prevented many further deaths, and the reports of it to the retreating party from Bologna ensured that this part of the story was at an end. Reports of it to Rome ensured that Aulus Vitellius, first hailed merely by soldiers at Cologne, was pronounced emperor by the senate and people, where emperors were supposed to be pronounced. The new emperor continued his march south.

46

WINE FOR THE BATTLEFIELD

In Lugdunum, to the west between Cologne and Bedriacum, stood a memorial to one of the most respected side-changers from the entire century of the Caesars. Lucius Munatius Plancus founded the colony in the year after Caesar's assassination while he was still trying to decide whether the assassins or one of Caesar's would-be heirs deserved his support. He was organising banquets for Cleopatra till only a few weeks before her defeat which brought the emperor Augustus to power. While he was flattering his way back to favour with the new regime, Horace wrote for him a wry ode reminding him of his mistaken past, the benefits of bureaucratic peace (not least his home by the waterfalls of Tibur) and of bygones being bygones. Plancus quickly became a pillar of the new order.

His past foundation of Lugdunum, beside a river so slow-flowing that no one could tell its direction, became just one of his achievements, a town of baths fed by foaming aqueducts, with a massive amphitheatre used by emperors on their frequent visits as well as a luxurious place of exile for unwanted eastern kings. Both Claudius and Germanicus were born there. It was a very Roman city where rich men's freedmen boasted freed slaves of their own.

Lugdunum's position on the gold road from Spain made it ideal for the minting of money for troops. This was the place where an incautious master coiner once declared the newly dead Tiberius a god before learning that the official designation by Caligula was maniac instead. It was the empire's only mint until Nero ordered his own coinage struck in Rome. A little more than a century after Plancus's statue first rose from the mud, this was the well-chosen site, still 500 miles from Bedracium, where Aulus Vitellius, moving slowly south, ordered the senior survivors of his victory to meet.

The newly unchallenged emperor did not yet look the part. While the tradesman of Cologne provided food fit for his station, no one offered suitable clothes. Only the governor of Lugdunum gave him the gold and purple that prevented him having to re-enter Italy in the shabby garb in which he had left. Once appropriately dressed, he was keen to congratulate his supporters, accommodate those who had fought against him and plan a long trip to Rome to claim what he already owned.

Vitellius was not alone in getting new clothes. He raised his stammering son to the imperial purple too and renamed him Germanicus, the heir to his father as the original Germanicus had once been to Tiberius. This must have seemed a doubtful double augury for the boy. Many remembered the murder of the first Germanicus and the trial which did so much for the new emperor's uncle. A few too might have recalled the role Plancina, wife of Piso, Plancus's granddaughter.

Once a man was emperor every event of his past became history, a piece of something that mattered as well as merely having happened. Publius Vitellius had not proved that Plancina's husband was a murderer, but now he was important again. That was the relevant truth. The daughter of Lugdunum's founder had been protected by her friendship with Augustus's long-surviving widow, Livia. That too was now part of the story of the Vitellii.

At Lugdunum power began with the personal. Showing a matrimonial jealousy unusual at the highest levels of Rome, Aulus ordered the pursuit and execution of the man who had married his first wife, Petronia. He promised a seemingly modest marriage for his young daughter, Vitellia. Her husband was set to be the governor of north-eastern Gaul, Decimus Valerius Atticus, wealthy and himself from a Gallic family. There was not yet a new web of imperial connections but, even without the Caesars, there were still many traditional roles for the family of an emperor, enemy, heir apparent, mother behind the scenes, brother as protector and maybe heir too if anything were to happen to the son.

Aulus commissioned coins that showed his father, Lucius, as he had never been portrayed in his lifetime, leaner-faced than his son, smug and smiling. Aulus's mother remained a reluctant convert to respect for the new emperor, especially dismissive of her grandson's new name. She had known the original Germanicus, not well but enough to know that the boy presented to the crowd at Lugdunum did not deserve the name. Nor did her son, who had added Germanicus to his own names. She had given birth, she said, only to a Vitellius.

As Aulus left Lugdunum there was already the clash of advisers for which the Palatine was well prepared. Cluvius Rufus, an historian and former supporter of Otho, joined the travelling court from Spain and immediately clashed with one of Aulus's freedmen, Hilarius. Cluvius, an eloquent orator too, found himself accused of trying to establish a breakaway province. Cluvius won his case. He was a supporter of Vitellius now. He understood the senate as he understood the theatre, and he knew the mood in still-faraway Rome.

Lines of responsibility were more fluid than in Rome, where courtiers had clearer roles – for answering letters, writing speeches, vetting appointments and negotiating with supplicants. In Rome only the very senior courtiers crossed boundaries into each other's areas of responsibility. On the road men might be masters of all trades. Cluvius became more than a supporter – a new senior courtier to the Emperor Aulus Germanicus Vitellius.

In Rome the palace guards were the only soldiers close to the men and women running the household. In a military camp there were soldiers in daily attendance. Neither group knew easily how to deal with the other. Aulus flattered his soldiers, and the soldiers flattered him in return by praising his freedmen. They called for one of the grandest of them to be promoted to the status of a knight with the right to wear gold rings on his fingers, the degree immediately below that of a senator. Aulus was reluctant and confused. He agreed the promotion but continued in private to address him as a former slave, soon crucifying him as a slave too for a crime of alleged corruption.

In place of some senior freedmen, Vitellius also promoted Roman businessmen of the class just below the senate, favouring especially those who had witnessed his initial elevation before the northern legions. To have been at Cologne was an honour, to be at Lugdunum too. Household roles were accepted by members of Rubellius Blandus's class as a promotion, an award of jobs which once they would have despised, an expansion of a policy that Claudius had cautiously begun. This began slowly to transform the way in which imperial courts were staffed, if less so the nature of the courts themselves.

The new emperor was keen to attend the gladiatorial games which Caecina and Valens were planning in his honour in local towns near Bedriacum. He also wanted to see the battlefield itself and the tomb of Otho at Brixellum, which he had been assured was suitably small. Word spread that he intended to continue the party of Cologne. Carriages of finest seafood queued to meet the imperial demand. Boxing bouts became drunken riots. The great survivor, Lucius Munatius Plancus, a general once prepared to crawl across Cleopatra's floors in the costume of a mermaid, was the perfect presiding spirit.

It was a long and slow journey into Italy. Not till he was at Bedriacum did Aulus see how he had won his victory – or at least how he might plausibly claim to have won it. He did not lack help. Caecina and Valens explained their exploits. Unusually for court life, despite the chaos, there was enough glory to go round.

Otho's men, he learnt, fought better than expected. Their guardsmen from Rome may have been reinforced with actors and dancers; they may have been more used to watching slaughter in the arena than fighting for a cause; but they had driven back Caecina's troops in the first battle for Placentia, dropping millstones and other heavy agricultural equipment on the heads of attackers who were drunk, hungover or both.

The final victory was clear enough: the enemy commander was dead. But there was great doubt, until a common story could be agreed, over who had fought for whom, how genuinely, how loyally and sometimes whether they had fought at all. Otho's troops had suspected that their own commitment was greater than that of their commanders. It suited those same former commanders for Otho, newly pardoned at Lugdunum, to suggest that this fear had indeed been justified: they had been sympathetic to Aulus Vitellius all along.

Caecina, it seemed, had been both at his boldest and weakest before Valens arrived. He had given no order to attack Otho's men in a single massive strike. He had had to move on to softer targets in order to claim a victory. It was hard to be sure if this had been right or wrong, but there were enough ambushes and raids to enliven the war stories on both sides.

Mutinies were just as numerous. Caecina had to show Aulus his firmness in dealing with a mutiny among his men without taking responsibility for the mutiny having happened in the first place. Valens had to explain his own mutinies. His escape from his men while disguised as a slave had to be turned into a triumph of adventure. The commanders vied with each other to show a valiant progress from risk to reward.

The coordination and final victory of Vitellius's forces had come most from the anxiety of Valens's soldiers that they might be deprived of victory's revenge, the profits of loot. They had raced and joined their comrades from the Rhine while Valens himself was still considering his options. The central truth was that the Rhine army was superior to that from the Danube, even if many of Otho's troops had the fiercer loyalty to their emperor.

Otho, however, had failed to match that loyalty – and doomed himself by his impatience. He was not an easy man to advise or control. His years as a courtier had inured him to most forms of flattery. While some men on the Palatine were forever addicted to false words, Otho in Lusitania remembered enough to make him sick.

Patience might have triumphed for Otho if he had allowed it. The Vitellians had pillaged the ground behind them and were short of supplies. Otho had access to provisions from the whole of Italy and Rome itself. He could have waited. Instead he ordered a mass assault before all his reinforcements were in place.

From the safety of Brixellum, with Lucius Vitellius uneasy at his side, Otho had waited for news of a battle that he need not have fought until his enemy was weaker. Caecina and Valens had subdued their rivalries for a final act of joint intimidation above their enemy's camp. It was this solidarity which persuaded Otho's commanders to surrender. These were all claims and controversies of the kind that battlefield tourists appreciated – and always have. Failings were forgotten, bravery remembered, blame distributed as far as possible to the dead.

Although the battle stories had been cleaned up for the victor from Cologne, the battlefield had not. Ears were more easily deceived than eyes. In civil wars the fallen were often quickly removed, their relatives near, the first scavengers knowing what the dead would have wanted as well as what the living might want from their corpses. But the fighters at Bedriacum were all far from home, not permitted to enslave or take prisoners for ransom, only intermittently obedient to their commanders.

Forty days after the final fighting there was still much around Bedriacum to show what had happened there, corpses of all ranks wearing what had once been the labels of life, faces with papery eyes, cavernous stomachs, severed hands, ditches of blood and spears, cheap dented helmets, arms and men smashed beyond use by any but farmers who would soon again be trimming their vines. Aulus Vitellius was later credited with the line, delivered after much use of medicinal alcohol, that dead enemies smelt sweet but dead Roman enemies even sweeter.

More than half a century before, Aulus's uncle, Publius, had seen the grim impact on Germanicus's men of visiting the Teutoburg forest, where Varus had lost five of Augustus's legions. That journey of expiation had been taken ten years after the *clades* that would forever bear Varus's name. At Bedriacum the evidence of war was fresher, the flat land black with gorging birds, black kites and vultures, black shrikes and crows, mountain birds in a long landscape stretching towards invisible peaks. The bloody fields would soon be vineyards again, but meanwhile the army of Vitellius began its slow progress south, a growing court of wine-sellers and cooks in close attendance.

The men deserved a mighty party to clear their minds. It was several weeks before Aulus finished his journey from Cologne to what became the greatest Roman banquet that anyone could imagine. Lucius Vitellius, conscious perhaps that he had not committed himself to the Vitellian cause as courageously and completely as he might have done, was ready to be the most enthusiastic master of ceremonies.

47

THE SHIELD OF MINERVA

Sea fish travelled alive in wooden barrels of saltwater, heavy cargoes requiring round-bottomed transport ships or carriages capable of dragging artillery to war or silver for soldiers, or whatever was needed at the time. It was a trade whose profits depended on assessing faraway demand. A red mullet from Marseilles might be worth a small fortune one day and nothing the next. A scorpion fish, washed up on the rock beaches of Germany where Publius had almost lost his men, could find a high price as long as it was where men were competing to feed an emperor with a reputation. So could prawns from the most prized Greek islands, anchovies from the Black Sea, the sea urchins of Egypt and the oysters of Britain, sometimes rushed to market by teams of runners if the boats and trucks were too slow. However exaggerated some of the stories of Aulus's gluttony became, there seems little doubt that the victory of Valens and Caecina at Bedriacum was good for the exotic fish trade.

Between Bedriacum and Brixellum there was at first little cause for a party. The roads showed fresher signs of savagery than the battlefield itself. While Caecina and Valens had been warily celebrating in Lugdunum, their men had begun a neighbourhood riot of plunder and destruction. The defeated too had joined in to take their share. For the families farming beside the Po, or fishing coarse carp or catfish in its streams, the aftermath of the battle was more brutal than the fighting. The wiser tradesmen kept their distance. The victorious armies were like an inland sea, controlled by no one but the distant tides. Only the returning commanders, with Aulus Vitellius newly at their head, restored the order of before.

At Brixellum there was the site of Otho's headquarters, closer to the battle than Aulus had ever been but arguably more a sign of cowardice. Here the emperor's brother could add to the family story.

Lucius could explain his frustration at being held behind the lines, even if not all believed him. He could report the stubborn loyalty of the enemy officers, not a group easy for a brother of Vitellius to live among. He could show Otho's personal tents and the remains of documents and letters. Otho had maybe destroyed his records in order that his supporters, or those undecided, should not suffer when Aulus was in power. Or maybe Otho had been burnishing his reputation in other ways; but the murder of Galba would not be so easily expunged.

Aulus and Lucius could discuss tombs, two brothers in a family which now had claims on grandeur. Otho's was small, his body burnt to ash to save it from desecration. Nero, the last of the Caesars, lay in the tomb only of his father's family. The mausoleum of Augustus was filled with many who had hoped to succeed and died too early. There was no such vault for the Vitellii yet.

Lucius was determined to allay any doubts about his own place in the new imperial family. His first marriage had been to Augustus's great-great-granddaughter, Junia Calvina; his second wife, Triaria, was ferocious for her new family's regime. The Vitellii of the third generation, like Lucius and Publius in the second, were a contrasting pair. But Lucius was already Aulus's fiercest defender as their armies swarmed, unopposed, upon the capital, a gastronomic march on Rome.

The most efficient way of cooking for successful troops on the march was to roast meat. As far back as the epics of Homer, this was the way. Roasting needed the fewest dishes and plates. It was not a lesson that the Vitellii brothers intended to apply. Chefs accompanied the soldiers as though they were the cavalry protecting their flanks, a parody, both in the act and in the telling, of the great imperial cavalcades through the countryside, the *comites*, by which Augustus and his successors had dispensed law and power.

The troops ate well off the summer lands, their officers from the wagons from distant seas, and all displayed the easy debauchery that Romans preferred to associate with foreigners. The standard fare may have been little more than *Pisa Vitelliana*, the eponymous paste of peas or beans, pepper, ginger, lovage, hard-boiled yolks and honey. The only memory for later writers was of vastly expensive food, regularly demanded, imported and consumed by Vitellius, sometimes four times a day, in his borrowed imperial regalia.

The finest food for the march was garlanded like the most successful general, wreathed in laurel like a conquering hero. The serving dishes were called *fercula*, the word once used for the carts that hauled the gold and silver in a triumphal parade. The feasting was a form of reward for Vitellius's flatterers, a substitute for the real power he had not yet achieved, and perhaps an obliterating therapy for himself.

Valens and Caecina were becoming even more like courtiers and less like commanders. Valens ordered from Rome a huge cast of actors to add to the entertainment, aiming to impress both Vitellius and, more importantly, all the other would-be members of the emperor's court who were presenting their credentials. The civilians created too much of a party atmosphere for some of the soldiers' tastes. Admiring applause was fine; stealing swords and belts was not. Swords were drawn and spectators killed, a spree that ended only when one of the dead was found to be the father of a man welcoming his son back from the wars.

Lucius began preparation for his brother's *Cena Adventica*, the banquet that would mark Aulus's arrival in his capital. The finest fish needed the finest plate. No pottery dish could be found that was large enough. When Apicius was making his pancakes of fish and thrushes' breasts, he recommended the added satisfaction that would come from a silver dish, not just because of its value but the possibility of its greater size. It was a horrible vice, said Horace, to pay a huge price at market only to squeeze the purchase on to a plate that was too small.

Silver was the favoured metal from which the rich should eat, mined in Spain, hammered and riveted into giant dishes decorated with what they were made to contain. There was no lack of such silver at Rome. Connoisseurs collected examples from the empire, exhibiting the treasures in their homes, buying antiques from the masters of the Greek workshops. In the reign of Claudius the freedman Rotundus Drusillianus, once the property of Caligula's favourite and most notorious sister, had been just one who collected tableware on this grand scale. Fruits of land and sea, dogs and dolphins danced around the rim of many a plate which a new emperor might acquire, or which might be offered for his use.

The Vitellii had not extended the empire, nor even visited very much of it, but on their 'Shield of Minerva', a gleaming dish of epic name and proportions, would lie the produce of everywhere from Parthia, still unconquered, to the Pillars of Hercules between the Mediterranean and the Atlantic, still passed only by the few. Aulus and his new court would dine off Spanish silver on pikes' livers streaked in red and yellow, sperm of lampreys, brains of pheasant and peacock, tongues of flamingos.

Much lesser food would be served to thousands of soldiers and citizens, roasts and fish stew, the lesser parts of the lampreys as once offered by Julius Caesar. Not everyone could celebrate with silver on the delicacies that showed Rome's reach beyond the Euphrates and the Ocean. But every rich variety, more like vomit to later minds, would become a metaphor for wider ills. When Agrippa Postumus was exiled by Augustus for excessive fishing in the guise of the god Neptune, it was a single charge against a soon-to-be forgotten man. The charge against Vitellius of excessive fish-eating would never die.

The final progress to the dining tables was as slow as Aulus's exit from Cologne. Some of the German troops, who had never seen Rome before, rushed ahead to see for themselves the Palatine, the temple of Jupiter Optimus and Maximus and between them in the Forum the place where Galba had died. The narrow streets were awkward for the new arrivals. They found Romans as bemused by their long swords and leather jackets as they themselves were surprised at the massed white togas of officials, and would-be officials, for the new reign. The abundance of ovens for the coming feasts was less of a surprise. Violence of a mostly good-natured kind was no surprise at all.

Behind these men of the Rhine army, as he had been ever since their departure, Aulus Vitellius had to make his own choice of dress. He had options. He was no longer dependent on the hasty packing at his house in Rome when Galba was still alive, nor on the generosity of the Roman governor at Lugdunum who had fitted him for the role he was about to take. His first thought was to wear the red cloak of a conquering general, to ride on a great horse with a conqueror's sword at his side. The theatre of war was beginning to suit him.

But Aulus had advisers too. Those who had fought at Bedriacum did not want their chances of wealth and power to be destroyed by a mad pretence that their leader was a Caesar. The Emperor Augustus had also been the victor in a civil war, but he had dressed his triumph against fellow Romans as a victory over Cleopatra, a dangerous alien. The people of Rome, perplexed and contemptuous as many of them were, might still revolt if Aulus pretended too far to be what he was not. Not yet crippled by the certainty of a Caligula or Nero, he wore the clothes that those who were waiting for him wanted to see.

Aulus Vitellius passed through the city walls on foot. He wore the toga that he had been entitled to wear while Nero was alive. His height made him easy to see, but his modesty was on view too. Behind him were the legions who had made him, their eagles gleaming against the summer sky. Around him were Caecina and Valens and their commanders. But togas took prime place among the armour. His leading centurions wore the white robes of priests. He had Germanicus, his son and heir. He had most of what a Caesar had ever wanted. It was a magnificent display.

Other members of his family were waiting. His elderly mother, no less sceptical of Aulus than on the day of his birth, no less clear that the Vitellii were not the Caesars, had to take the title Augusta. Continuity was what the Senate and People of Rome demanded, the SPQR that was all the more potent in letters than in fact. The Emperor Vitellius walked the broad path up to the Capitol, led the sacrifice to Jupiter and greeted his mother by her new name. He made a speech that flattered himself. Leaders of the popular assembly returned the flattery by urging that he become Augustus.

Meanwhile, Lucius was preparing his banquet. Sea creatures, so far from their home seas and so freshly dead, sprawled over the largest silver plate that Lucius could find. Light was able to pass through the piles of raw flesh, tiny shrimps and slices of mullet and turbot, showing the shadows of animals, vegetables, gods and heroes carved below. Crab and oyster were more solid elements of the gastronomic theatre, blocking the diners' view of any shining corn sheaves or acanthus. Silver was the metal that Apicius had commended for the best display of his cuisine. It enhanced the translucent and reflected what would not let through the light. It was precious but not so precious as to take all attention from the trophies of the Black Sea and Atlantic.

The plate was called the Shield of Minerva, after the protective armour for Rome's goddess of art and memory. This was not a shield for war. Minerva was a rival of the war god, Mars, mistress of flautists, not fighters. Those who were served from this shield would be unlikely to see even a scene of war, nothing more violent than the sword of a swordfish or the backward-pointing teeth of a pike. This *Cena Adventica* was a banquet for when battles were in the past. Neither Lucius nor Aulus had fought themselves to advance the name of Vitellius to barely below that of the Caesars. But when Lucius gathered the roes of rare fish alongside the tongues of rare birds and spread it all over a giant piece of theatrical armour, he ensured how his brother's arrival in Rome would always be remembered.

48

EMPEROR VITELLIUS

Aulus Vitellius found the same easy popularity with the people of Rome as he had with the troops of Cologne. He discovered that the memory of Nero, his long-time companion of the streets, was still warm in the places where they had played together. He ordered that an altar be built to the last Caesar in the Campus Martius behind the Capitol. Crowds outside the great temple to Jupiter were soon able to look out beyond the site of Julius Caesar's assassination and smell the smoke of the latest sacrifices. Nero's priests were to come from the order that Tiberius had established in memory of Augustus. Nero's poems were to be read aloud and admired as though their author were still seeking the flattery of his hearers. A flute-player was urged 'to render something from the Master's Book', and there was no doubt who was the master.

Aulus advertised his support for his favourite team of chariot-racers just as Nero and Caligula had done and as many Romans in the street liked to do. When the Blues triumphed on the racetrack he was as clearly content as when wine was in his cup or prime prawns on his plate. Julius Caesar had dictated routine letters while the horses were wheeling around the track. Everyone could see that Vitellius preferred the stadium to the office.

The offices of the emperor were vastly larger than when Augustus had ruled the Roman world from his tower. Offices, baths and banqueting halls extended out into Nero's Golden House. Aulus's wife disapproved of these additions to the imperial domain, her critics claiming that she deemed it not extravagant enough. The Palatine was still primarily the workplace of the slaves and ex-slaves of the emperor, responding to requests or queries from thousands of miles away as they had for 100 years.

There were no immediate shifts in tone towards the city or the empire between the summer and autumn of 69 CE. At the court of the new emperor were some who had accompanied him from Cologne, for his battlefield tour and on the gastronomic march south. He promoted more *equites* to posts which previously men of their class had been reluctant to take. But there were many more who occupied the same rooms in which they had served for Nero, Galba and Otho, answering letters, selling favours, feeding dogs, some of them even surviving since the reign of Claudius, remembering when Lucius Vitellius the elder ruled the staff and his sons were unruly children.

Aulus alienated some support that was dangerously close to home. There was a new class of impoverished senators whom Nero had exiled and whom Galba had allowed to return. Aulus was persuaded that these senators' freedmen, who had become as rich as his own, should pay a tax to help their masters, a policy which, with insufficient foresight, he imposed on the freedmen of the Palatine too. The people in the streets applauded yet another move which brought their emperor closer to themselves. For the courtiers there came the need for ever more elaborate tax evasion and a first sense that their master was not on their side.

The new emperor returned some of the goods of the damned that had been taken after the treason trials under Tiberius and Caligula. He left untouched the fortunes of those whom he had executed for supporting Otho. But there was no time for these sorts of administrative adjustment to succeed – or fail. Just as the Caesars had sometimes exiled all actors, Vitellius barred from Rome all impudent prophets of the kind that his mother had heeded at his birth. That did not stop them successfully prophesying his imminent death or, like the actors after every exile, slipping quietly back into the city.

The prosecutors still prospered. Nero's master lawyer of the treason trials, Vibius Crispus, joined the Vitellian cause and proved himself as flexible as his predecessors. Like Seneca he pleaded for a leave of absence through illness. If he had not fallen ill, he said, the banquets would have killed him. Though a reluctant glutton, Crispus showed all the survival skills that had been necessary for a public servant during the era of the *domus Caesaris* that had come to its end.

The soldiers who had put Aulus in power profited from higher pay. The new emperor was not about to repeat the mistakes of Galba. But the legions from Germany found their status undermined by the favouring of local recruits for prestigious posts in the palace guard. Some of them were living in swampy areas close to the Tiber, sharing their homes with malarial mosquitoes unfamiliar to them from the Rhine. The heat was the biggest killer since the battle of Bedriacum. The armies who had acclaimed Aulus at Cologne were still loyal, but less enthusiastic in their applause.

Caecina and Valens were also as loyal to Aulus as they had been before, but this did not make them loyal in the way that Augustus or even Nero would have expected. Both were consuls, but neither was the most reliable of aides to an emperor still finding his way. Each hated the other much more than they loved anyone else. Each competed with the other in promoting games across the city, paying the bills with the houses and lands of those who had died support- ing Galba and Otho. Valens, though as focused as ever on his varied personal pleasures, was more skilful than Caecina in rewarding his own troops.

Aulus had little time to watch and wait and eat and enjoy as he had done for so much of his life. At the beginning of September there were reports that a single legion in Moesia, modern Bulgaria and Serbia, was in revolt. At first this did not raise serious alarm but, quite quickly, it became clear that another Roman army was march- ing on Rome, aiming, it seemed, to do from the east what Aulus had done from the west.

This army contained the legions of Judaea and Syria that Lucius Vitellius had once held for Tiberius. It had a commander currently in Alexandria, Vespasian, who was a decorated veteran of Claudius's British campaign. If one army could impose its will on the Palatine court, so maybe could another. The rival force would have to be faced.

It was Caecina alone who led the Rhine legions back north to the battlefields beside the River Po; Valens was either too ill or too cunning to start the trip. Each of Aulus's commanders had to decide how serious was the threat, how likely it was to succeed and how best they should protect and advance themselves. The emperor, who was staying behind in Rome, had never been a totem for his commanders, never a cause in himself worth fighting for. He was liked by his men but not an object of devotion. He was that much more common kind of leader, the man in charge at the time. The question for Caecina, newly back on the road, and Valens, still in Rome, was how long that time would last.

The totem for the armies heading towards them was a man who had been in and out of the lives of the Vitellii for fifty years. Vespasian was more a soldier than a courtier, but he had skilfully trodden the fine line between those roles. He never had to pretend that Caligula was talking to the Moon, but he did once deliver a senate speech of exceptionally flattering thanks for an invitation from Caligula to dinner. Like Aulus's father he was part of the court of Augustus's niece, Antonia, also the long-time lover of her famously unforgetting secretary, Caenis. He was a protégé of Narcissus, and in Britain sixteen years before he had won a fearsome military reputation under Aulus Plautius.

Under Nero the career of Vespasian had seemed to be coming to an end. He had been an unlikely companion on the poetry tour of Greece. Though knowledgeable in courtly manners, he was notoriously hard-faced for musical evenings which required the appearance of relaxation. His expression seemed often held by wire, as though he were permanently adjusting his mask or, as the unkinder noted, just about to have a shit. Already almost sixty years old, he had a reputation for falling asleep during Nero's performances, on one occasion having to be abused for his yawning by Phoebus, one of Nero's freedmen. His elder brother, Titus Flavius Sabinus, the city prefect at Rome, was the head of the family.

Only an unusually serious revolt in Judaea brought Vespasian to the right place at the right time. He had been a hammer of the tribes of west Britain while Aulus's father was the top man at Rome.

In 66 CE Nero needed to choose a man to be a hammer of the Jews
when most of the group around him were more fitted for dancing.
Vespasian was the best prospect in the emperor's sight, and suddenly he was at the level in the Roman world from which, in 69 CE, he
could make a challenge for the throne.

Vespasian's family was only a little grander than the Vitellii
had been before the rise of Aulus's father. He was the grandson of
a centurion who became a debt-collector, a profitable but hardly
respectable trade whose members Aulus knew all too personally.
Like Aulus and his brother he had been a governor of Africa. He
was notoriously poor, less through excessive spending than by failing to acquire, and often dependent on Sabinus for support.

Aulus's first reaction to the news of an army loyal to Vespasian
was that it was fake. He made a speech blaming dissident supporters
of Otho for spreading alarm. He ordered troops to break up crowds
of potential gossips, an act which merely made the rumours more
believed. At the same time he ordered legions from Germany, Spain
and Britain to leave for northern Italy in case they were needed.

On the road north from Rome Caecina had many reasons for
confidence. Vespasian was not even with his men: his priority
was controlling the Egyptian corn supply. The soldiers of the east
would be fixed more on their own advantage than that of their
absent leader, just as those of the west had been. The Rhine armies
who had created Emperor Vitellius were well capable of defeating
their rivals.

But Caecina also knew that his troops were not any longer the
angry men of Cologne, nor even the banqueters of the march from
Brixellum. He could see, more clearly on the march than before he
left, that their armour was neglected, their horses tired and their
spirits low. They were fine fighters. They could face the jealous
armies of Vespasian or any other army. But they lacked the fire they
had had before.

A message came to Caecina from Valens in Rome calling for his
own soldiers in the army to halt and await his arrival as, he said,
had previously been planned. Caecina ignored it. The position, he
claimed, had changed. It was important that the Vitellians faced

the armies of Vespasian at full strength before any reinforcements made him stronger. Caecina had little faith in the arrival of the new troops that Aulus had ordered from the western provinces; their commanders would be wisely waiting to see which was the winning side. They would claim every sort of local unrest for staying at their posts. It was winter. The roads were hard to travel.

Only with the biggest possible force would Caecina have the chance to prevaricate too. He could then hold Aulus's future in his hand. If he were to defeat the legions of Syria and Judaea, he would have the glory which not even Valens could challenge. A second *Cena Adventica* would be even more splendid than the first. If he were to change sides and persuade the whole Vitellian army to follow, he would cleanly destroy Aulus's cause. Aulus would have nothing left with which to fight, Rome would have its fourth emperor in a year and Caecina would be owed the biggest debt by the new incumbent. Messages soon began to arrive from Vespasian.

49

NO TIME FOR A PARTY

Aulus Vitellius never much wanted to be emperor. Everyone who knew him knew it. His opinion of himself was not so far from that of his father and mother. He did not, however, want to be an ex-emperor. There had never been a living ex-emperor and Aulus was not an innovator, except perhaps in the kitchen, and maybe not even there. He had taken a role into which others had thrust him. He had discovered at Cologne his ability to motivate men by bonhomie and belching and understanding their needs. If the high-minded criticised him for enjoying an execution or a banquet, they were criticising most men of Rome. He was an everyman of Rome. He was happily doing the little that an emperor had to do.

For the second time in his life he had entrusted the same two men to manage his interests. His forces were gathering to repel the invaders. Caecina was ahead and Valens was on the road too, just as they had been on the march from Germany that brought him to the Palatine. Valens had eventually set off from Rome, without fresh troops but, or so it was said, with a generous accompaniment of women and eunuchs to lighten his nights. His pace had been slow, but the two were now manoeuvring in northern Italy as they had before. Beyond that Aulus knew little.

The emperor did not take up arms himself. There was no shame or bad strategy in that. He was closer than Vespasian to the battles about to be fought in their names. His heir was a child. His death would end his family's cause completely. Aulus retired to eat and drink amid the statues and pistachio trees of the villa that had once been his father's. While his protectors went north, he himself went south.

He retreated fifteen miles from Rome to his family estate at Aricia. This was where he had taken meals with his father and mother when he was young, eating simple food under the watchful eyes of their household gods, wooden statues of Peace and Plenty beside those of Pallas the accountant, Narcissus the master of the post, Callistus the sifter of petitions and Polybius the self-styled artist who had ignored Seneca's pleas for help.

In the autumn of 69 CE the shade of the trees was the same, though much else was not. The food owed more to Apicius than in the past and the threats to his peace of mind were more military than the papyri that had pursued his father from the small rooms of the Palatine. The need for the familiar deities was more acute. His boy, Germanicus, not only bore the name of a failure in the Julio-Claudian line; it was a reminder of his family's long service to that line. The Caesars were over, and the Vitellii were under threat.

He rested in his garden and waited. The unkind could compare him to an animal on a hot day before the circus, forever content as long as he was fed. But his loyalist soldiers on their way north would be more understanding. They had never served under his direct command. They would have been content that he was alive – and that they had someone to fight for and gain from. It did not matter whether Aulus was with Silius Italicus, discussing the restoration of Virgil's tomb, or with his cook considering the virtues of the spiny lobster, or by himself with Peace and Plenty. No soldier cared if his emperor was a glutton or an aesthete or neither. If they ever had cared, they did not care that summer.

Silius was important for Aulus Vitellius even though he did not yet have any readers. Augustus Caesar had had a name, a long reign and the poets Virgil and Horace to commemorate his ideals. Aulus Vitellius had a name that was still little known beyond the Palatine, only a short reign at the time he was relaxing in Aricia, and a poet companion who had not yet written what, like all poets, he was always threatening to write.

Yet Silius had plans for what would become the longest Latin poem to survive, the story of Rome's struggle against Hannibal 250 years before. The repetitive brutality of Silius's battle scenes would soon recall perfectly the year when there were four emperors. Aulus's poet was the master of horses toppling and writhing, swimming fields of gore, the dredging of bodies from ditches of blood as though they were the sea.

While Aeneas's shield, given to him by the goddess Venus, carried the weight of Augustus's hopes for Rome's future, Silius's shield for Hannibal was a common gift from man to man. Aulus himself had borrowed his own armour. His most famous shield carried flesh from the fishmonger's scales. But none of that meant much to the soldiers back around the flooded fields beside the Po.

After weeks of silence, news eventually came back to the dining tables of Aricia. There were more successes to toast, failures to ignore, loyalties and defections to note for the future. Near Bedriacum, where Aulus had toured the battlefield only weeks before, drinking to disguise the smell of death, there had been much more death, brutal clashes of sword and shield, each bout interspersed with hours for discussion among the commanders about whom the men were fighting for and why.

Aulus knew the chequerboard pattern of the battlefields, the squares of land which Augustus had awarded to his victorious veterans, a legacy as lasting as that of his poets. He knew what the ground was like, brown and gold and red, dogs licking the blood of the living and dead. He didn't need to see it. Caecina, it was said, had changed sides, or tried to, a man worse than a dog. He had made a speech praising Vespasian and tried to persuade his officers to join him. His men had not agreed. They had objected to being sold like slaves in a market. Caecina was the one now in chains, waiting for either Aulus or Vespasian to give him his reward.

The messages were confused. Aulus reluctantly felt the need to provide clarity where none existed. He returned from Aricia to Rome, addressed the city guard, praised the loyalty of their colleagues in the field, and removed their commander who was close to Caecina. He gave a longer speech to the senate on the healthy state of the empire and heard his brother, Lucius, commend a vote of censure on Caecina and his removal from the consulship.

There was one day left to run of Caecina's term of office. So, in a stately adherence to the motions of government, he promoted one of his friends for the shortest term since Julius Caesar did the same in the year before his assassination. That previous move had promoted the joke that Gaius Rebilus was so vigilant in his consulship that he never slept. The genuine consul for 45 BCE, Gaius Trebonius, had been so offended at the diminution of his office as to move closer to joining the assassins of the Ides of March. Aulus's friend became merely an object of ridicule.

Lucius tightened his grip on his brother's court. With no more knowledge than Aulus of their enemies around the banks of the River Po, he concentrated on those who might be enemies beside the Tiber. Lucius was still insecure about the part he had played at Brixellum. He had not left to fight beside Caecina and Valens. Those with betrayal on their own minds were particularly liable to pursue others on the same charge.

Top of Lucius's list was the man who had given Aulus his first set of emperor's clothes, Junius Blaesus, the governor who had hosted the victors and vanquished of Bedriacum at Lugdunum. Aulus had arrived at Blaesus's palace in the same state of dress that had taken him from bankruptcy in Rome to victory in a battle that he hadn't fought. He had left it in the scarlet cloak and military bronze of a successor to the Caesars.

Back in Rome after his tour of duty, Blaesus might have expected due gratitude. Instead Lucius saw an opportunity to bring him down. Blaesus was unlucky that a party to welcome him home was held on one of the rare nights when Aulus was not in the party mood, when the provider of his new clothes was perhaps not what he wanted to see.

By the standards of 69 CE there was nothing unusual about the homecoming. The host was the freedman son of one of Nero's nurses, a man famously once fired for using a lavatory erected for the sole use of the emperor. The event was the same kind of *Cena Adventica* that Lucius had given for Aulus. There may not have been a Shield of Minerva, but there were blazing torches and other normal signs of revelry, all of which Aulus could see and hear from an imperial villa in one of Nero's former gardens.

Aulus was feeling sick that night and all the less happy that anyone else should be celebrating. Lucius seized this moment when his usually genial brother was open to jealousy – and fanned that feeling into anger. Blaesus, he claimed, was one of those wealthy aristocrats always sneering at Aulus when they thought it safe: he had been close to Caecina from the start and might be so still: he was a threat not only to Aulus but to his son Germanicus. To stress the last point he brought the six-year-old to Aulus's sickroom.

Aulus was grateful for his brother's confidence in the future of the Vitellii. He was lying in a house he had once shared with Nero, and may have thought of what Nero would have done with much less reason than Lucius was presenting. Blaesus, he agreed, must be executed. The means should be poison. He would visit him when he was dying.

Lucius took on the task. He also took an empty space in the membership of the Brothers of the Fields, receiving his personal rose petal to mark his promotion, rolling a jar down a sacred hill, feasting on pork, beef and lamb in the menu order set out in stone.

50

A DRINK TO DEFEAT

While Caecina was in chains, the first news from Valens was a suspicious request for reinforcement. Aulus's remaining general wanted not legions but cavalry and light-armed troops. Aulus paused. What Valens wanted, and very rapidly wanted according to his dispatch, seemed more useful for an escape than for fighting Vespasian.

Further news followed of Valens's determined sexual exploits while he waited for the new troops to arrive, more defections and losses and reports of Caecina with their enemies. Vespasian was accepting allies and deserters. There had been a final battle on a field too blood-soaked and waterlogged for any forces to make camp. Valens had escaped – and his whereabouts were unknown.

Aulus did not give up. He had watched emperors and learnt from them even if he had never wanted to be an emperor. He assembled a band of cavalry and guards and sent it north to block the mountain passes which Vespasian's armies would need to cross to reach Rome. He called up a legion of marines from the fleet in the Bay of Naples. He put Lucius in charge of the defence of Rome itself. He began a programme of buying support with money that he did not have. He sold lucrative appointments, cutting taxes and granting greater freedoms, stretching the credulity of all recipients but flattering them nonetheless.

Behind every door in the court was a man who would normally say no – to a request for a consulship, a proposal for a new aqueduct, a plea that a city be given the same tax advantages as its neighbour. Suddenly the treasury was like a bath with every plug set to open. Some of the doors had no one behind them at all. The cautious and lesser-known had fled, newly prepared to risk their posts in the hope of claiming them back when the view was clearer.

Aulus sent spies north to assess the new balance of power, hoping for answers that would justify his generosity. Vespasian's officers identified the interlopers, organised meetings with their most determined fighters, tours of their disciplined camps, then sent them back to Rome. One was a centurion whom Vespasian's men took on a tour of the bloodiest battlefields beside the Po. From this vivid reversal of Vitellius's tour of Bedriacum it was undeniable that the armies of Caecina and Valens had been destroyed – by defection, but massively by death.

Bodies lay in piles once more in the ditches. Every farm on the chequerboard around the Po had its pieces of a defeated army. Reports from civilian survivors brought more horror than the sights of the dead, torture and burning, rapes of boys and girls, the tormenting of the old to reveal wealth they had long since lost.

When the centurion returned for his interview with his emperor, he found Aulus's confidence still high. To prove his worthlessness when so obvious a truth was not believed, he killed himself. Aulus heard all his spies' stories and ordered all their executions. Morale was his surest remaining strength and he did not want it sapped by truth.

Finally Aulus began his own march north with his cavalry and guards. A crowd of senators followed behind. Gradually their numbers fell. His senior courtiers encouraged him for longer, knowing that their own survival in power might not survive another change of control on the Palatine. The soldiers stayed loyal, but Aulus's military inexperience was insufficient for what became a complex test.

News arrived that the fleet at Naples had defected. Dividing his forces, he sent one half back to quell the revolt and the other forward to the passes of the Apennine mountains. His officers knew that this way both moves would fail. His courtiers panicked that their master was out of their control, and kept from him the advice that might have saved him.

Aulus was a man faraway out of his depth. Reportedly he was drunk much of the time. Drunkenness was a regular charge against failures, but that did not make the charge a falsehood. He was buoyed by the support of the local people who cheered his progress. He accepted their offer to take up arms themselves and registered the first volunteers himself.

These were the fantasies of a drowning man. It was a century and a half since Rome last had a citizen army. He ordered his personal band of gladiators to join the suppression of the naval rebels. He raised cash from freedmen and rich supporters who still saw their best future with Aulus if he could take a grip on events.

There was little sign of that. Ahead of him his soldiers were already defecting. His aides could not protect him from the news that Valens was dead. Hopes that his most loyal commander was raising new armies in Germany were as false as all his present hope. Valens's head on a spear, paraded among his former troops and camp-followers, was seen by too many for the fact to be doubted. There were no reprisals from Vespasian's commanders against the men and women who had supported Valens since Cologne. The testimony of their defeat was enough.

When Aulus had marched on Rome in April he was like a lottery-winner floating on a cloud of popularity and success. Making the return journey he was still popular, but on a darker cloud. Messages arrived in Vespasian's name offering generous terms for surrender, comfortable retirement homes near the town where his family had begun, safety for his family, for the next generation, his son and his future children, a life with money and slaves. He responded with queries about exactly where his houses would be, the quality of sea views and kitchen service.

51

IN AUGUSTUS'S TEMPLE

Tarracina was a high town by the sea, half way between Nuceria, where the Vitellii began, and Rome, where Lucius was charged with defending his brother's reign as emperor, between where Augustus had died after forty-five years in power and where Galba had died after seven months. Some fifty miles both from Naples and from the Palatine, Tarracina stood on a bright white rock, a marker for travellers, an inspiration for poets and, in the early winter of 69 CE, a place where Lucius, after surprising his soldiers by leaving Rome, was planning the next move in his family's fortunes.

Virgil and Horace had passed through Tarracina as part of a sensitive diplomatic mission more than a century before, Horace describing it as *inpositum saxis late candentibus*, 'perched upon the far-shining rock'. Lucius had to seize and fortify that high white rock and from there cow the naval revolt, protect the grain supply for the capital and maybe, if more defeats followed, leave Italy for Africa and renew the fight from where he and his brother had each once been the governor. With him was his wife Triaria, as keen as Lucius himself to defend the family honour with her sword.

Back in Rome Aulus learnt that their mother was dead. Sextilia had supported him as a son if not as an emperor. She was the last link to the second generation of his family's public life. Some soon claimed that he had starved her, in the tradition of Augustus and his daughter, in order to fulfil a prophecy that he would rule longer if his mother died first. Others said that his mother had asked for poison to commit suicide. A reputation as a devoted mourner or a murderous manoeuvrer for advantage: that was the difference between winning and losing.

While Lucius was besieging Tarracina, Aulus began to be besieged, rather more gently, by Flavius Sabinus, the brother of

Vespasian. Sabinus was a very different kind of brother from Lucius: he was older and quieter, the highest hope of a modest family, relied upon for loans in trouble, and, although himself a distinguished veteran of Claudius's British campaign, a conciliator in recent years more than a fighter. Nero had appointed him as city prefect and he had retained the job throughout the reigns of Galba and Otho.

Aulus too had kept him in charge of the city. Sabinus had supporters in Rome who thought him a better prospect for their quiet lives than Vespasian himself. Vespasian was far away. Sabinus was a man with whom Aulus might reasonably hope to do business, to save his life and family in some form of retirement. Offers continued of country homes by the sea and all the seafood that even he might want to eat.

The main negotiation between the two men was set for the Palatine temple of Apollo, Augustus's great addition to the house which would become his family's palace. This was still Aulus's domain. He could still invite Sabinus to look out from its broad colonnades and round-domed chamber to the *Circus Maximus*, where he had ridden chariots with Caligula, and to the banqueting halls which had been the love of his later life. Sabinus too knew the temple well. It was a public space in a private house, as Augustus had always intended it to be.

Aulus brought to the temple two of his most trusted friends, Cluvius Rufus, the historian and governor of Spain whom he had saved from a treason charge at Lugdunum, and Silius Italicus, who had been consul in the previous year. He needed a deal. This was not an occasion for freedmen trained to say no. His court was anyway much reduced, a shadow of that which had run the empire from the time of Tiberius to Nero.

Cluvius was already writing a history of the Caesars, and at the temple of Apollo he would be in the room when the next phase began, whatever that next phase was. He was an authority on the theatre as well as politics, the Latin farces cited by Augustus on his deathbed and the Greek songs preferred by Nero. Cluvius was a man with answers both on the origins of the histrionic arts and on their place in the history of all Rome.

Silius was younger, richer, a former governor of Asia for whom the past was just as important as the present, maybe more so. His passion was for the poetry of Virgil and, if he himself would only rarely match the skill of his hero, that did not stop his ambition or his hopes.

Together they stood with Aulus as he discussed terms with Sabinus. Observers watched as best they could, reading signs from the faces and gestures as though from a theatre's highest seats. Aulus, tall, tired and limping, seemed dejected, maybe humbled. Sabinus looked out more compassionate than triumphant. The outcome was surely an abdication, although when and how could not be known.

The next show for the onlookers in the Forum was a procession from the doors of the Palatine, headed by the emperor in the black toga of a mourner. Behind him was a closed litter, carried by slaves, and behind that a line of his remaining courtiers, listless, their faces lowered like that of their leader. Some citizens shouted encouragement to the man whom they still saw as their emperor. The soldiers of the Vitellian cause, the drivers of that cause since Cologne and Bedracium, kept a sinister, contrasting silence.

Aulus spoke to the simmering crowd. For the sake of peace, the state and his children he announced that he was giving up the throne. He held out a dagger to the most senior man in the crowd. The symbol was refused. At Cologne Aulus had taken a dagger from Caesar's altar to show his acceptance of the throne. In Rome he could not give a dagger back. His son, Germanicus, was in the litter lest anyone be in any doubt. An abdication, accompanied by wife, court and stuttering heir, was a first in imperial history and, unlike the monsters, freaks and other novelties greeted at the gates of the Palatine, was ungratefully received.

The abdicator tried to depart by way of the temple of Concord and leave the dagger there. Next he turned towards his family home on the other side of the *Circus Maximus*. Soldiers blocked every route bar that back to the palace. Aulus was back in the *domus Caesaris*.

It was not clear what this meant. Perhaps the party was changing its clothes: black togas for a funeral were traditionally exchanged for white before a banquet in honour of the dead. There were no reports of banqueting, but to the troops of Vespasian the retreat of Aulus to the Palatine did not look like the abdication promised to Sabinus. Perhaps Aulus was instead hanging on.

The news of uncertainty spread. There were soon two sets of forces in the Forum and surrounding streets, not always easy to distinguish even by each other. The biggest difference was that Vespasian's soldiers were subordinate to Sabinus, and Aulus's were taking orders from no one. The unled won the early skirmishes with ease.

Sabinus did not want to have to fight for Rome. That was neither in his character nor in his commission from his brother in distant Alexandria. He ordered a withdrawal to the heights of the Capitol, where he could consider his next move. The Vitellians followed in pursuit.

Rain poured through the night. Aulus and Sabinus succeeded in exchanging messages as though they were still preparing for the conference that had already happened. Aulus admitted that he had lost control. Sabinus accused him of negotiating in bad faith and never intending to abdicate. Aulus had even fewer powers of an emperor than when he was first hailed by his troops in Germany. Sabinus was in fear for his life and begging by letter for what Aulus was unable to give.

Aulus learnt of the aftermath only when Sabinus was brought before him in chains. The men who had fought for the Vitellian cause (hardly, in truth, his own cause any more) had been frustrated by piles of toppled statues which Sabinus had ordered as barricades. They had no machinery with which to clear their way. The stones were slippery after the storm. Both sides had thrown torches. The battle had spread across the Capitol to the temple that more than any other defined Rome itself. The ancient roof over the marble columns dedicated to I.O.M. Jupiter Optimus Maximus, Best and Greatest, was made of ancient wood. Each blamed the other for the fire that had dried, then cracked and roasted the sacred rocks.

Aulus still hoped to save Sabinus's life. But this was no longer a private meeting at which his advisers were a would-be poet and an historian of the theatre. He was hemmed in by the soldiers who had brought their captive and by citizens who had followed them for the sport of seeing a powerful man die.

Aulus's soldiers feared betrayal by their own leader. They had their emperor and the debts that he owed them – and they wanted to keep them both. Sensing further equivocation, they found their enemy's brother, severed his head and dragged his body to the top of the Capitol hill, treading their way through the ruins of what had only days before been the greatest temple in Rome.

A starfish of stiffening limbs tumbled down towards the Forum. A headless corpse fell faster than a faller who was still alive, bumping and streaking the stones with whatever last meal he had taken. Occasionally a dying man might accelerate his death – or delay it till a drowning in the Tiber. Aulus Vitellius had not seen precisely how his fellow negotiator had died.

He was away from the horror, banqueting in the halls where as a boy he had watched Tiberius. After sufficient men and women had seen that the cause of the Vitellians was still alive, the remains of Flavius Sabinus rolled into the river and out to sea.

In even the worst circumstances Aulus liked to see hope. Some said that Vespasian, the would-be fourth emperor, might possibly be pleased at his brother's death, thinking that even the most helpful member of his family might become a rival once the throne was won. But this was hardly a secure basis for future talks on Aulus's own safety. He had his own brother, still alive and working on his behalf. He was not sure exactly where.

52

OUT OF THE DOGHOUSE

News came to Aulus from inside Tarracina, where the forces of Vespasian were as keen to eat, drink, rape and plunder as were Lucius's besiegers. The defenders were in no state to hold the white rock. It took only a single slave to shift allegiance from one master to another for a gate to lie open and an assault to become a massacre. The forces of Vespasian fled to their ships. Lucius's wife, Triaria, put on her sword and stormed the streets as a victorious Vitellian soldier. For Aulus, unable to concede power, there was a new possibility that he might maintain it.

Yet, on the north side of Rome, his enemies, roused by the death of Sabinus and the destruction on the Capitol, were only ten miles away. Aulus sent towards them a band of guards and slaves and barely trained citizens whose local knowledge brought them further victory in the maze of gardens and narrow streets. He called on the senate to send emissaries, accompanied by vestal virgins, for a truce. The answer from Vespasian's officers was only a pause.

The next sight in Rome was of fierce fighting by troops of both sides, neither trusting their leaders to allow the fighting to last. Even in the season of Saturnalia, it was the most extreme of contrasts and reversals. Friends were enemies, and enemies friends. In one street there was a party, in another a welter of blood and maimings. Dogs fed on their usual scraps or on skulls. Prostitutes plied their trade in one corner, while in another they piled the corpses of their colleagues and their clients.

The Roman Forum, no longer a political museum or place for rhetoric, was a battlefield. Beneath the ruins of the great Capitol lay the wreckage of fighting street by street, damp dust that had once been the state records at the base of the hill. It was an accident, a spark in a musty library, a smoulder of pressed reeds, a flame over taxes and treaties, a new fire like the spread of a rumour around the Palatine and then a roar of destruction. The stuff of much history was gone.

There were tiny victories for both sides, cheered on by citizens watching from open windows as though this urban war were a parade. Soon it became clear that a force with leaders but less knowledge of the terrain was beating those with more knowledge but no leadership at all. Aulus knew no more than did these enthusiastic spectators about the last moves in his military career. Vespasian's cavalry included many who a week before had been its enemies. Legionaries still fighting for Aulus disappeared into a small camp by the city's north-east walls, determined that when Vespasian's main force poured into the city, it would not pass unopposed.

It seemed as though Aulus's troops were deliberately giving their leader time to escape. Whether or not that was true, Aulus did attempt the same route out of the Palatine that he had failed to take after his abdication, first to his family home and then out to the south towards Tarracina. At his side he had his baker and his cook, no longer an historian or poet. This time he was not prevented by force but by a collapse of his own powers to go on. Again he turned back towards the palace.

Behind him the Forum was no longer a battlefield. A few women picked over what the soldiers had left. Inside the gates he sought familiarity in the halls where the Vitellii had so long served, the rooms where his grandfather, Publius, had administered for Augustus, where his uncle, Publius, had argued for Germanicus, where his father, Lucius, had flattered Caligula's wish for worship and Claudius's to be the conqueror of Britain. All were empty, unrecognisable, without even their ghosts.

Every emperor had extended these halls. Nero's Golden House exceeded every predecessor and neighbour, spreading across the southern hills. Banqueters had so many more spaces than before to rouse a jaded palate. When filled, the rooms had seemed perfect for their purposes. When empty, they were vast. His cooks had gone. There was no one to reminisce over his Shield of Minerva. His baker had gone.

He found a smaller room where the guards once kept their dogs, African and British, the hunters from Syria and Spain. It was not so very small, but it was dark. He could not see in every corner. There was a bed and a mattress. He moved them against the door. He waited. He heard clanking from down below. There was the sound of soldiers' voices, the opening of gates and the acrid smell of blackened marble. He would be found if anyone cared to look. He would be recognised, though maybe not if the searcher was from the banks of the Danube and had never seen the Palatine before.

He would not be found dead. He had neither the will nor the sword for suicide. Nero and Otho had killed themselves. Otho had gained credit for that. Otho had stopped a war. Otho had saved lives. Aulus Vitellius Germanicus had tried to stop a war while also staying alive. He had failed. He was just waiting for the soldier who would remind him how far he had failed.

Hard footsteps hammered against mosaic. There was a crash against the door. His barrier fell back softly. The soldier's name was Julius Placidus. That was all he learnt. This Placidus knew whom he had found. Maybe the image on his coins was not so different from the face of Rome's third emperor for 69 CE. Aulus felt the tying of his hands, the tearing of his clothes and the bite of an emboldened dog. His dead master, Tiberius, had held the city like a wolf by its ears. Aulus had let the city go.

Outside in the corridor Placidus checked that he had the right prisoner and led Aulus from the palace. Rome's eighth emperor would have gained many more admirers in future if he had died before being dragged, hands tied behind his back, along the Sacred Way towards the Capitol. Instead he still tried to negotiate. He had important information, he said, too sensitive for anyone to hear except the man who wanted to replace him. He had for half a year wanted his successor to be the son whom he had named Germanicus. If he could not have that, he wanted Germanicus's safety to be assured and that of the Vitellii who were left.

The statue of his father was still standing in the Forum where the climb to the Capitol began, its inscription declaring the loyalty of Lucius Vitellius to the house of the Caesars. It had been no part of

Aulus Vitellius's own life to want to be a hero. Other statues that had for a century been the memory of Rome were piled as barricades. The ashes of laws and taxes blew along the streets. Marble arms reached towards the sky. There were still many stone dead standing, enough for many future street fights, but most of the living were gone.

Aulus Vitellius had few illusions about himself or why he was in power. The coinage of his brief time in charge of the mints made no claims in gold, silver or bronze for Justitia, Virtus or Pax. He did not present himself as a man of Justice, Virtue or Peace, still less as the son of a god or the father of the fatherland. An occasional gold coin which boasted his support from the SPQR was a mistaken use of old moulds, maybe those of the hopeful Galba. Aulus had been resistant to believing those who flattered him. His money offered mere assertions of the *consensus exercituum*, the agreed choice of the armies. A glance on one side showed his puffed cheeks, fleshy nose and double chins, on the other the slender figure of a youthful war god, naked except for a cloak. As soon as there was no consensus of the armies Aulus lost his power. He was a very ordinary man, with ordinary vices, an ordinary willingness to go with any flow – and a love of obliteration by food and drink which was ordinary, magnified by his opportunities and exaggerated in his failure.

News of his progress spread fast. Wound followed wound. Outside the palace gates was the place in the Forum where foreign supplicants to Tiberius and Caligula used to leave their gifts, their strange animals, dwarfs and giants. Aulus became just such an attraction himself. People prodded his belly and pulled at the hair on his unshaven face. He made a final attempt to attract the attention that an emperor better deserved. He had information, he said, that would save Vespasian's life. He had to be allowed to tell what he knew to the man who most needed to know it. His captor continued their shared procession to the Capitol. Soon there were more captors and a longer climb to the acrid remains of the ancient temple.

The descent was shorter. The soldiers did not sever his head at the top of the Groaning Steps. They placed a cord around his neck.

He was led like the companion of his kennel, stumbling before he fell. His last sight of the Palatine was in the smoky distance. His last words were a reply to a barracker in the crowd. He cried out that, whatever his failings and present fate, he had been that man's emperor: *ego tamen imperator tuus fui*. He died slowly by blows and cuts, torn to fat, fleshy pieces, tumbling towards the memorial to his father, a sword under his chin to make him face his torturers, his belly protruding forever to stand for his failure to control his appetites, his opportunities and himself. Galeria received what was left of his body. His head disappeared into the spreading crowd.

53

NEW COURTS FOR OLD

This book has been the story of a hill and its people, of a palace and a mostly forgotten palace family. To conclude first the family story, Lucius Vitellius did not try to escape to Africa. He marched his troops towards Rome from Tarracina, tried to negotiate for his life with those hunting for him, failed and died at the pleasure of the victors. The stammering Germanicus lasted only a little longer than his uncle.

The family name was as quickly degraded as the body at the bottom of the Groaning Steps. The name of Aulus Vitellius – and that of Lucius too – was expunged from the stone tablets of the Brothers of the Fields. The fabricated lineage from the local gods of Nuceria was replaced by a hardly less likely line of descent from a freed slave, a shoe-maker, an informer who had married the prostitute daughter of a baker. This was a jibe of farce, easily hurled against a glutton. Suetonius, the biographer of emperors in the early second century, born around the time of Aulus's death, left the truth of the divergent tales to be judged by his readers. Others were less generous. Once its refuge had changed from shady villas to a doghouse, so did the family's past and future.

Aulus Vitellius was left as an exemplary man of the Palatine, over-promoted like so many in administrative machines, the courtier son of a great courtier father, a flatterer's disciple. After he became the eighth emperor of Rome his name was glued to gluttony because he blasted away the madness of his world with peacock's brains and flamingo tongues. He didn't fall from power because he was a glutton; he was a glutton because he fell from power. After Aulus, no other Vitellius ever much mattered. It was a bad name to have.

Of all Aulus's many failings gluttony was merely the most memorable, the most vivid, the one word of abuse into which all others could be wrapped. His father Lucius earnt his place in the stories of his time by management, flattery and intrigue. His son ate his way into history. When Renaissance artists wanted characters for Roman orgies, his face was a favourite. The fat, fleshy marble bust, owned by the Grimani family of Venice, became one of the most repeated images from ancient Rome, coming to symbolise all the sins of the city and empire in which its subject had lived, worked, survived and so briefly ruled. Both gluttons and flatterers were characters of the Palatine that later state servants recognised nervously among themselves.

Many historians praised the civil peace brought by Augustus and the successor heirs to Julius Caesar. A few saw it as ruthless autocracy. But in films and other fictions the first phase of the Roman Empire ended only in stories of flattery, lies and excess. The Palatine was where gluttons sat at their top tables, guzzling and vomiting while regimes rose and fell faster than the plates could move from dormice to giraffe. Flatterers corrupted their masters, made the bad even worse and created the conditions in which anyone might eat themselves to death. Aulus and his father were in the rooms of power and represented that era's end.

The Palatine hill itself quickly lost prestige. The year 69 CE was like a long, low theatre show of the kind that Augustus had cited as he died – an unrolling sequence of uncomfortable, identifiable characters, the young madman, the old martinet, the libertine, the glutton, the soldier – all of them caricatures that Romans were happy to forget for a while. The new emperor Vespasian wanted to mark a difference from the past. His historians were happy to help him. Slaves, ex-slaves and other courtiers were easy scapegoats.

Vespasian took the name of Caesar, but preferred to rule from one of Rome's imperial gardens rather than the rooms left empty when Aulus Vitellius departed for the last time. He ordered the destruction of Nero's palatial extensions – and their eventual replacement by public spaces financed by the proceeds of another Roman repression of the Jews. The Colosseum arose where the

Domus Aurea had briefly stood. Banqueting declined. Cooks and clerks found it wise to choose more modest marble memorials. Vespasian showed virtuous clemency to Aulus's daughter, Vitellia, a reminder of the best spirit of Augustus. The aim of the new regime was to revive as much as was prudent of the simplicity affected by the founder of the empire, to promote beans as food for the poor, to expel the most flagrant wastrels from the senate, to preserve the best disciplines and leave the worst behind.

Yet the system of government did not – and could not – change for long. The Palatine's empty rooms rapidly refilled, many previous occupants returning to their old places or to promotions. Vespasian used courtiers, favourites, slaves and former slaves to run the empire as Claudius and Nero had done. He re-employed as his office gatekeeper the freedman Phoebus, who had rebuked him for yawning while Nero sang. He had ten more years of service from Caecina before, in his own dying days, he had him executed for conspiracy. Crispinilla, once the controller of Nero's new clothes, moved to the edges of political life and profited from the wine trade. Her name survived on amphorae as well as in histories written by those horrified by her role at court and the roles of other upstarts like her.

Caenis, once the slave of Antonia, survived for five years in even greater prosperity as Vespasian's long-time mistress, entrusted with selling priesthoods, governorships and other offices of profit under the empire, freeing her own slaves for office with the name Caenidianus. Famed in her youth for her beauty and powers of memory, she outlived Vespasian's wife and daughter, becoming the single heiress to the legacy of both Pallas and Agrippina, a courtier and a princess, less criticised than they within a court now accepted as a system.

The name of the veteran courtier from Smyrna freed from slavery by Tiberius, advanced by Caligula, Claudius and Nero, did not survive in any inscriptions. Or, if it did, no one has recognised it. But he himself lived till the age of around ninety, husband of a consul's sister, imperial procurator, father of two children, holder of the post once held by Pallas, each day deciding what to spend on soldiers, food supply and aqueducts. He had an administrative skill, in Rome and in the east, which Vespasian and his family appreciated as the heirs of Julius Caesar had done. Like Lucius Vitellius he suffered a demotion at the end of his life, but no fate worse than comfortable exile. Throughout his life on the Palatine he ate and drank modestly, or at least gained that valuable reputation.

Unlike Lucius, this quiet man from Smyrna saw neither of his sons ever become emperor. But the son known as Claudius Etruscus became massively rich, added to Rome's bath houses and commissioned a poetic tribute to his quiet father, a 'wearer of so many yokes and endurer of so much rough sea', a man never even quite securely named. The flattering poet was not Aulus's friend Silius, who under the rule of Vespasian found the peace to begin his epic of Hannibal, but Publius Papinius Statius, another figure of what would become a lesser literary age, a master of praising domestic architecture, public works and the madder of Vespasian's sons. The eulogist of Claudius Etruscus's father was a more than worthy successor to Clutorius Priscus, the praise-seller who had failed to survive his party night with Aulus's sister.

The Palatine title, *procurator*, held under Augustus by Publius, the first courtier of the Vitelli, grew in range and power. Those officials who were governors without needing to be from the senate became familiar, if not always welcome, to the emperor's distant subjects. The princes of Commagene exchanged their authority at home for status in the empire as smoothly as though swapping currency. Those Commagene people who hated government from Rome remained in exile, their complaints loudly made but only to the few who might listen, very few of those in the swollen rooms around the emperor.

Rome held its empire, tightened its rule and the bureaucracy of Rome spread just like the aqueducts. Like the *Aqua Claudia*, it was useful and survived. Below the princes and procurators more than 4,000 names and job titles have survived on memorial slabs, *Claudii* and *Julii*, *tabularii* and *dispensatores*, *adiutorii* and *pedise-qui*, proud bearers of a sometime emperor's name, account clerks and stewards, administrators and escorts. Graffiti appeared beside more formal engravings. The name of one Palatine wardrobe slave was commemorated with a donkey head and cross, scratched on a wall to mock his worship of a 'King of the Jews'.

Some inscriptions boasted progress through the ranks on what was almost a career path, others the satisfaction in stone of a life as the emperor's *pistor* or *dulciarius*, his *a lagona* or *a cyatho*, his baker, his sweet-maker, the man who held the silver, the wine jar or the cup. When an emperor needed to wear new clothes, he might use his *a veste privata*, his *a veste castrense* or his *a veste gladiatoria*, the choice dependent on whether he intended to be at home, out with soldiers or at the theatre. Vespasian curbed what he saw as excess but did not stop what others, not least his sons and successors, saw as normal. Much survived into later courts. So did the serious administration of empire with which the courts were inextricably linked.

The Palatine remained as an administrative palace even after the capitol of the empire moved to Constantinople in 330 CE. Later still it became much more than a place, more than any single hill or palace, surviving as a symbol long after there was any Roman Empire anywhere. In the sixteenth century the crumbled walls and terraces of the Caesars became one of the first botanical gardens and bird collections in Europe. Where thrushes and cranes had once been served on silver platters, there were new aviaries and exotic plants for peacocks to eat. But the ideas of the Palatine, codified because they were so useful, moved to wherever there was power. When Peter the Great was designing his new Russian capital in the early eighteenth century, he decreed imaginary hills in the swampy ground: his Palatine was what would become the Nevsky Prospect, the grandest street in the city. A Russian Caesar was already a Czar. A Palatine became the title for officials from Bohemia to Burgundy.

Nero's freedman Epaphroditus, the well-rewarded saviour of his master from assassins, had among his own slaves the philosopher Epictetus, who, even while the first dynasty of Caesars was fading, posed the question of what the court had become, how its members should behave to each other, an insider's guide to the lessons of the recent past. He showed the need for getting the work done, for doing the most good within the system, for recognising that those around an emperor were like fish alive in a tank, rising and falling in the water, promoted, demoted, but in the greatest peril only if they fell outside. Power was a circle, not a triangle, a globe, not a pyramid, a place where the provider and consumer were one, where a flatterer may be as much responsible for flattery's ills as the flattered.

Epictetus compared all human life to being a guest at a banquet of the gods. Men could take gratefully what is offered and be worthy of their invitation. Or they could refuse dishes and attempt perilously to share in the power of their hosts. The court was the model of the world. Everyone had different weapons. Flattery was a weapon of the weak. Exchange was everything. The courtier should expect nothing for nothing. Just as a small coin bought a lettuce, so too did flattery. No one should expect to have both the lettuce and the coin. Men exchanged invitations for personal attention, food for fawning over the host.

Courtiers and emperors were not so very different. The view of both was necessary for understanding history. Epictetus knew that all were liable to inflate their own importance, to believe they were worthy of their roles, to think that when a Caesar put a man in charge of his chamber pot he was suddenly a wise counsellor. But the banquet was theatre. Everyone, for Epictetus, was an actor in a play. Augustus at the end of his life was like all men and women at all times of their life. Their part might be as a grand consul or a lowly cripple, a fat fool or a subtle schemer. The play itself might be long or short. The aim was to be part of the whole.

Epictetus, like Phaedrus, parodied the behaviour of the court. He recognised the desire to worship any source of office or benefit. A god might be anyone who could deliver a favour. Divinity was just another status within a bureaucracy. Even gods were slaves to higher powers, as Statius, in his *consolatio* for the death of Claudius Etruscus's father, agreed. The former slave of a former slave understood the nagging doubts behind even the most successful servant. Epictetus knew the works of Phaedrus. He was a theorist grounded in practice. The court was the old normal and the new normal. It might change, but not change very much.

In the Middle Ages Epictetus was the most read of all ancient philosophers. He had been on the Palatine of the Caesars. He had seen how gluttons and flatterers accepted insults and expressed gratitude for them, how they ran around after favours like children chasing nuts at a wedding party, how they sensed what was necessary to live another day.

NOTES

1 In the palace doghouse

Cassius Dio (c.160 CE–c.235), one of the five main sources for the early empire, was a wealthy politician who wrote a history of Rome in Greek in eighty volumes, some of which survive intact and others in abridgement and quotations. His aim was to expound and explain the greatness of Rome, with a good eye for vivid detail and many sideswipes at those who disrupted his positive narrative. Dio devoted his books 63–5 to the Year of the Four Emperors, describing Aulus Vitellius's last days (64.16–20) and his last hiding place in a palace room where dogs were kept.

Suetonius Tranquillus (c.70 CE–c.130), who wrote biographies of Julius Caesar and every emperor up to Vespasian, was himself a courtier and imperial official. In his Life of Vitellius (*Vitellius* 16) he has the dog tied up outside the kennel door rather than inside. The exact site of the kennel, like so much about the sprawling imperial palaces, is clear in none of the sources. For the development of the Palatine see Wiseman (2019) and for the newer palace, the *Domus Aurea* built by Nero, see Ball (2003).

For the variety of dogs in Rome, as set out by the poet Grattius in the time of Augustus, see https://penelope.uchicago.edu/Thayer/E/Roman/Texts/Grattius/Cynegeticon*.html#ref38 p. 167

The pessimism of Aulus's mother, Sextilia, at her son's birth is described by Suetonius (*Vitellius* 3), who also reports Aulus's common touch as a belcher (*Vitellius* 7) and his final days (*Vitellius* 15–17).

Publius Cornelius Tacitus (56 CE– c.120), the most influential historian of the period, was damning of Aulus Vitellius at every point. He began his *Histories* (c.100 CE) with the Year of the Four Emperors and then went back to write his more famous

Annals, from the reigns of Tiberius to Nero, not least to explain how the antique greatness of Rome had decayed to such a state that Vitellius (*Histories* 3.84–6) might end his reign as a glutton on the Groaning Steps. Tacitus, an aristocrat with a strong sense of the virtues of Rome's senatorial government, is the source most responsible for prejudice against a bureaucracy of former slaves.

2 Mr Glutton and Mr Fool

Suetonius describes the death of Augustus (*Augustus* 97.3–100) and his actor's call for applause (*Augustus* 99). Augustus's apology for Tiberius's slow chewing (*Tiberius* 21.2) is echoed by Dio (56.31).

There is much controversy about the nature of Atellane farce, particularly its longevity and relation to other theatre. See Frassinetti (1967) and review by A. S. Gratwick in *Classical Review* (1970), 20. Also E. Fantham (1989), 'The earliest comic theatre at Rome: Atellan farce, comedy and mime as antecedents of the commedia dell'arte', in D. Pietropaolo (ed.), *The Science of Buffoonery: Theory and History of the Commedia dell'arte* (Toronto).

3 Succession

Dio (31.1) reports the claim of Livia delaying the announcement of Augustus's death.

For Augustan mythology of the Palatine see Virgil *Aeneid* 8.337–61.

For the Augustus and Tiberius cups in the Boscoreale Treasure, buried before the eruption of Vesuvius in 79 CE, see Kuttner (1995).

4 Care for what we eat

Suetonius (*Augustus* 101.1) names the trusted freed slaves who wrote out parts of Augustus's will, Polybius and Hilarion, successors to two of his earliest private servants for public duties, Thyrsus and Epaphroditus, who negotiated with Cleopatra and guarded her after the Battle of Actium (Plutarch, *Antony* 73.1–2). Thyrsus took a flogging from Antony for seeming to him to want from Cleopatra what he and Julius Caesar had already had.

The already-dead son of Augustus's sister, Octavia, was Marcus Claudius Marcellus (42–23 BCE).

Gaius Plinius Secundus, Pliny the Elder (23 CE–79), who died in the eruption of Vesuvius, was an encyclopaedist of the natural world. He notes the idea that Italy's farms were fertile from unmined precious metals in his *Natural History* (33.21:4). For Ovid on the sexual vocabulary of archery see his *Amores* (1.8:47) and Adams (1982) on strings and bows.

Gowers (1993), pp. 126–79 gives a subtle account of Horace and the dining table. Obesity embodied moral and literary excess. A fat book was a bad book. For an invitation to a modest meal see *Odes* 1.20 and for a critique of storks' legs, goose liver and roast blackbird *Satires* 2.8. Suetonius (*Horace* 1) describes Horace's father as a *salsamentarius*, a seller of cheap salted meat and fish.

The library with the treatises on flattery was owned by Julius Caesar's father-in-law, Lucius Calpurnius Piso, at Herculaneum on the Bay of Naples. The house philosopher, Philodemus, a friend of Virgil and Horace, had ample opportunities to see how theory matched practice. See *Herculaneum Papyrus* 222 and Obbink (1995).

5 A wolf by its ears

Suetonius was a master of using detail and quotation to paint his complex picture of Tiberius as emperor, avoiding the moralistic attacks by which Tacitus shows his disapproval of the court. The comparison between ruling Rome and holding a wolf by its ears is attributed directly to Tiberius (*Tiberius* 25); also the reply from the fake Agrippa Postumus that he had gained his title in the same way that Tiberius had – by fraud. Tacitus (*Annals* 2.40) has the same story about the slave who pretended to be Augustus's legitimate heir.

Ovid's comparison of the Palatine to the home of the gods is at *Metamorphoses* 1.168–76. For his pleading praise of the divine

Augustus from exile see *Tristia* (2.22, 4.4) and *Epistulae ex Ponto*
1.1:25–9. For a fine short account of the issues in Ovid's dealings
with the *domus Caesaris* see L. Morgan (2020).

6 Publius among the fishes

Sea conditions for the unwary have changed little in the Channel
over 2,000 years. Publius's two legions were the Second and
Fourth. The Second had fought on both sides in the civil wars
which brought Augustus to power, eventually gaining the title
Augusta for its service to the new regime. Tacitus reports the
drama of the march by the sea (*Annals* 1.70) and the earlier catastrophe for Rome in the Teutoburg forest (*Annals* 1.57–90). See
also Dio (56.19:1–22) and Murdoch (2006) for a modern account.
For Aratus's *Phaenomena* see note on Chapter 19.

7 Between the emperor and his heir

Suetonius (*Augustus* 23) gives Augustus's reaction to the losses in
the Teutoburg.

8 Flattery and fear

Dio (66.14) describes Caenis's reputation for memory. For a survey of Antonia's household, within a detailed account of inscriptions referring to imperial freedmen and freedwomen, see L.
R. Penner (2013), 'The epigraphic habits of the slaves and freed
slaves of the Julio-Claudian household' (University of Calgary).
Penner gives a good account of the opportunities and difficult-
ies of using inscriptions in the *Corpus Inscriptionum Latinarum*
(CIL) for understanding the court of the Caesars. Inscriptions
on stone are usually brief, broken and vulnerable to confusion
when, e.g., every female slave freed by Augustus, Tiberius or
Caligula can have the same name, Julia.

9 Words for a palace

For poetic grappling with the new Palatine see Ovid (*Tristia* 3.1, *Metamorphoses* 1.248).

PART TWO

10 The fox and the crow

For issues surrounding the life of Phaedrus see Henderson (2001) and E. Champlin (2005) in *Journal of Roman Studies*, 95, discussed by R. M. Edwards (2015) in *Rheinisches Museum für Philologie, Neue Folge*, 158. Champlin argues that Phaedrus was not a Greek slave but a Roman courtier writing in the persona of a Roman Aesop.

The philosopher who linked Aesop's tales to simple food was the vegetarian and abstainer from alcohol Apollonius of Tyana (*c*.3 BCE–97 CE), cited by Philostratus, *Life of Apollonius of Tyana* (5.14). Apollonius was said by Philostratus to have entered Rome in Nero's time in defiance of a ban on philosophers. The fable of the fox and the crow (1.13) is discussed by Kapust (2018).

11 Who killed the prince?

For Tiberius's nervousness at Germanicus being seen as a god in Alexandria see V. Ehrenberg and A. H. M. Jones (1955), *Documents Illustrating the Reigns of Augustus and Tiberius* (Oxford University Press), p. 320a.

Tacitus (*Annals* 3.9:3) describes the *irritamenta invidiae*, the incitement to resentment, of Piso's house on the crowded Palatine.

12 The only verdict that mattered

Marcus Aemilius Lepidus was set to lead for Piso's defence. Tacitus (Annals 1.13) describes Augustus's considering him, and others of the old aristocracy, as his successor instead of a member of his own extended family.

Tacitus (*Annals* 2.74, 3.13) reports Publius's speech in the Piso trial. See also Tacitus *Annals* 2.55:5, 2.57:3–4, 2.69, 2.75, 3.9, 3.15.

For the bronze tablets, which add substantially to the details in Tacitus's narrative, see W. Eck, A. Caballos and F. Fernandez (1996), *Das Senatus Consultum de Cn. Pisone Patre* (Munich). Also M. Griffin (1997), 'The Senate's story', *Journal of Roman Studies*, 87, and A. Cooley (2009), 'The moralising message of the *Senatus Consultum de Cn. Pisone patre*', *Greece & Rome*, 45(2).

13 Tiberius, Tiber and Tibur

For Tiberius on food subsidy and flattery see Tacitus *Annals* 2.87:2.

The builder of the *Via Appia* and *Aqua Appia* was Appius Claudius Caecus (*c.*312–279 BCE).

14 Hercules the herdsman

The night journey to Tibur is at Propertius 3.16.

Marcus Terentius Varro (116–27 BCE) was a politician and polymath who in a late work on agriculture (*De Re Rustica* 3.2:16) wrote of the threats to food prices from the demands of those providing banquets. See J. H. D'Arms (1995), 'Between Public and Private in Epulum Publicum', in *Horti Romani* (L'Erma di Bretschneider) (1998), Maddalena Cima and Eugenio La Rocca (eds).

Pliny (*Natural History* 14.97) credits Julius Caesar with serving four different wines for the first time at a public feast.

15 Care for cucumbers

Pliny refers to *triplatinum*, a luxury of lampreys, bass and other fish, at *Natural History* 35. 162. See Gowers (1993), p. 123 n.

Phaedrus's fable of the hand, foot and stomach is at 3.16.

16 Vitellia's night out

The family tree of the Vitellii is tangled and not everywhere clear. Vitellia was the sister of Lucius and Publius, thus the aunt of Aulus the emperor. She was also the grandmother of the Petronia who became briefly Aulus's first wife. She was the mother of Aulus Plautius, who would later lead Claudius's invasion of Britain.

Tacitus (*Annals* 3.49–51) reports the performance and trial of Clutorius Priscus. Also Dio 57.20:3–4.

Suetonius (*Tiberius* 42) notes Tiberius's appointments of fellow heavy drinkers and his commissioning of a dialogue between various courses of a banquet – a mushroom, an oyster, a thrush and a fig-eating warbler.

17 Pen and knives

Plutarch (*c.*40 CE–*c.*120), a Greek priest at Delphi, was one of the earliest sources for the first-century imperial court, author of the famous *Parallel Lives* of noble Greeks and Romans. He also wrote separate lives of the eight emperors from Augustus to Vitellius; only those of Galba and Otho, two of Vitellius's predecessors in the Year of the Four Emperors, have survived. Plutarch (*Cato* 56) describes Caesar's puritanical enemy, Marcus Porcius Cato, as vowing not to recline at dinner while Caesar's tyranny is still a threat. Cato is paired in the *Parallel Lives* with the Athenian general known, mockingly by his enemies, as Aristides the Just.

There are various versions of the fable of the bat who cannot decide between the birds and the beasts. Phaedrus's is fable 18.

Dio (57.195) and Tacitus (*Annals* 4.1) describe Sejanus's relationship with Apicius. The invention of foie gras is credited to Apicius himself by Pliny (*Natural History* 8.77). The attribution of recipes, then as now, is notoriously inexact.

Tacitus (*Annals* 4.12) has Agrippina as open-mouthed for power as for food. He is as hostile to women in public life as to slaves and former slaves. See M. Beard (1995), 'Imaginary Horti: Or Up the Garden Path', in *Horti Romani* and note on Chapter 32.

Tacitus (*Annals* 4.52) has Agrippina charging Tiberius with hypocrisy for the simultaneous worship of Augustus and prosecution
of his descendants.

18 The way of the guard captain

Phaedrus's fable of the fox and the peacock is 1.3 and of the frogs
complaining about the sun 1.6.

Suetonius (*Tiberius* 39) tells the story of Tiberius in the cave. See
Conticello and Andreae (1974). Reviewed by A. F. Stewart in *JRS*,
67 (1977). For a modern life of Sejanus see McHugh (2020).

19 Water on dust

For Phaedrus (2.5), the emperor and the watering can, see Henderson (2001).

There is much argument about the content, origins and influence of
the *phlyax* plays. See Trendall (1967) and Taplin (1992).

For discussion of Suetonius's account of Tiberius's sexual interests,
and the role of the *spintria*, see E. Champlin (2011), 'Sex on Capri',
Transactions of the American Philological Association 141(2), pp.
315–22. Also B. Gladhill (2020), 'Tiberius on Capri and the limits
of Roman sex culture' (McGill). Suetonius (*Tiberius* 45.1) reports
Tiberius as the goat lapping up the doe.

Parrhasius (*c.*430–350 BCE), from Ephesus and Athens, is sometimes described as the first pornographer in painting.

Suetonius (*Galba* 5) describes Livia's bequest. Plutarch (*Galba* 3)
says that he and Livia were related. Plutarch's *Galba* is one of the
most positive portraits of the period, highlighting the attempt by
the first of the four emperors of 69 CE to reject the court culture
of the Palatine.

20 Profits from propinquity

Suetonius (*Caligula* 19) reports Thrasyllus's prophecy about Caligula
being as likely to become emperor as to walk across the Bay of
Naples.

Dio Cassius (57, 21, 3) suggests that Tiberius banished all actors from Rome in 23 CE because they debauched women and caused 'uproar'. See also Suetonius (*Tiberius* 37).

For the redistribution of wealth through the confiscations from the condemned see E. Champlin (1992), 'Death and taxes', *Studi Italiani di Filologia Classica*, 10.

21 Death of the damned

For the significance of Rubellius Blandus see R. Syme (1982), 'The wedding of Rubellius Blandus', *American Journal of Philology*, 103(1).

Tacitus (*Annals* 5.8) reports the death of Publius Vitellius. The charges and the suicide belong in Book Six, but the incorrect numbering in Book Five goes back to the sixteenth century and still survives. Also Suetonius (*Vitellius* 2).

For Grattius's *Cynegetica* see J. Henderson (2001), 'Going to the Dogs', *Proceedings of the Cambridge Philological Society*, 47.

For the economic crisis of 33 CE see Tacitus *Annals* (6 16–17). For a modern account, see too P. Temin (2001), 'A market economy in the Early Roman Empire', *Journal of Roman Studies*, 91.

22 Lucius Vitellius and the Son of God

St John's gospel (19:12) has the line that 'If you release him you are no friend of Caesar.' For the limited Roman mentions of the crucifixion of Jesus see Tacitus (*Annals* 15.44) and Josephus (*Antiquities of the Jews* 18.3). Joseph ben Matthias (c.37 CE–c.100) (Titus Flavius Josephus) is the historian who wrote closest to Vitellius's time as emperor. He was born soon after Lucius organised the recall of Pontius Pilate and moved in his thirties from being a supporter of Jewish revolts to a recogniser of the power and authority of the Roman Empire. His account was later extended and enhanced by Christian sources.

Lucius's predecessor in Syria was Pomponius Flaccus. Suetonius (*Vitellius* 6) gives a dismissive account of Aulus Vitellius' wives.

23 Goat worship

See Dio (59.26:5–10) on Caligula's new god-like clothes for seducing
his sisters, and Suetonius (*Caligula* 22.2) for the emperor and the
statues of his favourite gods wearing the same clothes. Tacitus
(*Annals* 6.20) records Passienus Crispus on Caligula as servant
and master.

24 Ill will for the twin

Suetonius (*Caligula* 21) records the start of the *Aqua Claudia*.

25 Man talks to a Moon

Dio (59.27:6) and Suetonius (*Caligula* 22.4) describe Caligula's view
of the heavens. Phaedrus (1.26) tells the fable of the fox and the
stork.

For the idea that the *Fratres Arvales* had origins earlier than Rome
itself see Aulus Gellius (*Attic Nights* 7.7:7) and Pliny (*Natural
History* 17.2:6).

26 Good water, golden meat

Suetonius (*Caligula* 22) reports the gold statue and its regular
change of dress. Juvenal (*Satires* 6.615–20) jokes of Caesonia the
poisoner.

Phaedrus (5.7) tells the story of the actor and the emperor. See
Henderson (2001).

27 Torture of an actress

Philo (*c.*20 BCE–50 CE) was a pioneer in connecting Greek and
Jewish philosophy. His role (*Legatio ad Gaium*, *Embassy to
Caligula* 361) in the delegation to Caligula in 40 CE and its discussion on the benefits of pork and lamb is his only recorded
appearance in political history. Josephus (*Antiquities of the Jews*
19) recounts the death of Caligula. See Wiseman (2013).

28 Garden ornaments

Aricia as Horace's first stop on his diplomatic journey for the future Emperor Augustus is at *Satires* 1.5. Pliny (*Natural History* 33.145) reports Rotundus Drusillianus's ownership of a silver plate weighing 500 pounds (350 modern pounds) and eight others half the size but still substantial on any table.

The best account of Grattius, the dog poet, is by J. Henderson (2001) in *Proceedings of the Cambridge Philological Society*, 47, a witty defence of the poet against those who have treated him as barely better than a dog himself. Ovid's single mention of Grattius is at *Letters from Pontus* 4.16:34. The dogs from what is now Ukraine are the *Geloni*.

29 Lucius rules the world

Horace (*Odes* 3.5:2–4) echoes Augustus's British ambitions. Suetonius (*Claudius* 17) and Dio (60.19–23) recount Aulus Plautius's invasion of Britain for Claudius. Strabo (*c.*64 BCE–24 CE) in his *Geography* (4.5) gives an economic assessment for invading and holding Britain. For the best modern account see Hingley (2022).

Josephus (*Jewish War* 7.1.3) describes the award to officers of miniature spears and eagles of silver and gold. To some soldiers the award of a soft-tipped spear to a eunuch might have seemed less outrage than irony. The second-century lawyer and writer on strategy Polyaenus (*Stratagems* 8.23.5) describes the role of elephants in Britain.

Seneca (*Apocolocyntosis* 13.12) mocks Claudius's little white pet dog once its owner is safely dead.

30 Ashes of a swallow

Largus's recipe for Antonia's throat medicine is from the Oxyrhynchus Papyri (P.Oxy. 2547) and is in the Wellcome Library for the History & Understanding of Medicine, London. Largus's

Compositiones are at PHI Latin Texts. https://latin.packhum.org/
loc/1011/1/0#0

31 Flattery's textbook

Seneca's letter to Polybius (*De Consolatione ad Polybium*) is analysed
by L. Gloyn (2014), 'Show me the way to go home', *American
Journal of Philology*, 135 (3). Dio (31–2) refers to an embarrass-
ing letter from Corsica that Seneca later tried to suppress. See
Wilson (2015).

32 A bedroom slipper

Suetonius (*Vitellius* 2) describes Lucius's performance with
Messalina's slipper. Tacitus (*Annals* 11.1–3/ 5–8) reports the prosecution and death of Valerius Asiaticus and Claudius's siding
with Suillius in the argument over legal fees and the importance
of a law career not being restricted to the already rich.

For descendants of Pallas see CIL 6. 00143 and others listed by L.
R. Penner (2013), 'The epigraphic habits of the slaves and freed
slaves of the Julio-Claudian household' (University of Calgary),
p. 128. For the literary use of Messalina's open-mouthed lust for
gardens and lovers see M. Beard (1995), 'Imaginary Horti: Or
Up the Garden Path', in *Horti Romani*. Tacitus (*Annals* 11.29 and
37–8) reports Messalina' death.

33 Of unshakable loyalty to his emperor

Pliny (*Natural History* 12.12) tells how Dionysius from Thessaly,
a wealthy importer of plane trees, on one occasion pretended
to be a freedman in order to join the court in search of power.
Suetonius (*Claudius* 28) tells the story of Arpocras. See also note
on Chapter 35.

Tacitus (*Annals* 12.4) describes Lucius Vitellius's role in Claudius's
marriage to Agrippina. Ovid's version of the Judgement of Paris
is at *Heroides* 16.

The senator who wanted the new rights of Claudius and Agrippina for himself was Alledius Severus. Tacitus (*Annales* 12.7) reports this unusual form of flattery while suggesting that Agrippina had put Severus up to it.

For the Arval Brothers see M. Beard (1985), 'Writing and ritual: A study of diversity and expansion in the Arval Acta', Papers of the British School at Rome, 53.

Plutarch (*Galba* 9.1) and Tacitus (*Annals* 15.72) report the legacy of Callistus. His name on lead pipes is at CIL 15. 07500.

Pallas's younger brother suffered harsh criticism in Judaea from Christian and Jewish writers, some elements of which he may have deserved; others probably fell upon him because of his status within the court. He found it as difficult as his predecessors and successors to deal with the addition of Christianity to the tensions between Greeks and Jews (*Acts of the Apostles* 24.24).

Lucius's accuser on treason charges in 51 CE was Junius Lupus, an otherwise unknown senator whom Claudius, after an appeal from Agrippina, sent into exile (Tacitus, *Annals* 12.42). This last piece of courtly manoeuvring is Tacitus's last reference to Lucius. Suetonius (*Vitellius* 3) records Lucius's death and the honour of his commemoration in the Forum.

34 God-given mushrooms

See V. Grimm-Samuel (1991), 'On the mushroom that deified the Emperor Claudius', *Classical Quarterly*, 42(1).

35 Aulus the educator

Seneca (*Apocolocyntosis* 10, 13) gives the list of Claudius's freedmen, sent 'on ahead' to Hades, and mocks Claudius for killing as easily as a dog shits – also as the owner of a white pet dog, being terrified by the shaggy black hound guarding the gates. Tacitus (*Annals* 13.15) describes the poisoning of Britannicus. Pliny (*Natural History* 19.33) reports Nero's diet of leeks. Phaedrus (1.7) tells the fable of the fox and the mask.

Seneca (*A consolation to Helvia, his mother* 10. 3) consoled his
    mother during his exile by stressing the benefits of life away from
    the banqueting halls, his absence from those who eat to vomit
    and vomit to eat. The letter was written at about the same time as
    his pleading flattery of Polybius.

36 Oedipus and actors

The work of Cluvius Rufus was influential on later understanding
    of the fall of the Caesars. An enthusiast for the theatre as well as
    politics, he is arguably the best candidate to be what is known as
    the 'common source' for the Year of the Four Emperors, the lost
    contemporary account used by Plutarch, Tacitus, Suetonius and
    maybe Dio and Josephus too. The career of Aulus Vitellius, as
    recorded by those historians, provides some of the best evidence
    for this unrecognised eyewitness. For his life and scraps of iden-
    tifiable work see Wiseman (2013) and Cornell (2013).

The anonymous author of *Acts of the Apostles* (18.17) describes the
    refusal of Seneca's brother Gallio to involve himself in disputes
    between Jews and Christians. Seneca's advice to Serenus in dif-
    ficult times is *On Peace of Mind* (*c.*60 CE), a recommendation
    to steer a middle way between sobriety and drunkenness – also
    between other extremes.

The dating of Calpurnius Siculus is disputed. T. P. Wiseman (1982),
    'Calpurnius Siculus and the Caludian Civil War', makes a pow-
    erful case for the time of Nero (*Journal of Roman Studies*, 72).
    Calpurnius appears in J. W. Duff and A. M. Duff (1934), *Minor
    Latin Poets (Vol. 1)*, Loeb Classical Library.

The Greek epigrammatist was Lucilius. The object of Nero's penis
    poem was Claudius Pollio. Lucan's exceptional flattery of Nero is
    in his *Pharsalia* (1.33). Cicero wrote a poem praising his own con-
    sulship. For the mockery of Cicero the self-flatterer see Tacitus
    (*Histories* 2.36) and Seneca (*On Anger* 3.37:5). Tacitus (*Annals*
    12.59) reports Agrippina's lust for gardens. See M. Beard (1995),
    'Imaginary Horti: Or Up the Garden Path', in *Horti Romani*.

37 Dish of Minerva

The image of the Macellum magnum on Nero's coinage is at https://
www.britishmuseum.org/collection/object/C_1958-1101-1

Tacitus (*Annals* 14.1–28) gives a dramatic account of Agrippina's
murder, its causes and consequences.

For the need for a staging post between Rome and Sublaqueum
see B. Frischer (2010), 'The Roman Site Identified as Horace's
Villa at Licenza, Italy', in G. Davis (ed.), *A Companion to Horace*
(Wiley-Blackwell).

38 Blackened tables

Pliny the Younger (*Letters* 7.29:2) reports Pallas's tomb on the *Via
Tiburtina*. Paul of Tarsus on the Romans for whom 'their god is
their belly' is at Philippians 3:19. Tacitus (*Annals* 14.29) gives the
name of the short-lived governor of Britain as Quintus Veranius.
Suetonius (*Nero* 32) reports the inheritance tax of five-sixths
instead of one half for freedmen who died with false imperial
names. For Nero's fears of Rubellius Plautus see Tacitus (*Annals*
13.9:3.), for the comet (14.22:21) and for Plautus's death (14.58:9).

39 Food and fire

Cluvius Rufus is the likely source for the main historians' shared
and detailed account of the relationship between Poppaea, her
husband Otho, and Nero. For the popularity of Nero's marriage
to Poppaea, as opposed to the view of it by ancient historians,
see the graffiti, *Neropoppaenses*, cited in Opper (2021). For the
Domus Aurea see Farinella (2020).

40 Tutor in vice

Suetonius (*Vitellius* 5) reports Aulus being accused of swapping gold
for brass in temples. Suetonius (*Nero* 49) reports Nero's dying
words. See too M. F. Gyles (1962), 'Nero: *Qualis artifex*', *Classical
Journal of Middle West and South*, 57(5).

PART THREE

41 Mr Stingy

Depending on who was telling his story, Galba was either prudent with public funds or mean towards the pay demands of his army, an enemy of the Palatine court or an emperor whose fewer advisers pillaged much more money. His mostly good reputation was a product of the wholly bad reputation of Vitellius. Plutarch, who prized moral comparisons over other duties of a biographer, began a lasting trend.

Suetonius (*Nero* 50) describes the loyalty of nurses and mistresses at Nero's funeral. Dio (63.22) and Josephus (*Jewish War* 4.440) recount the Vindex revolt. See too P. A. Brunt (1959), *The Revolt of Vindex and the Fall of Nero* (Latomus).

Suetonius (*Vitellius* 6) describes Vitellius's son as a stammerer and (*Galba* 13) reports Galba being mocked with a line attacking meanness from an Atellane farce.

42 A good job for a glutton

Aulus's relative in Pannonia was Lucius Flavianus. Suetonius (*Vitellius* 7) describes Aulus's appointment to Germany and popularity for belching. For the Nero drain cover in Cologne see Wolff (2003). Tacitus (*Histories* 1.46–55) describes Aulus's adoption by the German armies.

For a commemoration of freedmen's freedmen, see the tribute to Scurranus and his business manager, Venustus, his household accountant, Deciminianus, his doctor, Agathopus, his dresser, Primus, and Tiasos, his cook. CIL 6. 01597, cited by L. R. Penner (2013), 'The epigraphic habits of the slaves and freed slaves of the Julio-Claudian household' (University of Calgary).

43 Fill me up!

Dio (64.3) reports Galba's view of the Palatine court. For Acte's own court see L. R. Penner (2013), 'The epigraphic habits of the slaves and freed slaves of the Julio-Claudian household' (University of Calgary), p. 228 and Appendix K.

For street plan of Cologne see Wolff (2003). Suetonius (*Vitellius* 8) reports Aulus's wit following the fire at his headquarters. Tacitus (*Histories* 1.15, 1.48) explains Galba choosing Piso over Otho as a strike against flatterers.

44 A hard man to flatter

Suetonius (*Otho* 6) reports Otho's password. Tacitus (*Histories* 1.76) tells of the feast in Carthage given by Crescens in support of Otho.

45 Brother behind the lines

Tacitus (*Histories* 2.47–8) describes the suicide of Otho and (2.54) reports the first flattery of Lucius Vitellius as the brother of the next emperor.

46 Wine for the battlefield

Horace's ode (1.7) is addressed to Plancus. For a discussion of Horace's attitude to Plancus and to Tibur see J. Moles (2002), 'Reconstructing Plancus', *Journal of Roman Studies*, 92.

For the site of Lugdunum see J. F. Drinkwater (1975), 'Lugdunum: "Natural capital" of Gaul?', *Britannia*, 6. Tacitus (*Histories* 2.54) reports Aulus's execution of Gnaeus Cornelius Dolabella, the husband of his first wife, Petronia.

Plutarch's narrative of Bedriacum and the battles of 69 CE focuses on the unusual independence of Roman legionaries from their chains of command. Tacitus agrees, while putting somewhat more emphasis on the orders of their officers. For a discussion of these shades of difference see G. Morgan (2006), pp. 5–8. See too E. Manolaraki (2005), 'A picture worth a thousand words: Revisiting Bedriacum', *Classical Philology*, 100. Plutarch toured the battlefield himself; see R. Syme (1980), 'Biographers of the Caesars', *Museum Helveticum*, 37(2).

47 The Shield of Minerva

Pliny (*Natural History* 35.163) and Suetonius (*Vitellius* 13.2) report the Shield of Minerva. Tacitus (*Histories* 2.95.3) gives the cost. Dio (65.2) explains that the silver was necessary not to show extravagant luxury but to make a dish of sufficient size. For Rotundus Drusillianus's silver plate see note on Chapter 28.

48 Emperor Vitellius

Dio (65.2) reports Vibius Crispus's gratitude for the illness that took him away from the table and saved his life. The expulsion of astrologers is at 65.4.

Tacitus (*Histories* 2.82, 3.8) shows Vespasian prioritising control of Egyptian corn and the ability to starve Rome over being with his army in the field. To be in Alexandria Vespasian had the support of the imperial prefect, Tiberius Julius Alexander, a proof that Augustus's policy of banning ambitious senators from Egypt and using personal appointees instead had failed.

49 No time for a party

Rosius Regulus was the consul for one day. The party-giver was Caecina Tuscus. Tacitus (*Histories* 3.12–14) reports Caecina in chains.

50 A drink to defeat

Tacitus (*Histories* 3.42–62) reports the death of Valens.

51 In Augustus's temple

For a discussion of Sabinus, Vespasian's elder brother, see K. Gilmartin Wallace (1987), 'The *Flavii Sabini* in Tacitus', Historia, 36. Tacitus (*Histories* 3.68–79) reports the negotiations with Sabinus and his death.

52 Out of the doghouse

Tacitus (*Histories* 3.71) reports the burning of the records.

53 New courts for old

On Aulus's very public humiliation see Pliny (*Natural History* 34. 24). Tacitus and Cassius Dio record Aulus's last words.

On the father of Claudius Etruscus Statius (*Silvae* 3.3) see Weaver (1965). For Caenis's legacy see CIL. 6. 04057.

See A. Sillett (2018), 'The Prince and the Pauper', whatwould cicerodo.wordpress.com for the Roman procurator in the adaptation of Roman government for empire. For the continuing lamentations of anti-Roman exiles from Commagene see Josephus (Jewish War 7.231–6).

Suetonius (*Vitellius* 1) begins his Life with contrasting accounts of the origins of the Vitellii, the flattering and the dismissive, and does not choose between them, a scepticism which improved his reputation among later writers, such as Vopiscus (fourth century). See H. W. Bird (1971), 'Suetonian influences in the later lives of the *Historia Augusta*', *Hermes*, 99, p. 131.

For representations of Vitellius in art and the donkey-headed Christian graffiti see Beard (2021). The late punishment of Ephaproditus for his role in Nero's suicide is described by Suetonius (*Domitian* 14.4) and Cassius Dio (67 14.4).

Suetonius (*Vespasian* 4) and Dio (66.11–12) recount the story of Vespasian and Phoebus.

Tacitus (*Annals* 3.55) describes approvingly Vespasian's attitude to banqueting. See also Mommsen (1996).

For the sixteenth-century Palatine see N. Nonaka (2015), 'The aviaries of the Farnese Gardens on the Palatine', *Memoirs of the Academy in Rome*, 59/60 (University of Michigan Press). For the Palatine of St Petersburg see Larmour and Spencer (2007).

Epictetus compares life to banqueting with the gods (*Handbook* 15), arguing that any superior is divine (*Discourses* 4.1). He describes life as a play (*Handbook* 17) and the danger of wanting both the lettuce and the money, the ancient equivalent of having one's cake and eating it (*Handbook* 25). Statius (*Silvae* 3.3:50) in his poem on the father of Claudius Etruscus describes the hierarchy in which everyone is a slave to a higher power.

BIBLIOGRAPHY

Adams, J. (1982), *The Latin Sexual Vocabulary* (Duckworth)

Baldwin, B. (1992), *The Career and Work of Scribonius Largus* (Rheinische Museum für Philologie), Neue Folge, 135, pp. 74–82

Ball, L. F. (2003), *The Domus Aurea and the Roman Architectural Revolution* (Cambridge University Press)

Balsdon, J. P. V. D. (1934), *The Emperor Gaius* (Clarendon Press)

—(1979) *Romans and Aliens* (Duckworth)

Beard, M. (2021), *Twelve Caesars: Images of Power from the Ancient World to the Modern* (Princeton University Press)

—(2015) *SPQR: A History of Ancient Rome* (Profile)

Bédoyère, G. de la (2017), *Praetorian: The Rise and Fall of Rome's Imperial Bodyguard* (Yale University Press)

Brothwell, D. and P. (1998), *Food in Antiquity: A Survey of the Diet of Early People* (Johns Hopkins University Press)

Conticello, B. and Andreae, B. (1974), *Die Skulpturen von Sperlonga* (Mann, Berlin)

Conybeare, F. C. (1911), *Philostratus: The Life of Apollonius of Tyana* (Harvard University Press)

Cornell, T. J. (ed.) (2013), *The Fragments of the Roman Historians* (Oxford University Press)

Corpus Inscriptionum Latinorum (CIL) 1863– (Berlin)

Davidson, J. (1997), *Courtesans and Fishcakes: The Consuming Passions of Classical Athens* (HarperCollins)

Eden, P. T. (ed.) (1984), *Seneca, Apocolocyntosis* (Cambridge University Press)

Farinella, V. (2020), *The Domus Aurea* (Electa)

Frassinetti, P. (1967), *Atellanae Fabulae* (In Aedibus Athenaei, Romae)

Garnsey, P. (1988), *Famine and Food Supply in the Graeco-Roman World: Responses to Risk and Crisis* (Cambridge University Press)

Gowers, E. (1993), *The Loaded Table: Representations of Food in Roman Literature* (Clarendon Press Oxford)

Griffin, M. T. (1984), *Nero: The End of a Dynasty* (Routledge)

Hard, R. (ed.) (2014), *Epictetus, Discourses, Fragments, Handbook* (Oxford University Press)

Henderson, J. (2001), *Telling Tales on Caesar: Roman Stories from Phaedrus* (Oxford University Press)

—(2004) *Aesop's Human Zoo: Roman Stories about Our Bodies* (University of Chicago Press)

Hingley, R. (2022), *Conquering the Ocean: The Roman Invasion of Britain* (Oxford University Press)

Kapust, D. J. (2018), *Flattery and the History of Political Thought: That Glib and Oily Art* (Cambridge University Press)

Kuttner, A. L. (1995), *Dynasty and Empire in the Age of Augustus: The Case of the Boscoreale Cups* (University of California Press Berkeley)

Laes, C. (2018), *Disabilities and the Disabled in the Roman World: A Social and Cultural History* (Cambridge University Press)

Larmour, H. J. and Spencer, D. (eds) (2007), *The Sites of Rome: Time, Space, Memory* (Oxford University Press)

Levick, B. (2001), *Claudius* (Routledge)

—(1999) *Tiberius, the Politician* (Routledge)

McHugh, J. S. (2020), *Sejanus: Regent of Rome* (Pen & Sword)

Millar, F. (1997), *The Emperor in the Roman World* (Duckworth)

—(1964) *A study of Cassius Dio* (Clarendon Oxford Press)

Mommsen, T. (1996), *A History of Rome under the Emperors* (Routledge)

Mooney, G. W. (ed.) (1930), *Suetoni Tranquilli De Vita Caesarum Libri VII–VIII* (Longman)

Morgan, G. (2006), *69 A.D.: The Year of Four Emperors* (Oxford University Press)

Morgan, L. (2020), *Ovid: A Very Short Introduction* (Oxford University Press)

Mouritsen, H. (2011), *The Freedman in the Roman World* (Cambridge University Press)

Murdoch, A. (2006), *Rome's Greatest Defeat: Massacre in the Teutoburg Forest* (History Press)

Obbink, D. (1995), *Philodemus in Italy* (University of Michigan Press Ann Arbor)

Opper, T. (2021), *Nero: the man behind the myth* (British Museum)

Romm, J. (2014), *Dying Every Day: Seneca at the Court of Nero* (Knopf)

Rowe, G. (2002), *Princes and Political Cultures* (University of Michigan Press)

Spawforth, A. J. S. (ed.) (2007), *The Court and Court Society in Ancient Monarchies* (Cambridge University Press)

Sullivan, J. P. (trans) (1986), *Petronius, The Satyricon / Seneca, The Apocolocyntosis* (Penguin Classics)

Taplin, O. (1992), *Comic Angels: and Other Approaches to Greek Drama through Vase-Paintings* (Clarendon Press)

Trendall, A. D. (1967), *Phlyax Vases* (University of London Institute of Classical Studies)

Vehling, J. D. (1936), *Apicius: Cookery and Dining in Imperial Rome* (Walter M. Hill, Chicago)

Vickers, M. and Gill, D. (1994), *Artful Crafts: Ancient Greek Silverware and Pottery* (Oxford University Press)

Wallace-Hadrill, A. (1996), 'The Imperial Court', in the *Cambridge Ancient History, Vol. 10, The Augustan Empire 43 BC–AD 69* (1996) (Cambridge University Press)

Weaver, P. R. C. (1964), 'The slave and freedman 'cursus' in the imperial administration', Vol. 10 (Cambridge Philosophical Society)

—(1965) 'The Father of Claudius Etruscus: Silvae 3.3', *Classical Quarterly*, Vol. 15(1) (Cambridge University Press)

Wellesley, K. (1989), *The Year of the Four Emperors* (Routledge)

Wilson, E. (2015), *Seneca: A Life* (Allen Lane)

Wiseman, T. P. (2013), *The Death of Caligula* (Liverpool University Press)

—(2019) *The House of Augustus: A Historical Detective Story* (Princeton University Press)

Wolff, G. (2003), *Roman-Germanic Cologne* (Bachem, Cologne)

ACKNOWLEDGEMENTS

To Mary Beard, Joanna Evans, Ed Lake, Caroline Michel, Ruth Scurr, Andrew Sillett, Stefan Vranka, Paul Webb, *Optimi Lectores*, the very best of readers.

ACKNOWLEDGMENTS

INDEX